NORTH PUGET SOUND

AFOOT & AFLOAT

SECOND EDITION

NORTH
PUGET SOUND

AFOOT &   AFLOAT

SECOND EDITION

Marge & Ted Mueller

THE
MOUNTAINEERS

 Published by
The Mountaineers
1001 SW Klickitat Way, Suite 201
Seattle, Washington 98134

First edition 1987. Second edition: first printing 1995, second printing 1997, third printing 1999, fourth printing 2002

Published simultaneously in Great Britain by Cordee,
3a DeMontfort Street, Leicester, England, LE1 7HD

Manufactured in the United States of America

Edited by Kris Fulsaas
Maps by Marge Mueller
All photographs by the authors unless otherwise noted
Cover design by Watson Graphics
Typesetting by The Mountaineers Books
Book design and layout by Gray Mouse Graphics

Cover photographs: Mount Baker rises above Padilla Bay and Hat Island; *insets:* Blaine Marina; Walking the beach at Ebey's Landing State Park, Whidbey Island

Frontispiece: Marine pyrotechnics at Tongue Point Marine Life Sanctuary

Library of Congress Cataloging-in-Publication Data

Mueller, Marge.
    North Puget Sound, afoot & afloat / Marge & Ted Mueller. — 2nd ed.
        p.   cm.
    Includes bibliographical references and index.
    ISBN 0-89886-435-6
    1. Outdoor recreation—Washington (State)—Puget Sound. 2. Outdoor recreation—Washington (State)—Puget Sound—Directories. 3. Marinas—Washington (State)—Puget Sound—Guidebooks. 4. Puget Sound (Wash.)—Guidebooks. I. Mueller, Ted. II. Title. III. Title: North Puget Sound, afoot and afloat.
GV191.42.W22P846   1995
796.5'025'7977—dc20   94-49399
                                                              CIP

CONTENTS

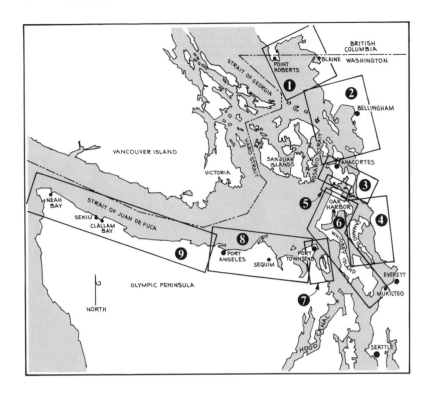

Fun on North Puget Sound: kayaking, fishing, and sailing

PREFACE

Many guidebooks are written with a specific activity in mind, telling people such as bicyclists, paddlers, or clam diggers where to go to better enjoy their favorite recreation. While the books of our *Afoot and Afloat* series do cover some activities and areas strictly limited to boaters, we recognize that boaters frequently leave their vessels to walk beaches, dig clams, or hike trails in nearby forests, and that some boaters even bring bicycles with them to widen their explorations.

At the same time, many people who do not own boats love roaming beaches or hiking bluff tops, enjoying the bite of salt air, the cries of seabirds, and the rush of waves. The one common thread in this book is shorelines, and all the activities associated with them, no matter how one arrives there.

Descriptions of facilities are kept brief, because we feel that such things as marinas and campgrounds are not ends in themselves, but merely places that enable one to enjoy the shorelines and water.

Attractions are described in order to entice visitors to out-of-the-way spots they might otherwise pass by. Because exploration of any region is more enjoyable if spiced with some of its history and ecology, we have included information on the historical background and natural life of some of the areas.

The areas in this book were surveyed over a period of several years and rechecked just prior to publication of this second edition. Changes to facilities do occur, however. The authors and The Mountaineers Books would appreciate your letting us know of any changes to facilities so future editions can be updated. Please address comments to: The Mountaineers Books, 1001 SW Klickitat Way, Suite 201, Seattle, Washington 98134.

Marge and Ted Mueller

Overleaf: *Spectacular scenery makes Salt Creek County Park one of the most popular recreation sites on the Strait of Juan de Fuca.*

INTRODUCTION

Before the arrival of European explorers, the Native Americans who lived along the shores of what we now call Puget Sound already had a name for all of this inland sea: *whulge* (loosely translated as "big saltwater"). Because early explorers were not given to paying much attention to the desires of the residents, this early name has largely been ignored. That may be just as well in this case; while the white man's tongue may have learned to embrace such Indian names as Swinomish and Sequim, whulge may be more than most English-speaking mouths can handle.

When British sea captain George Vancouver first visited the Pacific Coast in 1792 and charted these inland waters, he gave the name of "Puget's Sound" to the channels lying south of the Tacoma Narrows that had been explored by his lieutenant, Peter Puget. Over the years, usage of the Puget Sound name has been creeping northward, and today most maps and charts show it as the waters running south from the entrance to Admiralty Inlet—or south of a line drawn from Port Townsend on the Olympic Peninsula to Admiralty Head on Whidbey Island.

Commonly, however, many local people (as well as some state agencies) today consider Puget Sound to be all of Washington's inland waters running north from Olympia to the Canadian border, and west to the Pacific Ocean. In time the name may be accepted for the entire area by the State Board of Geographical Names, and a long-running problem will be resolved.

In this book, the area that we are calling "North Puget Sound" might, by strict definition, not be considered part of Puget Sound at all. The problem is that there is no other tidy name for these waters lying at the entrance to what is "officially" known as Puget Sound. Yet that's an awful lot of water to go nameless; so, by virtue of common usage and by the necessity for this book to have a concise term for the area it covers, "North Puget Sound" it is.

The North Sound in a Nutshell

This area is, in many ways, the most interesting and varied of all the inland waters. It ranges from the harsh, wave-worn, rocky shoreline of the Strait of Juan de Fuca to the seeping saltwater marshes of the Skagit delta. Its attractions include beautiful turn-of-the-century towns, unique nature preserves, fascinating old army forts, parks for every possible taste, and the best stretches of boating waters to be found anywhere on the West Coast.

A recurrent theme throughout this book is the dominant presence of the military on North Puget Sound over a long span of time. We didn't set out to write it that way—it simply became obvious after reading countless bronze plaques and informational displays, browsing dozens of museums, and standing on scores of escarpments gazing out over vulnerable waterways.

The legacy of the military to the recreational public is far more than a few old cannons for delighted 8-year-olds to climb on, or a spate of concrete emplacements picturesquely surrendering to thickets of wild rose at several state parks along the sound. The legacy is the precious land itself, uniquely preserved from early-day claim-stakers and latter-day developers and eventually delivered into the hands of government agencies for wildlife preservation and public use.

THE HISTORY OF MILITARY PRESENCE IN NORTH PUGET SOUND

At various times in the past, military reservations, forts, and naval installations have occupied thousands of acres of prime Puget Sound shoreline and, as strange as the concept may be, many of these have become part of our recreational heritage. While this chain of events may not have been intentional, it is still cause for the beachcomber and bird lover to celebrate—and to look hungrily at other military lands we may yet claim.

But how did this come about?

The First Fortifications

Early North Sound settlers, fearing raids by hostile Haida Indians from Vancouver Island, built strong, two-story blockhouses surrounded by log stockades. Some of these blockhouses, dating from the 1850s, are now in a National Historical Reserve on Whidbey Island.

In 1855 the usually peaceful Puget Sound Indians, angered at being relegated to reservations and encouraged by uprisings east of the Cascades, took part in the short-lived Indian Wars. These hostilities brought the first federal troops to the North Sound the following year, and Fort Townsend, the first such fortification on the North Sound, was established. A second fortification was established at Fort Bellingham in 1856. The Fort Townsend contingent soon had a different adversary, however, when a company of these troops, as well as a detachment from Fort Bellingham, were hustled to San Juan Island in 1859 to counter the British threat during the Pig War boundary dispute. (This, too, eventually resulted in a magnificent park, but that's a different story.)

Fort Bellingham, which had been considered only temporary from the beginning, was abandoned in 1860. Fort Townsend was never a hit with military brass, who found it poorly located and with precious little to defend along the sparsely settled shores of Puget Sound, and it was fitfully garrisoned until 1894 when the barracks were accidentally destroyed by fire. It was decommissioned a year later, probably with great relief on the part of the Army, but remained a military reservation.

Military Land Acquisition

During the early 1850s, as our nation grew in size and importance, the government became concerned with the defense of its shores, and a Fortifications Board recommended the establishment of land reservations at key locations that might be used for future military defenses. In 1866 President Andrew Johnson set aside 25 such parcels of land scattered along the shores of Puget Sound. After the San Juan dispute was settled in 1872 and those islands officially became part of the United States, seven additional tracts were reserved, commanding the entrances to Griffin Bay, which was to serve as a future harbor of refuge for the Navy.

Military apathy at building forts in such a remote corner of nowhere to defend a mere handful of citizens was further increased by the technical problems involved. The smooth-bore, muzzle-loading coast artillery pieces of the Civil War era had neither the range nor the accuracy to make effective fortifications possible—in short, at a distance they couldn't

Battery Downs at Fort Flagler State Park

hit the broad side of a brigantine. To compensate for artillery deficiencies, proposals for lines of defense north of the Tacoma Narrows required one or more forts to be built in the middle of Admiralty Inlet. Needless to say, such expensive fortifications were never cost-justified. By the late 1880s larger, breach-loading, rifled guns improved the range and accuracy of artillery, and coastal defense of Puget Sound became feasible.

At this same time the major navies of the world shifted from sailing vessels to faster steam-powered battleships and cruisers with armor up to 18 inches thick and supporting as many as ten 12-inch guns. Range finding and fire control on the bobbing ships was still primitive, however. Land-based guns were technically superior and were now even more necessary to defend against the threat of these iron-clad leviathans.

In the government's view, Puget Sound was still sparsely settled and of no economic value, thus the Endicott Board, commissioned by Congress in 1885 to develop a comprehensive plan for coastal defense, recommended no fortifications for this unimportant corner of the country.

The Naval Presence on Puget Sound

Shortly after the end of the Civil War, a board of Army engineers recommended the establishment of a naval station and drydock in the North Pacific. This may have been brought about by the embarrassment of large naval and commercial vessels being forced to use the drydocks at Esquimalt, on Vancouver Island—a facility of the British, with whom relations were somewhat strained. Between 1878 and 1880 the Navy surveyed possible sites along the U.S. coast, and after 10 years of commissions, studies, and pork-barrel infighting, finally confirmed a site on the southwestern reach of Port Orchard on Puget Sound. Land was acquired in 1891, and the following year construction of the first drydock at Bremerton began.

Ultimately, the presence of the Navy shipyard, the arrival of a transcontinental railroad at Tacoma in 1883, and the recognition of the increasing economic importance of commercial shipping to the Orient and Alaska combined to lead to the approval in 1896 of the fortification of the first line of defense for Puget Sound at Point Wilson, Admiralty Head, and Marrowstone Island. By mid-1897 work had begun at Marrowstone Island, followed shortly by construction at the other locations. The Spanish–American War in 1898 gave added impetus to the need to protect the Pacific Coast.

Fortifications on Admiralty Inlet were completed by 1907, and were turned over to the Coast Artillery as Forts Worden, Flagler, and Casey. The three forts, poised at the entrance to the sound, became known as the "Triangle of Fire," which reputedly could blow to smithereens any enemy ship.

Even before the fortifications were completed the military began to realize that the forts had serious drawbacks. The guns on Marrowstone Island were poorly placed and had a limited sector of fire, and at the other forts visibility was often severely limited due to fog or smoke from frequent forest fires. Even under the best of conditions it took several minutes to load, aim, and fire each gun, and hitting a fast-moving ship ducking in and out of the fog was nearly impossible. The forts could prevent the enemy from anchoring offshore on a nice sunny day, but any ship that chose to slip up the sound in the fog could probably do so unchallenged.

An inner line of defense was planned to protect the sensitive Navy shipyard, and in 1898 land was acquired at three sites on Rich Passage: Beans Point, Middle Point, and Orchard Point. In anticipation of enemy attack, mine fields, protected by smaller-caliber rapid-fire guns, were to be laid here and at a fourth planned location on Agate Passage. Although the fortifications at Beans Point eventually became Fort Ward, the other sites reverted to caretaker maintenance and never saw the troops originally planned.

Technology Marches On

In the 20 years following the work of the Endicott Board, technology and defensive requirements changed markedly, and in 1905 President Theodore Roosevelt appointed a successor, the Taft Board. This board classified Puget Sound among the ports of first importance and recommended both additional fortifications and heavier armaments at existing forts. Recognizing the visibility problems at Admiralty Inlet, a second line of defense was proposed at Foulweather Bluff and Double Bluff, where military reservations had existed since 1866.

The local artillery officers hotly debated these locations and suggested such alternatives as Old Fort Townsend, Nodule Point, Bush Point, Lagoon Point, and Partridge Point for additional armament. However, before the second line could be approved and implemented, the recommended fortifications became obsolete because of technology advancements during World War I, and they were never built.

The Taft Board also recommended arming Deception Pass to prevent enemy access to Saratoga Passage. Although the pass itself was never fortified in this period, a new fort—Fort Whitman, located on Goat Island—was built and commissioned in 1911 to defend Saratoga Passage.

World War I on Puget Sound

With the onset of the first world war, Puget Sound military installations took on a new role as tens of thousands of young men were shipped here for training for the European front. Armament was removed from some of the batteries at the forts to be mounted on railway flatbed cars for use in Europe, or as defensive guns aboard troop ships. The Navy shipyard at Bremerton tooled up for ship construction as well as repair and was also a training site for Navy recruits.

Battleships now carried 16-inch guns and displayed a dramatic improvement in fire-control techniques and high-angle firing capabilities. As a result of these improvements and the introduction of precision aerial bombing, the coastal forts became not only ineffective, but also very vulnerable.

With the cuts in military funding following the "War to End All Wars," coastal forts reverted to a caretaker status. Only the naval facilities continued to grow as the Pacific Ocean gained an importance once reserved for the Atlantic. The 1920s also saw the disposal of most of the unimproved military reservations in the area; some of these were turned over to local governments for public recreational use. A tract of over 1,000 acres at Deception Pass was dedicated as a gorgeous new state park.

In the 1930s many of the older guns and mortars were removed from the Admiralty Inlet forts and melted down. The only additions were antiaircraft batteries, which were effective against both airplanes and torpedo boats. The inner defense lines on Rich Passage ceased to exist when Fort Ward was deactivated and turned over to the Navy in 1930 for its use as a recreation site. Only the Navy shipyard at Bremerton continued to expand, partially because it was a convenient funnel for funds to address the critical unemployment conditions of the Depression.

World War II Brings Military Revival

The rumbles of impending war once again breathed life into the Puget Sound military bases in the early 1940s. Major maintenance took place at the remaining batteries at the Admiralty Inlet forts, and they were beefed up with additional searchlights and antiaircraft batteries. A new Harbor Entrance Control Post was activated at Fort Worden to coordinate harbor-defense activities and monitor new secret underwater detection and radar systems. Searchlights and guns were installed at Deception Pass on land requisitioned back from the state park, emplacements for mortars were dug at Cape George, and searchlights were placed at Middle (McCurdy) Point. Long-debated plans for defenses at Point Partridge finally became a reality with the construction of Fort Ebey in 1942. The last in a series of fixed coastal guns was installed when 6-inch and 16-inch batteries encased in impregnable bunkers were built at Fort Hayden on Striped Peak, west of Port Angeles.

At the Navy shipyard a fourth drydock, large enough to accommodate any ship in the fleet, was completed in 1940. Old Fort Townsend was resurrected as a Naval Explosives Laboratory. A new mine and bomb storage facility was constructed at Indian Island in 1941, and in three years was supplemented by another ammunition depot at Bangor on Hood Canal. Dabob Bay became a torpedo test site. Whidbey Island saw the construction of a seaplane base at Oak Harbor and a naval air station at nearby Ault Field.

As the U.S. Navy drove the conflict far into the Pacific, the waters of Puget Sound never saw an enemy vessel, and none of its protective guns were fired in anger. The only known damage inflicted occurred when guns at the forts were fired in practice, and the concussion caused local windows to break, plaster to crack, and pictures to fall from walls. At the conclusion of the war, most of the military installations quickly reverted to peacetime caretaker status—many for the last time.

The Era of the Park

A major benefactor of the demobilization was the Washington State Parks and Recreation Commission, as between 1949 and 1972 it acquired Middle Point (Manchester) and Forts Townsend, Casey, Flagler, Ward, Ebey, and Worden. Fort Whitman was acquired by the State Game Department, and Fort Hayden by the State Department of Natural Resources. Most of Fort Lawton became a Seattle city park (Discovery Park). Other properties, or portions thereof, went to the management of other governmental agencies for public use.

The Navy presence is still felt in Puget Sound, however, as the Navy shipyard has continued its growth at Keyport, Bangor, Indian Island, and Whidbey Island. The newest naval presence, the Nimitz carrier group, has overcome political and environmental barriers and has come into existence as a naval base in Port Gardner at Everett. Who knows? If history is prologue to the future, we may now be witnessing the creation of a spectacular waterfront park for Everett citizens of the 21st century. One cannot help but wonder, wistfully, if it might not be wiser to skip the time and tax money involved in the military undertaking and go directly to a park.

Clam digging on Scow Bay Spit at Fort Flagler State Park

GETTING AROUND IN NORTH PUGET SOUND

To Puget Sound pioneers the network of waterways was a tremendous asset. The land was covered with forests so thick that even walking was difficult and road building was a Herculean task; however, any of the homesteads and infant milltowns along the shore could be reached by boat with a minimum of effort.

In time, as communities were established, the rowboats and sailing ships of early settlers were joined by steamboats—reliable workhorses that churned through the waters of the sound transporting people, mail, and goods with little concern for the vagaries of weather. The number of little steamers grew to such a number, swarming hither and yon across wide channels and up narrow rivers and sloughs, that one observer referred to them as the Mosquito Fleet.

Although the automobile and the network of mainland roads it inspired brought to an end 70 years of activity by the steamers of the Mosquito Fleet, the sound still serves as a primary avenue of transportation for Puget Sound residents. A fleet of state-operated superferries, assisted by a few county-run and privately operated vessels, now carries goods and passengers to cross-sound destinations. Commercial ships fill the major channels, transporting goods to and from foreign markets. And every year hundreds of thousands of pleasure boaters use the sound to take them to fabled vacation destinations, such as those described in this book.

For boaters in large craft, most of the areas in the North Sound are within a day or two's cruising distance from any other point on the sound, via protected waterways. The 15-mile-wide Strait of Juan de Fuca, with its winds and waves sweeping in from the Pacific Ocean, can be a serious challenge at times, and its outer reaches present some difficulty in navigating and finding secure anchorages during bad weather.

Trailered or cartop boats and increasingly popular kayaks are easily transported to any of a multitude of public or commercial launching facilities for quick access to recreation destinations. For those who want to enjoy the shorelines by foot or bicycle, most points on the North Sound are but a half day away from the major metropolitan areas via highway and ferry. Interstate 5 is the main north–south route along the east side of the sound; in this book, most driving directions on the east side of the sound are keyed to exits from this thoroughfare.

The Olympic Peninsula—the westernmost point described in this book—can be reached by driving south around the end of the sound, then north on US Highway 101. A shorter, but multistep, process involves taking ferries from either Seattle or Edmonds, then driving across the Hood Canal bridge and looping around the peninsula on US Highway 101. The Olympic Peninsula can also be reached via the Keystone ferry from Whidbey Island.

Public Accesses

Public shorelines along Puget Sound rest in the hands of a variety of agencies. Most parks are either city-, county-, or state-owned. Another major landholder is the state Department of Natural Resources (DNR), which has an extensive inventory of beaches lying below the mean high-water level, although in a few cases the adjacent uplands are also included. The U.S. Fish and Wildlife Service controls most wildlife refuges; in the area covered by this book, the refuges at the mouth of the Skagit River and on Dungeness Spit are included in these lands. The state Department of Fish and Wildlife, which owns some boat launch ramps, and the U.S. Bureau of Land Management (BLM), which maintains Coast Guard-operated lighthouses, are responsible for some of the smaller segments of public shore lands.

Boat Launching Facilities

Public launching facilities are found at some state, county, and city parks, at city marinas, and at sites owned by the state Department of Fish and Wildlife. If there are no public ramps nearby, many commercial resorts have either ramps or hoists. In nearly all cases a fee is charged for the use of commercial facilities. A number of public ramps have an honor box for depositing fees for use of the facility.

The quality and safety of launch facilities range from the sublime— with excellent surface, drop-off, and protection—to the ridiculously hazardous, where boaters risk getting stuck in mud at low tide or having boats reduced to splinters by ever-present winds or waves.

Ramps are not always paved at the extreme tide levels; others are frequently choked by debris. Some ramps open out onto a long tideflat; some drop off very abruptly. Boaters should explore the surface of a ramp before launching to avoid miring the tow vehicle or launching it along with the boat. At times of wind or surges, extra care must be used to avoid damaging the boat or injuring boaters.

Launch facilities tend to change occasionally. Some are neglected due to lack of public funds and become unusable. Commercial ones close down for the season, or even go out of business. On the plus side, sometimes new ones are built or old ones improved.

Marina Facilities

Boating facilities on Puget Sound run the gamut from meager wooden docks clinging to ancient piers to posh resorts complete with full dock hookups for boats and hot tubs for salt-encrusted crews. The information summary listed at the beginning of the various public-access areas in this book includes those items that are of the most interest to captain and crew. "Complete boat and crew facilities" are considered to be guest moorage with water and power, diesel, gas, marine supplies and repair, groceries, a restaurant, restrooms, and showers. Marinas that have more or less than these amenities are noted.

Commercial marinas are operated by local port districts or private individuals. In either case a fee is usually charged for any use of the facilities, including launching. "Private marinas" that are mentioned in the text are open to members only and do not have facilities for visiting boaters.

Department of Natural Resources Beaches

Within the area covered by this book, the Department of Natural Resources owns in excess of 80 miles of public shore lands at over 50 separate sites. The majority of these are accessible only by boat, and their usability varies. In some cases boat landing can be so difficult, or the beach drops off so steeply, that it precludes any degree of public use. However, at a few beaches, such as those lying east of Sequim Bay, the DNR beaches are exquisite tideflats offering extensive walking, beach-combing, and clam-digging opportunities.

When Washington was first established as a state, all tidelands were in the public domain, regardless of upland ownership. The state gradually sold off these tidelands to private individuals until 1969, when the practice was discontinued. The remaining beaches that are suitable for public recreation have been inventoried by the DNR and are described in detail in booklets published by that agency. These booklets are listed in appendix D, Selected References.

For most DNR beaches, the public area is the tideflat below the mean high-water line. On nearly all beaches, this is the region just below the layer of driftwood or below the end of grass, trees, or other terrestrial vegetation. When uplands are public, it is specifically mentioned in the text.

The Nature Conservancy

The Nature Conservancy, a private conservation organization supported by membership and donation, has identified and purchased some environmentally important property on Puget Sound. Most of these areas are held by the organization as nature preserves. Occasionally land is acquired when it becomes available, with the intent to resell it at cost to an appropriate government agency when public funds become available. Through the efforts of this group some vital properties have been saved that might have been lost due to the slow turning of bureaucratic wheels. A portion of the Department of Natural Resources land at Eagle Cliff on Cypress Island was acquired by this means.

In general, lands owned by The Nature Conservancy are considered biological preserves and are open to the public for limited use—nature walks are fine, but camping and picnicking are not permitted. In some cases the area may be so sensitive that public visits are not permitted.

RECREATION IS DIVERSE

One of the most remarkable aspects of Puget Sound is the variety of activities the water and shoreline engender. It offers something for all ages, from tots experiencing the first squish of sand through toes, to senior citizens enjoying retirement with leisurely beach strolls or boat cruises. Although boating in its various forms is one of the major considerations in this book, it is by no means the only one. Recreation also includes bicycling, beachcombing, hiking, scuba diving, sightseeing, wildlife watching, nature walks, photography, and—the most delightful of all pastimes—harvesting and enjoying delectable fish and shellfish.

Boating and Paddling

On Puget Sound, boaters take to the water in everything from multi-million-dollar fiberglass "Ferraris" to lung-inflated plastic rafts from the neighborhood drugstore. The majority of local boaters, however, fall well between these two extremes. Along with a variety of craft comes a variety of points of view and areas of concern. The skipper of a high-powered cruiser is less interested in the strength of the tidal current than is a sailboater or a kayaker, but the cruiser captain breaks out in a sweat about water depths that kayakers breeze over.

Renting a boat for a day of fishing or exploration, or chartering one for an extended cruise, is common on Puget Sound. This book notes places where such boats are available. No matter what size the boat, to attempt boating without somebody on board who is experienced is folly. Most charter operators will check out clients before turning the boat keys over to them; if prospective boaters are obviously unqualified to operate a vessel safely, the charter operator may give them a quick course, or may insist that an experienced skipper go along—for a fee.

Particular mention is made of places that are appropriate for paddling—that is, muscle-powered boating in kayaks, canoes, dinghies, or inflatables. While this is the ideal way to reach many of the beaches along the sound, extreme care must be used, with an eye to tide rips and currents, the weather, and even larger boats. Kayaking recently has become extremely popular along Puget Sound; however, crossing channels can be quite hazardous for the inexperienced. Many places offer

Kayaking in Admiralty Inlet, off Ebey's Landing State Park

classes, and guided trips are available to a number of destinations; this is an ideal introduction to the sport for newcomers, or for those with some experience who want the safety and camaraderie of a group.

The Washington Water Trails Association has been a leading force in creating the new "Cascadia Marine Trail," a paddle-oriented water trail with convenient overnight stopping places from Olympia to the Canadian border. Many of the trail campsites have been allocated from existing county, state park, or DNR property.

A boater's best ally in navigating Puget Sound waters safely is "sea savvy": a generous helping of common sense augmented by boating safety courses and instruction in safely operating one's vessel. The U.S. Power Squadron's classes in small boat handling are excellent; information regarding the courses can be obtained through the U.S. Coast Guard.

This book attempts to address major boating concerns, but it is not possible to cover all navigational hazards that might affect all kinds of boaters. In some places water depths and particular current problems are noted; however, this book cannot take the place of a good *navigational chart* and the knowledge to use it properly. The best chart for close-in navigating is the one with the largest scale—that is, showing the greatest detail. Charts for the areas covered in this book are listed in appendix B, Nautical Charts and Maps.

Rocks and Shoals. Most hazardous rocks and shoals lying in well-traveled areas are marked with lights, buoys, or similar navigational devices. In less-frequented places these hazards may be unmarked, although they are shown on large-scale charts. Local boaters occasionally mark notorious keel-killers with a vertical pole; these aids are not always maintained and do not show on charts. Another warning of a rock or reef is long streamers of bull kelp floating on the surface—approach any bed of kelp cautiously.

The tidal range in Puget Sound is about 14 feet, except for extreme tides. The lowest low tides run about minus 4 feet, the highest high tides about 12 feet. During extreme low tides, rocks and shoals that are normally well covered suddenly are close enough to the surface to cause grief to the unwary skipper. During minus tides use special care to consult navigational charts, and, if mooring, check tide tables to be sure the night will not find you mired on the bottom.

Tidal Current. Tidal current is *not the same as the tide*, although one does give rise to the other. Tides measure the vertical distance that water rises and falls above the sea floor due to the gravitational attraction of the sun and moon, as well as more obscure influences. Tidal currents represent the horizontal flow of water resulting from the rise and fall of the tide. Tidal currents in Puget Sound vary from 1 to 10 knots, the most infamous being those through Deception Pass.

Tidal currents must be a concern for small boaters. Obviously a kayaker would rather be going in the direction of the current rather than struggling to make way headed into it. With long water passages such as are found in Rosario Strait, the Strait of Georgia, or the Strait of Juan de Fuca, a typical tidal current of 2 knots abeam can make as much as a 15-degree difference in the course to be steered—a difference that can be critical in conditions of fog and low visibility.

Tidal current tables (*not* tide tables), which are printed annually, are keyed to station points on the small-craft portfolio of charts. The approximate time of maximum velocity of the current can be computed by referencing the tidal current tables to the station point. Although many other factors enter into the actual surface velocity, and even the direction of the current, general knowledge of the predicted velocity is invaluable to safe navigation.

Tide Rips. Navigational charts typically bear a notation of "tide rips," off points between channels. Tide rips are caused by either the impact of tidal currents meeting from different directions or the upwelling of currents as they meet underwater cliffs. In either case the surface appearance is the same: the water appears to dance across an area in small to moderate choppy waves and the water appears to swirl like a whirlpool. A boat crossing a tide rip area may find it difficult to maintain course as erratic currents spin the boat first one way and then another. Kayaks and small boats may find rips an uncomfortable experience—one that should be avoided. The positive aspect of tide rips is that the upwelling current also brings to the surface food-chain elements that attract game fish, so they are ideal fishing spots.

Weather. In sections of North Puget Sound, steep terrain that forces winds along the direction of a waterway can produce an effect called channeling, which causes the speed of the wind to increase by as much as double. In the Strait of Juan de Fuca, winds near the west entrance have reached as much as 65 knots as a result of channeling.

In the North Sound the price often paid for warm sunny summer days is morning fog created by the temperature differential between the sun-warmed land masses and the perpetually chilly waters of Puget Sound. Fog generally lifts by midday, but early departure plans should also include a well-plotted compass course to destinations that may disappear in the sea-level morning mist.

In the Strait of Juan de Fuca, early morning fog can, on occasion, be accompanied by winds of 25 to 30 knots—an unpleasant combination.

Choppy Waters. A phenomenon peculiar to long, open channels such as Rosario Strait or the Strait of Georgia is a very short, steep wave form that generally occurs when a strong breeze comes from the direction opposite to the tidal current. Long, relatively shallow channels with moderate to strong tidal currents build this wave form, in contrast to the broader swells built in the deep channel of the Strait of Juan de Fuca or the open ocean. These short, choppy waves chew away at forward boat speed and provide those persons prone to seasickness an excellent opportunity to head for the lee rail. Passage for small boats can be downright dangerous in choppy seas, because they can be swamped or overturned. A close watch on weather reports and tidal current predictions can help a skipper avoid these unpleasant experiences.

Walking and Hiking

Very little of the footbound exercise described in this book is vigorous enough to be categorized as hiking. For the most part it involves easy strolls to viewpoints, short nature loops through forested glades, or walks along beaches. With time out for birdwatching, flower smelling, rock skipping, or any of many other diversions, most of the walks described are ample enough to fill an afternoon. For extended walks, many of the public areas can be linked by walking the beach at low tide, or following railroad tracks or city streets at high tide.

The incoming tide, which laps benignly at tenny-runner toes, can pose a considerable hazard for persons lured into an extended beach walk beneath high, vertical bluffs. Walkers may suddenly find themselves trapped between a rock and a wet place, and be forced to either climb up or wade out—either of which can be very hazardous. The solution is prevention. Before undertaking beach walks, check a tide table to find out when the predicted high will occur and how high it will be, then plan your walk accordingly. Tide tables are published in small books that are available at boating supply shops as well as book stores. The daily tidal prediction is also published in newspapers, along with the weather.

Some trails follow the shoreline along the top of vertical bluffs ranging up to 150 feet high. Typically such bluffs are of glacial till that is soft and frequently eroded and undercut. To compound the problem, the tops of many such bluffs are covered with a particular grass that is quite slippery, especially for smooth-soled shoes. Avoid walking near the edge of any bluff.

Bicycling

Nearly all the area encompassed in this book is well suited to bicycle exploration. Many of the roads are lightly traveled, yet are level and smoothly paved. Whidbey Island offers the best array of bicycle-to beaches, along with several fine campgrounds.

The most difficult bicycling route in the area described in this book is Highway 112 along the Strait of Juan de Fuca between Port Angeles and Neah Bay. Some venturesome bicyclists tackle this route as part of an Olympic Peninsula tour; however, the road has numerous ups and downs, curves, narrow shoulders, and occasional logging trucks and hell-bent motorists. Compensation for this is some of the finest scenery on the face of the earth—if you survive.

On any public road in Washington, bicyclists must ride on the right side of the road (in the same direction as automobile traffic), and travel in single file, or no more than two abreast. If several cars become stacked up behind them, cyclists must pull over, but do *not* do this at the crest of a hill or a bend in the road. Bicyclists need to stop where motorists can see them. Bicycles are welcome on any of the ferries. On state-operated ferries, they are loaded and unloaded ahead of vehicles; other ferries will give boarding instructions.

Camping

In addition to city, county, and state parks that have campgrounds, a number of resorts also have camping facilities. As of 1995 Birch Bay, Fort Flagler, and Fort Worden state parks will accept reservations; they are required between Memorial Day and Labor Day at these parks. Campsites are on a first-come, first-served basis at the other state parks. Most state park campgrounds are gated at dusk, picnic areas are open only for day use, and parking lots cannot be used for overflow camping. If the campgrounds are full, the park ranger may be able to suggest alternative space.

Beach Exploration

For many people, a visit to the beach is like a visit to another planet, with alien landscapes and a menagerie of strange life forms to marvel at. Unfortunately, some feel the need to cart buckets of these life forms home where they immediately die, create an ungodly stink, and in due time are thrown into the garbage.

All state parks and some county and city parks have regulations protecting nonfood forms of marine life such as starfish and sand dollars. Even in those areas that are unprotected by environmental regulations, beachcombers should avoid removing or destroying any of these animals. All play an important part in the food chain, and all add to the educational and aesthetic richness of the beaches. Many tidelands in populated areas along the sound were once a bright tapestry of marine life, but are now virtually barren due to longtime abuse by beachcombers, coupled with the effects of pollution.

Even nonliving beach objects such as driftwood and empty shells are an important part of the marine environment, forming growing sites for marine plants and homes for small creatures, and helping control erosion. If you must have a treasure from the sea as a souvenir of your trip, make it small, and check to be sure it is not harboring some tiny living marine creature.

Harvesting Seafood—Beach Foraging, Fishing, and Scuba Diving

One of the greatest enticements of the seashore is the prospect of gathering food fresh from the water for a seaside feast or a quick trip home to the dinner table. In many areas on Puget Sound this is possible, but it is regulated, and regulations change from time to time.

Licenses and Limits. The Washington State Department of Fish and Wildlife requires the following licenses:

- *Personal Use Food Fish License* to fish for halibut, herring, lingcod, rockfish, perch, cod, shad, tuna, shark, salmon, and sturgeon, and related species. No license is required for smelt, carp, or albacore tuna.
- *Personal Use Shellfish/Seaweed License* is required to harvest crab, clams, oysters, shrimp, sea cucumbers, sea urchins, squid, abalone, scallops, barnacles, cockles, mussels, octopus, crayfish, and seaweed.
- *Game Fish License* is required for freshwater game fishing at such locations as Pass and Cranberry lakes in Deception Pass State Park and Lake Pondilla at Fort Ebey State Park.

It is the responsibility of the fisherman or seafood gatherer to be aware of all regulations. Pamphlets on salmon, shellfish, and bottomfish sport fishing, as well as game fish regulations, are published by the Department of Fish and Wildlife and are available in most sporting goods stores. They list size and catch limits, seasons, and other restrictions for all types of shellfish as well as sport fish.

Digging Holes. State regulations dictate that holes dug in beaches in pursuit of clams *must always* be filled. Do not rely on the incoming tide to do the job; it may take several turns of the tide for displaced sand to be completely leveled. In the meantime, small marine animals trapped atop the pile may be exposed to the sun and may die of dehydration.

Oyster Shells. Removal of oyster shells from the beach is unlawful. Large shells frequently hold several oyster larvae that will die if the shells are discarded on land. Take a sharp, sturdy knife or oyster pick and plastic containers to the beach and shuck oysters where they are found.

A horse clam from a North Puget Sound beach

Marine Sanctuaries. State and county parks generally permit the taking of those edible forms of marine life that are defined and regulated by the Department of Fish and Wildlife; however, some parks have marine sanctuaries where such taking may be prohibited. Many underwater reefs are closed to spear fishing by scuba divers. At any park check the local regulations before gathering a meal.

Paralytic Shellfish Poisoning (Red Tide). When the state Department of Health periodically issues a "red tide warning" and closes particular beaches on Puget Sound, the public usually reacts with confusion or skepticism. A clearer understanding of the phenomenon of red tide leads to a greater respect for its dangers.

The name "red tide" itself contributes to some of the public's confusion, for it is not always visibly red, it has nothing at all to do with the tide, and not all red algae are harmful. Paralytic shellfish poisoning (PSP) is a serious illness caused by *Gonyaulax catenella,* a toxic, single-celled, amber-colored alga that is always present in the water in small numbers. During spring, summer, and fall, certain environmental conditions may combine to permit a rapid multiplication or accumulation of these microscopic organisms. Most shellfish toxicity occurs when the concentrations of *G. catenella* are too sparse to discolor the water; however, the free-floating plants sometimes become so numerous that the water appears to have a reddish cast—thus the name red tide.

Bivalve shellfish such as clams, oysters, mussels, and scallops, which feed by filtering seawater, may ingest millions of the organisms and concentrate the toxin in their bodies. The poison is retained by most of these shellfish for several weeks after the occurrence of the red tide; butter clams can be poisonous for much longer.

When the concentration of the toxin in mollusks reaches a certain level, it becomes hazardous to humans who eat them. The toxins cannot be destroyed by cooking, and cannot be reliably detected by any means other than laboratory analysis. Symptoms of PSP, beginning with tingling of the lips and tongue, may occur within a half hour of ingestion. The illness attacks the nervous system, causing loss of control of arms and legs, difficulty in breathing, paralysis, and, in extreme cases, death.

Shellfish in all counties on Puget Sound are under regular surveillance by the state Department of Health. Marine toxin/PSP (or red tide) warnings are issued and some beaches are posted when high levels of toxin are detected in tested mollusks. Warnings are usually publicized in the media; the state toll-free hotline listed in appendix A, Emergency Phone Numbers and List of Contacts, has current information as to which beaches are closed to shellfish harvesting. Crabs, abalone, shrimp, and fin fish are not included in closures because there have been no recorded cases of PSP in the Northwest caused by eating any of these animals.

Safety Considerations

Boating and beach travel entail unavoidable risks that every traveler assumes and must be aware of and respect. The fact that an area is described in this book is not a representation that it will be safe for you. The areas described herein vary greatly in the amount and kind of preparation needed to enjoy them safely. Some may have changed since this book was written, or conditions may have deteriorated. Weather conditions can change daily or even hourly, and tide levels will also vary considerably. An area that is safe in good weather at low or slack tide may be completely unsafe during inclement weather or at times of high tide or maximum tidal current. Many of the shores and waterways of North Puget Sound are the most exposed of any on the sound, and conditions can vary widely. Storms can make the channels hazardous to small craft, and bad weather and incoming tides can make beaches impassable. Be cautious when storms are in the offing.

You can meet these and other risks safely by exercising your own independent judgment and common sense. Be aware of your own limitations and those of your vessel, and of conditions when or where you are traveling. If conditions are dangerous, or if you are not prepared to deal with them safely, change your plans. Each year many people enjoy safe trips in the waters and on the beaches of North Puget Sound. With proper preparation and good judgment, you can too.

Not all walks described in this book are suitable at all times, or for all people. Do not approach too close to the edges of bluffs, because they may crumble. At no time should hikers attempt to climb or descend a bluff if there is no trail, and even when trails are present they can become treacherously slippery. The old army bunkers are especially enticing to children, but can be dangerous to the unwary. Do not allow youngsters to roam unsupervised; adults should use care where they step.

Emergency Assistance

Overall legal authority in all unincorporated areas of the state rests with the county sheriff. Emergencies or complaints should be referred to the local county sheriff's office at the number listed in appendix A, Emergency Phone Numbers and List of Contacts.

Within state and county parks, the park manager assumes emergency assistance responsibilities. Not all parks have resident managers, however; appendix A indicates the locations of managers responsible for smaller parks.

The U.S. Coast Guard has primary responsibility for safety and law enforcement on Puget Sound waters. Marine VHF channel 16 is continuously monitored by the Coast Guard and should be the most reliable means of contact in case of emergencies on the water. The Coast Guard monitors Citizen Band (CB) channel 9 at some locations and times, but it has no commitment to a full-time radio watch on this channel. Several volunteer groups do an excellent job of monitoring the CB emergency frequency and will assist as best they can with relaying emergency requests to the proper authorities. With the advent of fairly complete cellular telephone coverage of Puget Sound, cellular service providers offer a quick dial number, *CG, that will immediately connect the cellular telephone user to the Coast Guard Vessel Traffic Center in Seattle. This center coordinates all marine safety and rescue activities for the region.

Right: *Orca whales can sometimes be seen in the Strait of Georgia off Point Roberts.*
Middle: *A trail leads to the beach at Semiahmoo County Park.*
Bottom: *The Blaine Marina has moorages available for visiting boaters.*

CHAPTER ONE

THE STRAIT OF GEORGIA

The waters of the Strait of Georgia span the boundary between the United States and Canada. In summer this 10-mile-wide channel sees a steady flow of Canadian boaters headed south to fabled Washington islands and Yankee boaters headed north to island treasures in British Columbia—proving that even cruisers subscribe to the adage that the grass is greener (or in this case, the water is bluer) on the other side of the fence.

The several marine developments near the border on the U.S. side provide facilities and recreation to cruisers in transit, as well as permanent moorage for boaters who like to have their vessels within easy striking distance of vacation waters. Customs check-ins for boaters entering U.S. waters are at Point Roberts and Blaine marinas.

Boaters will note three sets of range lights in Semiahmoo and Boundary bays marking the international boundary at the 49th parallel. The 60-foot-tall white-concrete Peace Arch that straddles the boundary on shore is also visible from the water during most weather. The Strait of Georgia is free of obstructions except for Alden Bank, a 3-mile-long shoal marked by buoys that lies northeast of Sucia Island. Tidal currents in the channel rarely exceed 3 knots; however, a hull-jarring chop can occur when the direction of the current opposes that of the wind.

POINT ROBERTS

Point Roberts is something of a geographical anomaly: a political island created by a quirk in an early treaty. During the time of pioneer settlement both the United States and Great Britain vied for the territory between Oregon and Russia-owned Alaska. The Yankee cry in the 1840s of "54–40 or Fight" meant that the U.S. wanted to claim sovereignty over all the territory south of a latitude of 54 degrees, 40 minutes. The British insisted on an international boundary at the Columbia River. In 1846 a compromise was reached, with the 49th parallel established as the international boundary from the crest of the Rocky Mountains west to the Strait of Georgia where the boundary dipped south, down the center of the Strait of Georgia, giving the Gulf Islands and all of Vancouver Island to the British.

The lawmakers back in Washington, D.C., due perhaps to inadequate maps, failed to note two geographical problems: The 5-square-mile tip of the Point Roberts peninsula that hung below the 49th parallel became isolated from the rest of the United States, and the exact boundary through the San Juan Islands was not clearly defined. The oversight on the San Juan boundary brought the two nations to the brink of war in 1859 during the Pig War standoff. Point Roberts however, although a bit awkward, has created no major problems, and the U.S. citizens living there have learned to cope, and perhaps to enjoy their unique status.

Point Roberts is reached by land by crossing the border at Blaine on Interstate 5 and continuing north on Highway 99 for 13 miles to Exit 20, signed LADNER, TSAWWASSEN, HIGHWAY 10. Follow B.C. 10 east for 4¾ miles, then turn left (south) onto B.C. 17. In 3½ miles turn left again onto 56th Street, signed to Tsawwassen and Point Roberts. All intersections are well signed. The customs check at Point Roberts is a total of 24¼ miles from the border at Blaine. Crossing the border at either loca-

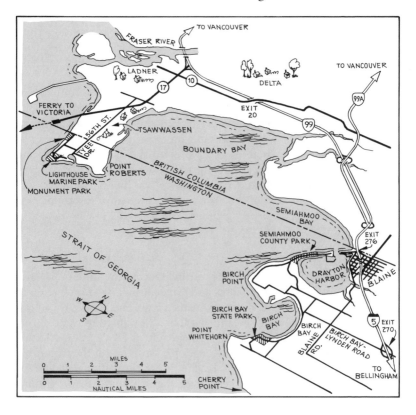

tion is usually a very quick process, except on weekends and holidays in B.C. or Washington, when heavy traffic may be encountered.

Point Roberts Marina

Facilities: Complete boat and crew facilities, laundromat, U.S. Customs, boat pumpout station, boat rental and charter, marine chandlery, restaurant, picnic tables, boat launch (hoist)

Convenience, both in facilities and location, is the byword at the Point Roberts Marina. The large comma-shaped yacht basin features the latest in moorage amenities as well as a wealth of fishing and cruising waters within a few miles of the entry breakwater. The basin, which holds more than 1,000 boats, is slightly inland, giving it maximum protection during even the most severe weather.

The marina is reached by water via a 200-yard-long dredged channel, which is in itself guarded by an angled jetty that serves to prevent shoaling of the channel. Fuel and groceries are found on the dock just inside the entrance, and guest moorage is at the extreme end of the basin. By land, the marina is reached by driving south from the border on Tyee Drive for 1½ miles, turning west on A.P.A. Road, and in another ¼ mile heading south on Simundson Road, which leads to the marina in ¼ mile.

Monument County Park (Whatcom County)

Park area: 8 acres; 500 feet of waterfront on the Strait of Georgia
Access: Land, paddle-craft
Facilities: Hiking trail
Attractions: Historical marker, viewpoint, beachcombing

Although this tract of county-owned land is undeveloped, it offers some nice views of the Strait of Georgia from the uplands. Unfortunately, English Bluff, the 150-foot-high cliff on which the park is perched, is so steep and treacherous that approaching the beach from above cannot be recommended. The park's extensive tideflats can be accessed by small, shallow-draft boats.

After crossing the border, continue south on Tyee Drive, and in 1¼ miles turn west on Gulf Road. As you near the beach, in ¾ mile head north on Marine Drive for 1¼ miles to Roosevelt Way, where there is a small parking lot at the U.S.–Canada boundary.

Adjacent to the parking area is a stone obelisk marking the boundary between Canada and the United States—the first, both historically and geographically, to be placed on the 49th parallel, in 1861. Views through the trees are of the long causeway at the Tsawwassen ferry landing nearby and the green stretches of the Gulf Islands in the distance.

Dense brush encroaches on a beaten path that follows the crest of the

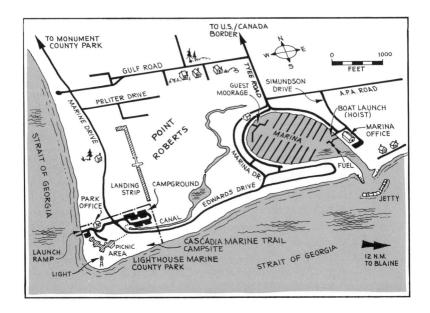

bluff south for several hundred yards. Trees obscure all views, and the few steep, slippery, boot-and-butt-built tracks that descend the face of the bluff are for the foolhardy. From the water the public beach is easily identifiable by a navigational marker on shore. The tideflat extends out for more than ½ mile before plunging steeply downward.

Lighthouse Marine County Park (Whatcom County)

Park area: 22 acres; 4,000 feet of shoreline on the Strait of Georgia
Access: Land, boat
Facilities: 25 campsites, picnic tables, fire grates, boardwalk, picnic shelters/windbreaks, drinking water, restrooms, view tower, fire rings, informational display, snack bar, boat launch (ramp) with boarding float, Cascadia Marine Trail campsite
Attractions: Camping, picnicking, boating, fishing, beachcombing, whale watching, clam digging

A spectacular site for a park: a gravelly cape of land thrusting into the surging waters of the Strait of Georgia, with views sweeping the length of the strait and out to emerald Gulf Islands. To the southeast rises Mount Baker, queen of all. The lighthouse, after which the park is named, is a metal framework tower with a rotating beacon.

The strong winds that sometimes buffet the point dictate a different approach to the usual assortment of park tables casually distributed along the beach, and the Whatcom County Parks Department has risen admirably to the challenge. Picnic sites are in angular wooden covered shelters on a long boardwalk; numerous fire rings near the beach are in the protection of shallow log-rimmed pits. When winds permit, there is ample space on the beach to spread a blanket for lunching or sunbathing.

On one corner of the boardwalk a 30-foot viewing tower increases the sightseeing possibilities. Whales, which travel in the strait, can sometimes be spotted. An enclosed shelter midway along the boardwalk has a display showing photos of orca whales (the ones most commonly seen) and describing fin characteristics, family pod identification, behaviors, how they make sound, and other fascinating information. Other enclosed shelters on the boardwalk hold restrooms and a snack bar.

The underwater shelf drops off sharply at the tip of the point, but to the north and east the tideflat flares out more gradually, providing opportunities for clam digging and beachcombing at low water. At the north edge of the park is a two-lane boat launch ramp; an adjacent line of floats, which is in place in summer, is used for boarding boats. Temporary anchorage can be found along the north side of the point in 5 fathoms of water, but wind and current conditions make this impractical for long-term stops.

By land, Lighthouse Marine Park is reached by continuing south on Tyee Drive for 1½ miles after crossing the border at Point Roberts. Just beyond A.P.A. Road turn right, and follow the road around the yacht

Bicyclists enjoy the boardwalks of Lighthouse Marine County Park.

basin, which becomes Marina Drive. At a T intersection in ½ mile turn west on Edwards Drive and reach the park in another ½ mile. The day-use area is on the south and west sides of the road, the campground to the east. A few low pines and a slight hill give the campsites some protection from winds off the strait. Owners of large RVs may prefer using one of the two commercial trailer parks located a few blocks inland because the campsites are a bit snug; they are ample, however, for tenters and small RVs. None have hookups.

Non-county residents are charged a fee for day use of the park on weekends and holidays from May 1 to October 31. Fees for boat launching or overnight camping vary, depending on type of boat and whether you are a county resident.

BLAINE

Blaine is best known as a border town, offering a rest stop and refueling station to motorists going to and from Canada. South-bound boaters also sometimes stop here at the marina to check through customs, although several other ports near the border provide the same service. Town businesses are geared to persons passing through—heavy on restaurants, lodging, and northbound duty-free shops.

Blaine lies on Drayton Harbor, a large shallow bay cut off from Semiahmoo Bay on the southwest by a 1½-mile-long sandspit and on the northeast by a man-made landfill jetty containing the town's marine industries. Only the dredged harbor by the jetty and a small portion of the bay near the entrance are navigable—the rest of it dries at the merest hint of low tide. The tideflats of Drayton Harbor, as well as those north of the marina jetty, are excellent for clam digging and oyster picking.

Shoals in Semiahmoo Bay spread outward for some distance on either side of the narrow entrance to the harbor. Boaters should give Semiahmoo Spit a wide berth and stay in the marked channel when entering.

During the Fraser River gold rush of 1858, Drayton Harbor was a staging site for prospectors

At Blaine, the Peace Arch marks the Canada–United States border.

headed to Canada. The gold boom was short-lived, however, and the town quickly dwindled away. At the turn of the century, fishing was the economic mainstay. The largest private salmon fishing fleet in the U.S. was centered here, and some 30 fish traps in Semiahmoo Bay and Drayton Harbor provided a steady supply of salmon to large processing plants on Semiahmoo Spit and Point Roberts. The enormous salmon runs became depleted, and after 30 years of operation the canneries closed. Today some fishing and crabbing boats still operate out of Blaine and there are processing plants here, but the industry is a shadow of its former glory.

Blaine Marina

Facilities: Complete boat and crew facilities, boat pumpout station, fuel, laundromat, barbecue, restaurant, fishing pier, U.S. Customs, boat launch (ramp), tidal grid, marine chandlery, shopping (nearby)

The 400-slip Blaine boat harbor, which is operated by the Port of Bellingham, is a favorite with boaters looking for good mainland moorage within easy striking distance of the San Juans and Gulf Islands. A rock breakwater along its south side encloses the dredged basin, giving it excellent protection.

To reach the boat facilities by land, turn west off Peace Portal Drive onto Marine Drive. The boat launch ramp is on the east, at the end of Milhollin Drive, inside the breakwater. The two-lane concrete ramp has an excellent slope into the water. A loading pier separates the two ramps; a large parking lot is nearby. A small float lashed to pilings in the channel off the boat ramp is part of the port's guest moorage.

A complex of small businesses, mostly marine related, occupy the landfill pier. Marina offices and accommodations for pleasure boaters are in the middle section, while commercial fishing facilities are at the far western end. The road terminates at a broad wooden pier where public fishing and crabbing are permitted. Downtown Blaine is about a ¾-mile walk from the visitors' floats.

An interesting feature of the marina is a tidal grid—a "poor man's drydock." It consists of a stable platform below the water level and some adjoining pilings where boaters tie their craft. As the tide goes out, the keel of the boat settles on the platform and the pilings support it for the duration of the low tide. The bottom of the boat is thus exposed for maintenance and repair. Numbers painted on the side of the pier or pilings (the "grid") indicate the depth of the water to the platform.

A shoreside barbecue, in the grass area near the Seafarers Memorial, is available for public use. Other swaths of grass across the road, facing on Semiahmoo Bay, have picnic tables and gazebos on the bank above the beach.

Semiahmoo Marina

Facilities: Complete boat and crew facilities, laundromat, boat pumpout station, propane, groceries, boutique, casual clothing, chandlery, boat launch (hoist)

Much of the property on Semiahmoo Spit that was once owned by the fish packing plant, as well as a large portion of land on the Birch Point peninsula, is a major resort community. It includes a tournament-class golf course and a fine yacht basin protected by a floating-log break-water on the eastern side of the spit, at Tongue Point.

Boating facilities here are new and nice, with concrete floats, power, water, and security gates. There is no designated guest float, so check with the harbormaster for any available slips. The marina store has some necessities.

By land it is 11¼ miles around Drayton Harbor from Semiahmoo to Blaine; however, the town can be reached by a short dinghy jaunt to the launch ramp at the east end of Blaine Boat Harbor. Enter the rock break-water at its west end and follow it to the ramp. Downtown shopping is a short walk away. By land, Semiahmoo Spit can be reached by follow-ing Peace Portal Drive south out of Blaine for 3½ miles. Turn right onto Bell Road, which shortly becomes Blaine Road. In 1 mile turn right again onto Drayton Harbor Road, then at a Y intersection in another mile bear left (south) on Harbor View Road. In ½ mile turn right (west) on Lincoln Road, which soon becomes Semiahmoo Parkway. Follow this road as it snakes past gated residential enclaves fronting on the re-sort golf course, pass through Semiahmoo County Park, and reach the resort in 4¾ miles from Harbor View Road.

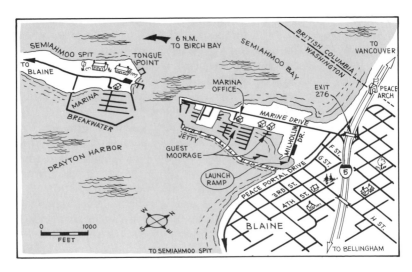

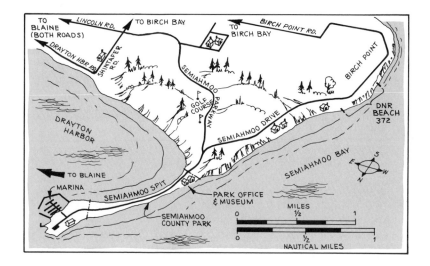

The commercial marina shares the sandspit with Semiahmoo County Park, which is within walking distance of the boat basin.

Semiahmoo County Park (Whatcom County)

Park area: 322 acres; 6,700 feet of shoreline on Semiahmoo Bay and Drayton Harbor

Access: Land, boat

Facilities: Picnic tables, drinking water, restrooms, museum, conference hall, handicapped beach access

Attractions: Clam digging, crabbing, beachcombing, swimming, birdwatching, fishing, paddling

This county park, which lies on the south end of Semiahmoo Spit between the residential and marina areas of the Semiahmoo resort, offers a nice combination of the natural and the historical.

The natural part of this park is a pair of wonderful beaches—one a windswept, driftwood-laced strand facing west on Semiahmoo Bay, the other a more protected tidal flat that spreads into Drayton Harbor. Both beaches offer the opportunity to capture crabs in the eelgrass beds; clam digging is best on the Drayton Harbor side.

The park's historical offering is in a group of buildings once used as bunkhouses for the salmon cannery. The museum in one of the buildings displays photographs, models, and artifacts that recall the era when the waters were filled with the graceful Bristol Bay sailboats used for gillnetting. A scale model of the bay shows how it looked in 1917 when it was filled with traps to snare the silvery deluge of salmon. A second building contains a gift shop and restrooms, and a third is rented as a conference hall.

Boats can be hand launched at either of the beaches; use care in Drayton Harbor to not become mired when the tide recedes. Semiahmoo Bay also offers paddling possibilities south around Birch Point to Birch Bay, 5 miles away. En route, DNR Beach 372 can be explored. That 2,000-foot-long gravelly beach, lying beneath a steep 70-foot bluff ½ mile north of Birch Point, is a likely spot to find some clams. There is no upland access; only the beach below the mean high water level is public. Strong winds off the Strait of Georgia can be a danger.

BIRCH BAY

Birch Bay is best known for the summer resort communities edging its shoreline. The cabins and condos at the towns of Cottonwood Beach and Birch Bay host families that come to revel in the sun and sand as well as enjoy the nearby golf course, water slide, and other recreational offerings. Even the weather collaborates to make this a summer playland, as this section of Washington's inland waters receives far more sun than upper Puget Sound.

While entertainment at Birch Bay tends toward the upbeat rather than the sedate, the area has its placid side. Once the summer crowds are gone it becomes a quiet retreat, both for off-season guests and for flocks of migrating waterfowl that gather in the bay. Black brants, loons, oldsquaws, and harlequin ducks are frequent visitors.

Driftwood on the beach at Birch Bay is a great place to play.

The bay itself is a shallow open bight holding less than 2 fathoms of water throughout much of its extent—great for swimming, but offering little to deep-draft boats. A few spots to drop a hook can be found well out in the bay in 4 to 5 fathoms of water. As compensation, a minus tide exposes a 1,000-foot-wide mudflat with good opportunities for seafood harvesting.

Birch Bay Village, a private residential community on the north side of the bay, has a small dredged basin, but it is only for the use of residents. Cartop boats can be put in at numerous signed public access spots along the shore.

Birch Bay is reached by land by leaving I-5 at Exit 270 and following Birch Bay–Lynden Road west for 4 miles. By water, the bay is 7 nautical miles south of the marine facilities at Blaine, where the nearest boat launch is located.

Cottonwood Beach and Birch Bay Public Accesses

From Cottonwood Beach south to Birch Bay State Park, the beachfront is public, broken only by a few sections of privately owned (well-posted) property. The road paralleling the shoreline has numerous parking areas along the side.

Each is equipped with a Sani-can. From a narrow band of driftwood, the tideflat recedes gradually into the water, remaining at wading level out for nearly ½ mile. The beach is so wide and glorious that not one, but three, sandcastle competitions are held here every summer, with dozens of competitive teams shaping the fine sand into flamboyant architecture or bizarre creatures.

Kayakers or canoeists can enjoy some 7 miles of near-shore paddling within the protected arms of the bay. Strong winds that occasionally sweep in from the west off the Strait of Georgia can pose problems in open water.

Birch Bay State Park

Park area: 193 acres; 8,255 feet of saltwater shoreline on Birch Bay, and 14,923 feet of freshwater shoreline on Terrell Creek
Access: Land, boat
Facilities: (Reservation campground) 147 standard campsites, 20 RV campsites with hookups, picnic tables, fire rings, drinking water, restrooms, bathhouse, 3 group camps (1 primitive), trailer dump stations, nature trail
Attractions: Camping, picnicking, boating, paddling, fishing, beachcombing, clam digging, crabbing, scuba diving, hiking, birdwatching, kite flying, water skiing

The climax of the Birch Bay shoreline is the state park at its southern end. Here the magnificent beach is complemented by grassy shores with picnic tables and ample space for playing volleyball, tossing Frisbees, or flying kites, or for any of the other sports that go so well with sun and sand.

The state park can be reached from the town of Birch Bay by continuing south on Birch Bay Drive to the park boundary. The entrances are gated at sunset to discourage nighttime partying and the kind of recreation inspired by moon and sand. The east entrance is reached by turning off I-5 at Exit 266, and heading west on Grandview Road for 5¾ miles, then turning north onto Jackson Road. Drive north for ½ mile and turn west on Helwig Road, which runs directly through the

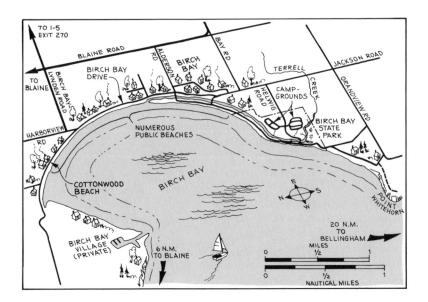

park in another ¼ mile. The route is well signed.

The park's upland section, where the camping area is located, is in stately old-growth forest of cedar and Douglas-fir. Two loop roads branch off on opposite sides of Helwig Road. Sites on the north are in fairly open forest; a few have views of the bay through the trees. The park's 20 RV sites with hookups are on this side of the road. Campsites on the south are more secluded in heavier timber with some undergrowth.

From the campground entrances, the road passes by picnic tables in grassy fields shaded by large cedar and hemlock. The road then winds downhill past a large parking area to the beach, where more picnic tables are strung along the shore.

Terrell Creek drains into a narrow estuary at the south edge of the preserve before bending north to flow parallel to the beach for a distance. The marshland here provides habitat for beaver, opossum, muskrat, and a variety of birds. A ½-mile nature trail loops through the forest to the edge of the marsh. Flora at nine marked stations along the trail are identified in a pamphlet available at the park. The trailhead, unmarked on the park road, starts at a kiosk just east of the trailer dump stations. The nearest parking is at the entrance to the campground loops.

Scuba divers entering the water at the park swim west to Point Whitehorn where the bottom drops off more rapidly and the rocky shoreline hosts a diversity of underwater life.

CHAPTER TWO

BELLINGHAM BAY

The several islands clustered around the edge of Bellingham Bay and Bellingham Channel suffer somewhat from an identity crisis. Although they are frequently referred to as part of the San Juans (which they strongly resemble geologically), they are not part of San Juan County and therefore, by bureaucratic measurement, are not "real" San Juan Islands.

In spite of the fact that they lie within a stone's throw of the major population centers of Bellingham and Anacortes, these half-dozen large islands and their entourage of smaller islets have managed to escape industrialization, although real estate developments have made some minor inroads, and the threat of development is constantly present.

Boaters seeking to avoid the heavy crowds and hoopla of the San Juans will find this area makes a nice cruising destination, with enough channels and tucked-away coves to hold their interest for a weekend. The city of Bellingham has full marine facilities.

Two of the islands, Lummi and Guemes, can be reached by car as well as by boat, making them accessible for persons with cartop craft or those who want to explore the shores by foot or bicycle. Larrabee State Park, south of Bellingham, is largely inland, but it does have a campground and a short beachfront with a boat launch ramp.

LUMMI ISLAND AND HALE PASSAGE

Lummi is the most dramatic of the islands in the Bellingham vicinity—more than 9 miles long and 1 mile narrow, with bluffs at its southern end rising precipitously for 1,500 feet, while at the north end of the island the terrain abruptly flattens into rolling farmland. Its striking silhouette is visible from many of the northern islands and channels, further adding to the misconception that it is one of the San Juan group.

The island can be reached via a small Whatcom County-operated ferry. By car, leave I-5 at Exit 260 and follow Slater Road west for 4 miles, then turn south on Haxton Way. In another 6¾ miles arrive at the

The marina at Gooseberry Point has launch facilities for boaters.

ferry landing at Gooseberry Point, on the Lummi Indian Reservation. On weekdays, the ferry runs half-hourly during times of heavy traffic, hourly when traffic is lighter. Crossing time is about 10 minutes.

A small general store on the island is on Nugent Road, ½ mile south of the ferry landing; an adjacent gift shop rents bicycles to persons touring the island. The only other tourist amenity is a cafe a short distance north of the landing. Be forewarned: there is no gas pumped on the island—tank up before you go!

Most of the island's beachfront homes and acreages are distributed on the flat, northern half of the island. The road that follows this northern shoreline offers motorists and bicyclists temptingly scenic views of Lummi Bay and the Strait of Georgia; however, there is no public access on the west side. On the south end of the island, roads penetrate for only a short distance before the steep and wild take over.

Hale Passage, a mile-wide channel, runs between Lummi Island and the mainland. The channel is unobstructed; however, a sandbar that runs north from Lummi Point to Sandy Point, on the west side of Lummi Bay, is covered by only 2 fathoms of water at mean low water. Current in the channel runs up to 2 knots; canoeists and kayakers should time their ventures for a favorable tide.

Gooseberry Point Marina

Facilities: Boat launch (hoist), gas and outboard mix (on shore), marine supplies and repairs, groceries, restaurant, gift shop

A commercial marina on the mainland, immediately north of the Lummi Island ferry landing, provides some boating amenities and a hoist for launching trailered boats.

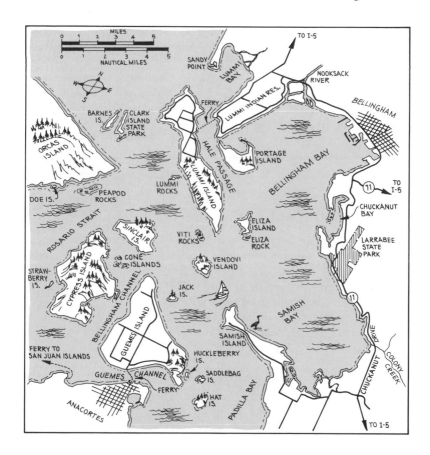

The marina has a short float on the side of the launch pier that facilitates loading and picking up fuel and supplies, but no overnight moorages. At minus tide the float sits on dry land. Boats launched here have ready access to the popular salmon fishing grounds along the end of Lummi Island and near Eliza and Vendovi islands.

Lummi Stommish Ground

Gooseberry Point and Portage Island are part of the Lummi Indian Reservation. An early Indian village was located at Gooseberry Point, and the natives portaged canoes from Hale Passage to Bellingham Bay across the sandbar that joins Portage Island to the mainland. Only members of the Lummi tribe are permitted to remove clams, crabs, or oysters from the tidelands of the reservation. One weekend in June the Lummi tribe holds war canoe races and other festivities during its annual Stommish (meaning "Old Warrior"). The Stommish is open to the public. From Gooseberry Point, take Lummi Shore Road south for 1 mile to reach the Stommish Ground.

Members of nearly a dozen Northwest tribes take part in the colorful event, which also includes a salmon barbecue, arts and crafts sales, and traditional games. The brightly painted racing boats, ranging up to 52 feet long and holding from two to 11 people, are paddled on a round-trip course that begins at the park, runs south past Portage Point, and then ends back in front of the judge's stand at the park. The men's course is 5 to 6 miles long; women and youngsters paddle shorter distances.

Portage Point and Portage Island

Cartop boats can be put in at the sandy beach at Portage Point, ½ mile south of the Lummi Stommish Ground. Technically, this can only be done at high tide, because crossing Lummi tidelands is not permitted without tribal permission. Much of Portage Bay is dry at a minus tide; at extreme high tide even the sandbar is covered.

For very shallow-draft boats, Portage Island is an interesting circumnavigation in protected waters. Beware of rocks that ring the south end of the island at Point Frances.

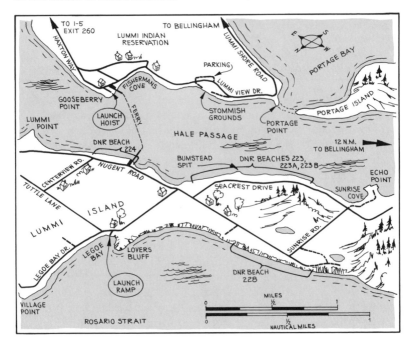

Lummi Island Recreation Site (DNR)

Area: 42 acres; 2,125 feet of shoreline on Hale Passage
Access: Boat
Facilities: 5 campsites, fire grates, latrines, hiking trail, *no water* (Designated Cascadia Marine Trail campsite)
Attractions: Camping, paddling, hiking

The eastern shore of Lummi Island, facing on Hale Passage, has a number of attractive little pocket coves offering some limited anchorages for large boats and some delightful exploring for paddlers of small ones. The shorelands are densely forested wildland, ensuring a quiet overnight stay interrupted only by the hooting of owls.

Three adjacent, unnamed coves 1¼ miles from the southern tip of the island are the site of a primitive DNR campground. The largest, most southerly of the little bays is just a few hundred feet across, and has a nice steep gravel beach below a line of driftwood. The second, smaller pocket on the north side of the headland faces east and is fairly open, with a gently tapering gravel and cobble beach. There is a baring rock in the very center of the cove. The third tiny cove, the smallest of the three, is oriented to the northeast and has very little beach—in most places the enclosing rock walls drop abruptly to the shoreline.

The coves, all of which are bounded by steep rocky walls, are linked by wooden steps and a steep trail that climbs to the campground above. The DNR campsite is a favorite for kayakers because it is part of the Cascadia Marine Trail system. A large sign onshore marking the campground is visible from the water.

About ½ mile north of the DNR Recreation Site, the open bight of Reil Harbor provides space in calm weather for a couple of very scenic anchorages; however, there is no protection whatever from southerly storm winds. The narrow gravel and rock beach, lined by bleached driftwood, quickly gives way to steep, wild bluffs.

Inati Bay

Access: Boat
Facilities: 2 mooring buoys, pit toilets, picnic tables, fire grates
Attractions: Camping, picnicking, boating, paddling, hiking, swimming

The best anchorage on this side of Lummi Island lies ¼ mile around the rock knob to the north of Reil Harbor. Here, at Inati Bay, the north-facing cove offers a pocket of protection for almost any weather, with ample space for a dozen or so boats. The two mooring buoys in the bay are for public use, but are privately maintained—their continued existence may not be as predictable as one is accustomed to with state-main-

Picnic tables are on the shore at Inati Bay.

tained public buoys. The Bellingham Yacht Club has leased land at the head of Inati Bay and has located pit toilets and fireplaces there for the use of boaters.

The bay has a rock shelf offshore about 500 yards, marked on the south by a white can buoy and on the north by a black post. From the south, enter south of the white buoy to avoid rocks and kelp in the entrance; from the north, closely follow the shoreline inboard of the marked rocks.

The last of the bays along the southeast shore, Smuggler's Cove, marks the end of the wilderness and the beginning of Lummi Island civilization. A gravel operation occupies part of this bay, but boaters may still find space to anchor.

Sunrise Cove, 1¾ nautical miles farther north along the shore, has space for some anchorages in the open, north-facing bay. The float and launch ramp on shore are owned by a private beach club, and all beaches in the vicinity are private—stay off.

Lummi Island DNR Beaches

Large portions of the tidelands along the east side of Lummi Island are DNR beaches. Beach 224 has a staircase access; the others must be reached by boat. Only the tidelands below mean high water are open to the public, except for Beach 220, which fronts the Lummi Island Recreation Site.

The northernmost of these tidelands, Beach 224 runs for 2,805 feet

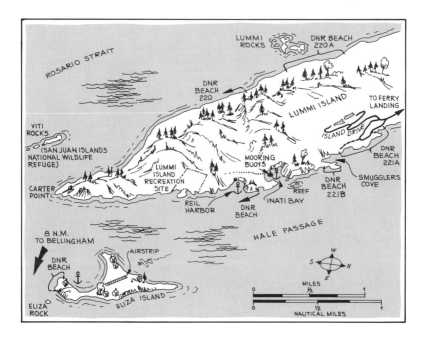

north from the ferry landing. The beach lies below a high bank and is quite wide at low tide. At its north end there is a wooden viewing platform overlooking the beach and ferry landing, and a staircase down to the beach. You will have to park at the ferry landing and walk along South Nugent Road to the staircase, because there is no parking in the immediate vicinity. The shore immediately north of the staircase and south of the ferry landing is private—do not trespass.

DNR Beach 223 (2,574 feet long), Beach 223A (1,188 feet long), and Beach 223B (1,014 feet long) are all south of the ferry landing, in the vicinity of Bumstead Spit. These three beaches, along with Beach 224, lie on sand and gravel flats that offer good opportunities at low tide for clam digging. They must be approached by boat, however, because all uplands above the mean high tide level are private.

The rocky shores on the south end of the island also have extensive DNR beaches, but they are much less hospitable. Beach 221A (4,812 feet long) runs north from Smuggler's Cove, and Beach 221B begins at the point east of the cove and runs south for 4,481 feet. The longest section of public tidelands is Beach 220, a 23,533-foot strip that wraps around the end of the island and extends northwest nearly to Lummi Rocks. All of these shorelands are rocky, with a scattering of gravel at the heads of occasional pocket coves.

Beach 220A, on the west side of the island, is a 3,188-foot tideland opposite Lummi Rocks. Use extreme care approaching this beach by boat because there are submerged rocks in the vicinity and the tidal current is much stronger on this side of the island.

Beach 228, which is broken into several short sections, stretches for ¾ mile along the northwest shore of the island, south of Legoe Bay. Numerous homes are perched atop the steep 50-foot-high bank. The public shorelands, which lie below the mean high-water level, are not marked. Use care not to stray onto property that is signed as private.

Legoe Bay Public Boat Launch

Legoe Bay, on the northwest side of Lummi Island, offers the only public boat launch on the island. The bay is open to winds from the south and west, making it poor for layovers in all but calm weather. A surfaced launch ramp is located at the end of a road stub at the east end of the bay, just below Lovers Bluff. All other ramps and rail launches along Legoe Bay Road are private.

To reach the bay from the ferry landing, head south on Nugent Road and turn west on Legoe Bay Road. In ¾ mile the road reaches the bay, then curves along its shore.

The bay is used by commercial reefnetting fishermen who spread nets between skiffs in shallow water. Lookouts on ladderlike towers on the bow of the boat watch for salmon to swim into the net. When a school of fish is spotted, the corners of the net are drawn in and the fish are scooped up. This method was first devised centuries ago by early Native Americans. Modern technology has added outboard motors and synthetic nets, but the basic method remains the same.

Reefnetters on Legoe Bay practice a centuries-old method of fishing.

BELLINGHAM AND BELLINGHAM BAY

One of the first things a visitor notices when wandering about Bellingham is its oddly mismatched sections of streets. This came about in pioneer times when early settlers along the shores of Bellingham Bay established four separate, rival communities. Whatcom, the first settlement (and the county seat when Whatcom County was established two years later), was the site of a sawmill in 1852. Shortly after the tiny mill on the shores of Whatcom Creek began churning out lumber, the discovery of a seam of coal brought the area a new industry and a new community: Sehome.

For some 25 years, Whatcom and Sehome were the only towns on Bellingham Bay. The Fraser River gold rush and the coming of the transcontinental railroad, along with the supply-and-demand vagaries of the lumber, coal, and fishing industries, kept the area in a constant state of boom or bust. In 1858, at the height of the gold rush, the local population was 15,000, but within a year it had dropped to a few hundred and in 1878, when the Sehome mine was closed, it was a mere 20 determined individuals.

When some 600 Kansans arrived in 1880, they established a third town on the bay: New Whatcom. Three years later the community of Fairhaven was founded. As the boundaries of the four burgeoning towns meshed, consolidation became inevitable, but selection of a name for this new metropolis was hotly disputed, with local residents all fervently pushing the name of their town. In 1903 voters chose a name that pleased few, but offended none: Bellingham, after the bay named some 200 years earlier by Captain George Vancouver to honor some obscure British nobleman.

Today Bellingham is the fourth-largest city on Puget Sound. The pride of the city is Western Washington University, at the base of Mount Sehome. Established in 1899 as one of three state "normal schools" for the training of teachers, it has grown in scope and recognition over the years to become a fully accredited university.

Downtown Bellingham is dominated by the Victorian brick building at 121 Prospect Street that served as a city hall from 1892 to 1936 and that now houses the Whatcom Museum of History and Art. The first ordinance enacted in this building by the city council banned cows from walking the streets between 7:30 P.M. and 6:00 A.M.—the mayor's cow was the first to be incarcerated for violating the law.

A full range of goods and services is available in city stores and nearby malls. Old, ornate turn-of-the-century buildings in the Fairhaven business district have been restored and now house restaurants, craft shops, art galleries, and other interesting places to browse.

A historic building in Bellingham's Fairhaven district

Since earliest times Bellingham has served as a portal for the San Juan Islands. Settlers routinely rowed the 30-plus miles from their island homesteads to Bellingham for supplies, mail, and even a Saturday-night date. With the advent of the steamboats of the Mosquito Fleet, a steady stream of goods and passengers flowed between the islands and their closest mainland point of commerce. Although many visitors now reach the San Juans via the ferry from Anacortes, Bellingham still maintains a strong tie through its marine businesses, with numerous boats chartered or berthed in Bellingham heading regularly for the San Juans.

Bellingham Bay is spacious and deep, and has no navigational hazards. The extreme north end of the bay dwindles into mudflats, but south of these flats anchorages can be found in 6 to 15 fathoms.

Squalicum Harbor (Port of Bellingham)

Facilities: Complete boat and crew facilities and supplies, bait and tackle, laundromat, restrooms, showers, boat launch (ramps and slings), boat rentals and charters, restaurants, educational display, shopping, day-use park, sewage pump-out station

In recent years Bellingham has undertaken a revitalization program. The city's efforts are especially evident at its waterfront on Squalicum Harbor, where spiffy new facilities provide everything a visiting boater may desire. Squalicum Harbor is on the northwest side of the town, west of the industrial area as one enters the bay.

The harbor consists of two large basins, separated by a landfill jetty, that provide moorage for pleasure craft and the local fishing fleet. The moorage to the east is a dredged basin behind a short rock breakwater. Guest moorages are on the two outer floats of the center dock; the first 24 hours are free. Floats by the adjacent boat launch ramp may also be used for overflow moorage.

By land, Squalicum Harbor is reached by leaving I-5 at Exit 253 and proceeding west on Holly Street. On C Street, at the downtown water-

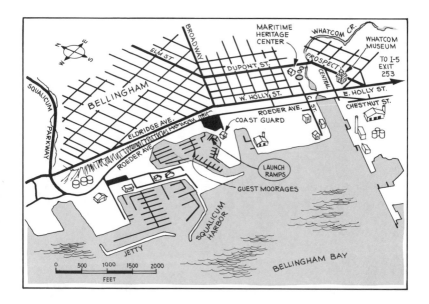

front, turn left, then in one block turn right on Roeder Avenue, which can be followed all the way to the boat basin. The Coast Guard station is located a little before the harbor.

A four-lane concrete launch ramp is adjacent to the Coast Guard station, just off Roeder Avenue on Thomas J. Glenn Drive. Its protected location makes it excellent for launching in all weather; ample parking is nearby.

At the head of this basin is Harbor Marine Center, where visitors can view acres of pleasure boats from planked walkways and elevated decks. A restaurant and other businesses occupy the building. Showers, restrooms, and a laundromat are available for use by visiting boaters. A large open tank at the center of the mall displays local marine life for youngsters to squeal and giggle at.

The boat basin to the west is protected by two overlapping rock jetties; entry is in the center or at the northwest end. All of the commercial fleet is moored here, as well as many permanently berthed pleasure craft. Some guest moorage may be available on the floats at the head of the bay, immediately below the two-story Squalicum Esplanade. The upper level of the elevated walkway affords a panoramic view of the harbor and its bustling activity.

Behind the esplanade are Squalicum and Harbor malls, which house the port offices, a restaurant, and a number of marine-related stores and services, and restrooms with showers. City bus service provides transportation to downtown shopping.

East of this harbor complex, on the jetty protecting the east boat

A rock breakwater protects Squalicum Harbor.

basin, is pleasant little Harbor Point Park. A large grass knoll, with a viewing telescope atop, is surrounded by park benches overlooking the bay and the boat basin. This is a great place to watch the boating activity on all sides and slip goodies to the bevy of squawking gulls that freeload in the area.

Maritime Heritage Center

Access: Land
Facilities: Restrooms, children's play equipment
Attractions: Educational displays

An interesting educational display near the mouth of Whatcom Creek tells you all you may ever have wanted to know about salmon. The facility shows the complete life cycle of the fish, with rearing ponds, a fish ladder, adult holding pens, and a spawning channel arranged around an open concrete terrace. Eggs are fertilized and hatched in an adjacent building. Most activity is in the late fall when fish are spawning.

The center is located on C Street, east of the intersection of Astor, four blocks from the downtown waterfront.

During the rainy season Whatcom Creek pours into the Heritage Center in a dramatic waterfall. Children's play equipment nearby makes this a nice spot for a family outing.

Boulevard Park

Park area: 14 acres; 2,800 feet of shoreline on Bellingham Bay
Access: Land, paddle-craft
Facilities: Picnic tables, shelter, fire grates, restrooms, drinking water, children's play equipment, viewpoint, hiking trail, craft studio
Attractions: Picnicking, beachcombing, paddling, swimming, hiking, fishing, crabbing

Every city should be so fortunate as to have a park as gorgeous as this! Bellingham has made the most of a steep bluff and a swath of beach, by developing it into a two-level showpiece that seems even more spacious than its 14 acres.

The upper section of the park lies along South State Street, on a bluff 75 feet above Bellingham Bay. A display at the overlook tells how British explorer Captain George Vancouver first sailed into the bay.

A path leads from the overlook past a gazebo, over a bridge, and then down a winding wooden staircase to the lower park area. This lower section can also be reached by turning off South State Street, at its intersection with 11th Street, onto Bayview Drive, which curves steeply downhill to the park. At the north end of the park is a short pier, handy for trying your luck at fishing or crabbing. The park closes at 8:00 P.M.

A path from the park goes north, paralleling the railroad tracks, all the way to Wharf Street on the south side of downtown Bellingham. Heading south, a trail crosses an old railroad trestle that has been converted into a fishing pier and viewing site. After continuing along the shore for about two more blocks, the trail dead-ends at a small cove where the stork-legs of old pilings that once supported railroad tracks continue south along the beach.

Harris Avenue Launch Ramp

A second boat launch facility is maintained by the Port of Bellingham on the southwest side of town, within a stone's throw of the Fairhaven business district.

If driving from I-5, turn off at Exit 250 and head west on the Old Fairhaven Parkway. At 12th Street turn right (north), and in three blocks turn left (west) on Harris Avenue. As the street approaches the water-front, a small, inconspicuous sign points to the right to Alaska Ferry auto loading and the public launch ramp. Follow this road; in a short distance it turns right again, paralleling a chain-link fence, and finally arrives at the small launch area.

The single-lane concrete ramp is not as good as the facility at Squalicum Harbor, but it does provide quick access to this side of the bay. Rentals of canoes, kayaks, dories, sailboards, and small sailboats are available at a nearby business.

Bellingham Cruise Center

Access: Land
Facilities: Ferry terminal, restaurant, viewing areas, gift shop, restrooms
Attractions: Historical displays, ferry viewing

In 1989 the Alaska Ferry System pulled up stakes from Seattle's waterfront and moved its southern terminus to Bellingham, lured by the promise of a new terminal. The city made good on its promise with a stunning $6.4 million facility covering 5½ acres on the Fairhaven waterfront. Ferries arrive and depart from here every Friday throughout the year; during the last two weeks of May and the first two weeks of June there are additional sailings on Tuesdays. The terminal is also the home base for other cruise ships, such as the Grayline Tours to Victoria, B.C., and the San Juan Shuttle Express to Orcas Island and Friday Harbor on San Juan Island.

The activity on the ships can be watched from the adjacent pier or from the enclosed glass dome of the terminal. Even if the ferry is not in port, the terminal provides fine views of Bellingham Bay. Historical displays located around the edge of the pier give interesting vignettes of early exploration and development of Bellingham and Fairhaven.

The terminal is reached by continuing west on Harris Avenue past the turnoff for the auto loading area and launch ramp.

Marine Park

Park area: 3 acres; 730 feet of shoreline on Bellingham Bay
Access: Land, paddle-craft
Facilities: Picnic tables, shelter, fireplaces, restrooms, drinking water
Attractions: Picnicking, beach walking

Harris Street continues west past the boat launch turnoff and the Cruise Center, and in about a block dead-ends at Marine Park, another example of Bellingham's dedication to fine parks. The beautifully land-scaped park has tables for picnicking and grassy lawns for afternoon siestas. Strategically placed benches look out to Bellingham Bay and passing marine traffic.

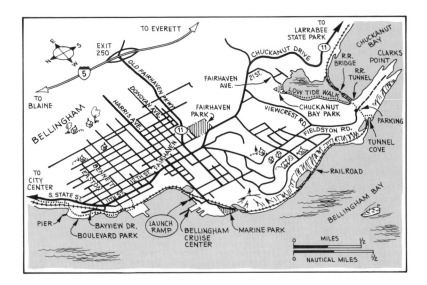

Although there are no boating facilities, small boats can be landed on the gravel beach at low tide, or hand-carried ones could easily be launched. From here you can take to the streets for a brief stint and walk west and north to connect with trails to Boulevard Park.

Chuckanut Bay Park (Undeveloped)

Although this city park is undeveloped at present, it represents an important potential link in the system of trails interlacing Bellingham. When the tide is in, cartop boats can be launched here, and paddlers can duck beneath the railroad trestle that crosses the bay to gain open water. At low tide the long mucky tideflat makes launching impossible.

The site is reached by turning off Chuckanut Drive at 21st Street. In one block, turn right on Fairhaven Avenue and follow it for ½ mile to the park.

After following a narrow, brambly path west from the park, at minus tides inveterate hikers can skirt the edge of steep sandstone cliffs to reach the railroad causeway near the Clarks Point tunnel. The wave-carved sandstone formations at the base of the cliffs, similar to those found on Sucia and other San Juan islands, seem out of place adjacent to this shallow muddy section of bay. Before the railroad causeway was built, however, this section of Chuckanut Bay was a deep, clear basin where winter storm-driven waves lashed against the base of the cliffs. The construction of the trestle and then the causeway, combined with silt generated by logging and the construction of I-5, has altered the bay, changing it to a low-tide mudflat.

Clarks Point Trails

Two short trails at the north end of Clarks Point offer public access to Chuckanut and Bellingham bays. Both start from a day-use parking area on a rocky bluff above the bore of the railroad tunnel. A sign at the parking area describes public lands and parks in the vicinity, and tells the history of Clarks Point and the Great Northern Railroad's Chuckanut cutoff. Public access is limited to the trails.

The trailheads can be reached by leaving I-5 at Exit 250 and taking Old Fairhaven Parkway west to Chuckanut Drive; turn left onto Chuckanut Drive. Follow Chuckanut Drive to 1¾ miles south of the Old Fairhaven Parkway and turn right (west) onto Viewcrest Road. Follow the road for 1 mile, then turn left (south) onto Fieldston Road and reach the trailheads in ½ mile.

The trail to the east wanders through thick brush and a canopy of overhanging small trees to the edge of the bluff at the northwest corner of Chuckanut Bay. Here the trail steepens, and finally a staircase leads down to the railroad causeway at the east end of the tunnel. This is the west end of the low-tide hike from Chuckanut Bay Park, described above.

The trail to the west is more open, and ends at a grass-covered rocky bluff with a smattering of second-growth timber that frames views across Bellingham Bay. A steep path on the south side of the bluff drops down to a very narrow, rocky beach.

A delicate flower clings to a rocky niche on Chuckanut Bay.

Chuckanut Bay

A *Chuckanut* is not some kind of local tree, as one might suspect, but an Indian word believed to mean "small cliffy bay next to big bay"—certainly an appropriate description for this site.

Paddlers who gain access to Chuckanut Bay by hand-carrying boats to the beach at Chuckanut Bay Park, or the launch ramp at Larrabee State Park just around the corner to the south, can explore rocky shorelines and tiny islands that dot the long bay.

Larger boats, too, will find the bay was made to order for gunk-holing, with several little bays offering ample space for anchoring. Aptly named Pleasant Bay, at the extreme south end of Chuckanut Bay, is well protected from southerly winds. A rock ledge, 3 feet below the surface, has been reported just south of Chuckanut Island.

At the center of the bay, Chuckanut Island is a wildlife preserve of The Nature Conservancy. The island's thick vegetation includes grand fir, madrona, western red cedar, and some Douglas-fir that are more than 250 years old. Two bald eagles nest on the island, and numerous other species of birds frequent its shores and uplands. The intertidal regions serve as a study area for marine biologists. The 5-acre island was donated to The Nature Conservancy by the family of the late Cyrus Gates; the preserve is named in his honor.

Larrabee State Park

Park area: 2,501 acres; 8,100 feet of shoreline on Samish Bay
Access: Land, boat
Facilities: 53 standard campsites, 26 RV sites, 8 walk-in sites, 3 primitive sites, group camp, group day-use areas, picnic tables, fireplaces, kitchens, picnic shelters, amphitheater, restrooms, showers, trailer dump station, boat launch (ramp), hiking trails
Attractions: Camping, boating, paddling, fishing, swimming, crabbing, tidepools, waterskiing, scuba diving, hiking, bicycling

Although most of Larrabee State Park lies inland, embracing the steep slopes of Chuckanut Mountain, a small corner of it touches the shoreline of Samish Bay. This corner contains most of the park's facilities, including the campground, picnic area, and amphitheater. The boat launch ramp is in an adjacent section of the park, reached by a separate road.

The state park is 5 miles south of Bellingham on Chuckanut Drive, or it can be reached by leaving I-5 at Exit 231 (signed to Highway 11 and Chuckanut Drive) and driving north.

The camping and picnic area lies in a narrow section between Chuckanut Drive and the railroad tracks. RV sites with hookups are spaced fairly closely together; tenting sites have a bit more privacy. Trails to the beach cross the railroad tracks or reach the shore via a tunnel.

At the intersection with Cove Road, ¼ mile north of the park entrance, a sign points west to the boat launch. The single-lane ramp is very steep, but well surfaced. Parking nearby is adequate for a dozen vehicles with trailers. Vault toilets are located beside the parking area. Wildcat Cove, into which the ramp empties, is small and rock-rimmed—unsuited for large boats. The cove has two sections separated by a rocky rib. At moderate to low tides, enough gravel beach is revealed to permit beach towels to be spread for sunbathing, or the waters to be tested for wading.

Another corner of the park touches the shore a mile to the south, but at this point the bluff is so steep that there is no upland access from the road. The beach below can be reached by boat or by walking the shore at low tide. Explore tidepools along the way, and marvel at the variety of wondrous creatures.

Steeply tilted layers of sandstone interbedded with lenses of shale are exposed along the shorelines of the park. Fossils of large palm leaves believed to be 60 million years old have been found in the shale deposits.

Larrabee State Park offers several miles of inland hiking trails on the slopes of Chuckanut Mountain. The trail up the mountainside is steep, gaining over 1,500 feet, but the reward of crystal mountain lakes and lookout points with panoramic vistas makes the effort worthwhile. For low-level leg stretching, the Interurban Trail, which begins in the park, runs north for 5½ miles all the way to Bellingham with no appreciable elevation gain. The wide, surfaced path is suitable for both hikers and bicyclists. The trailhead for both the route up Chuckanut Mountain and the Interurban Trail is on the east side of Chuckanut Drive, across from the state park entrance.

To gain the views without the exercise, drive a mile north of the park entrance and turn east on High Line Road, which becomes Fred Cleator Road after crossing the Interurban Trail. This rough gravel road winds uphill for 3½ miles to the Cyrus Gates overlook, a parking lot with views across Bellingham Bay to the San Juan Islands. A short trail from the first switchback below the overlook leads to a viewpoint looking east down a steep wooded face to Lost Lake and, in the distance beyond, Mount Baker.

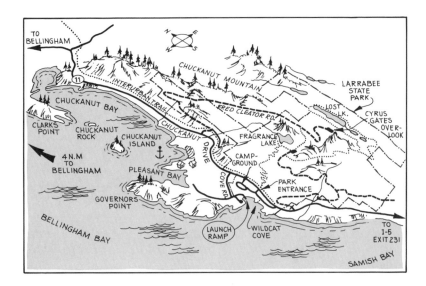

A canoeist surveys the rugged shoreline of Larrabee State Park.

The state park holds a distinctive spot in history—it was established on 20 acres of land donated by the Larrabee family, and was Washington's first state park. Additional donations and land purchases over the years have brought it to its present size.

ELIZA, VENDOVI, AND SINCLAIR ISLANDS

Three moderate-sized islands lying at the front door to Bellingham Bay are privately owned and have little to attract tourists, although their bays and shorelines offer some interesting boat exploration.

Eliza Island

This island, which lies closest to Bellingham, is the most settled of the three. Small planes that land at an airstrip down the middle of the island bring landowners to their vacation retreats. Shoals and numerous rocks lie off the east and west sides of the triangular-shaped island—visiting boaters should approach with care. A large open bight at the south end, facing the southern tip of Lummi Island, offers some anchorages, although the holding ground is poor and the bay is exposed to southerly blows.

The only public area on Eliza Island is a DNR beach at the extreme southern tip; however, the shores are so rocky, and the beach so small, that few boaters would care to approach, even in small craft. Eliza Rock, which lies just offshore to the south, and Viti Rocks, ¾ mile southwest of the southern tip of Lummi Island, are both part of the San Juan Islands National Wildlife Refuge. Avoid approaching so close to either area that nesting birds are disturbed.

Vendovi Island

The most primitive of the three islands is Vendovi, lying 2 nautical miles southwest of Eliza. Its shorelines are smooth and rocky, except for a small bay on its northwest point. All of the island's shorelines, with the exception of those facing immediately on the bay, comprise DNR Beach 214; the public area lies below the mean high-water level. The beaches are rocky, with some pretty little pocket coves. All the uplands are conspicuously posted with no trespassing signs—inland, snarling mastiffs presumably lie in wait.

Sinclair Island

Sinclair Island, which at about 1½ square miles is the largest of the three, is the only one to have real roads. It lies at the north end of Bellingham Channel, 1½ miles west of Vendovi Island.

Although most of the island property is private, some limited access to the uplands is possible. A short county dock protected by a piling breakwater is on the southwest end of the island at the community of Urban. Overnight moorage is not permitted on the dock, but anchoring in the open coves to the north and south of the dock is possible. There are no commercial facilities on shore.

The island was named by the Wilkes Expedition of 1841, although locally it was known as Cottonwood Island for the number of those trees that were found there. In the 1890s settlers arrived at the island,

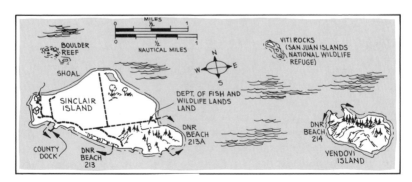

claiming property under the Homestead Act. Most were fishermen and farmers; gnarled fruit trees from orchards planted by these early farmers can still be found on the island.

Rocks and a large shoal extend out from Sinclair Island on the north and west, reaching almost to Boulder Reef, ¾ nautical mile away. This dangerous reef, which bares at half tide, is marked by a lighted bell buoy. Kelp that surrounds the reef, giving further warning of danger, is often towed under by the current.

DNR Beach 213 extends east from the Sinclair Island dock for about a mile. It includes some tiny pocket coves and rocky beaches below a 60-foot bluff—when the uplands dip down and shorelines gentle, the public beach ends. Public beach is only that area below the mean high-water level.

DNR Beach 213A encompasses 2,831 feet of shoreline at the southeastern tip of the island. The northern portion of this beach joins to Washington State Department of Fish and Wildlife lands, where visitors can extend their beach explorations with an upland nature walk through a small marshland. The Department of Fish and Wildlife lands can also be reached by walking east from the county dock for about 1½ miles. The public land lies south of the road near the east shore.

CYPRESS ISLAND

The natural riches of Cypress Island include six small spring-fed lakes, several marshes, three excellent harbors, magnificent fortresslike cliffs and forested mountains reaching to 1,500 feet. More than 80 species of birds and a dozen species of mammals are known to live here, including bald eagle, hawk, deer, fox, river otter, raccoon, porcupine, muskrat, and weasel. An important peregrine falcon nesting site is in the vicinity of Eagle Cliff. The unusual geological strata of the island support a great variety of flora; however, one notable tree is missing—there are no cypress on Cypress Island. Captain George Vancouver erroneously named the island when he identified the local juniper trees as cypress.

Ferry travelers have an excellent view of the island as the boat leaves the Anacortes ferry terminal; the island's southern tip lies just 2½ nautical miles to the north, across Guemes Channel. The northwest shore is a popular salmon fishing ground, and cruising boaters sometimes drop anchor along the eastern shore in Eagle Harbor or Deepwater Bay. Beaches and uplands on Deepwater Bay are privately owned.

At Eagle Harbor, roads that head inland from the concrete launch ramp at the southwest side are open to public access. A 2-mile road hike to the northwest reaches Duck Lake. To the southwest, a rather steep climb passes Reid Lake and continues uphill to the west to a spur road that in 1¾ miles reaches Phebe Lake (shown as Cypress Lake on some maps). Soaring, 100- to 200-foot-high cliffs surround the 15-acre lake, except at its drainage. Venturesome hikers can follow a road spur found 500 feet east of the lake road that swings east, then branches. The right fork climbs another 1¼ miles to a forested pocket enclosing Bradberry Lake, while the fork to the east traverses the hillside ½ mile to the site of a former airstrip, with wide views down the step wooded hillside to the east to Bellingham Channel. Additional road walks lead south across the steep wooded hillside for another 2½ miles to reach the south end of the island. Views along this road are few, but the hike is pleasant.

Land ownership on Cypress Island has had a controversial history. The island escaped early settlement due to its steep terrain and scarcity of water. Attempts at mining failed, and the land proved too harsh for agriculture. Over the years, private individuals acquired some small sections, and a few residences were built, primarily on Strawberry Bay.

Between 1960 and 1978 a Seattle realtor purchased property totaling about half of the island's 5,500 acres. Although he considered developing it as a site for a nuclear plant or oil port, in the mid 1970s he began negotiations for sale of the land to the state DNR. A plan was set forth by the DNR, requiring a then-staggering $10 million for purchase of the property and other holdings on Cypress Island.

Negotiations stalled, and in September 1978 another private entrepreneur purchased a majority of the property for $1.8 million. In the ensuing years plans were set forth first for a 1,000-unit exclusive residential development, then for a posh resort with a 200-room lodge, condominiums, a marina, and an 18-hole golf course. Both proposals eventually received initial permits by the Skagit County commissioners; however, they were fiercely opposed by local people and environmen-

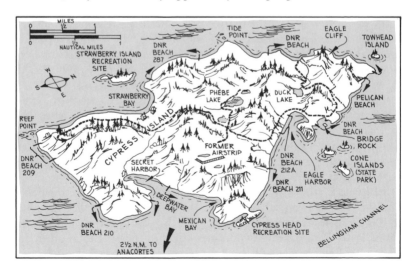

talists who realized the tragic effect such a large commercial development would have on the pristine island and the surrounding area.

In 1987, due largely to this public pressure, the land was offered for sale to the state. The Legislature approved funds for its purchase and 3,176 acres of the island were acquired for $5.3 million— well below its appraised value. This, along with an additional 1,000 acres that the state acquired later, and previously owned property and tidelands, gives the state title to 42,000 acres—nearly 80 percent of the island. Cypress Island is at last saved for the future. Current state plans are to have only limited recreational development. Existing jeep roads are used as trails. Camp

Anchorage at Cypress Head

ing is permitted only at three existing campgrounds at Strawberry Island, Pelican Beach, and Cypress Head.

Strawberry (Loon) Island Recreation Site

Area: 11 acres; 4,000 feet of shoreline on Rosario Strait and Strawberry Bay
Access: Boat
Facilities: 3 campsites, picnic tables, fire grates, vault toilets, *no water* (Designated Cascadia Marine Trail campsite)
Attractions: Boating, paddling, scuba diving

A ¼-mile-long narrow ridge of an island just off Strawberry Bay on the west side of Cypress Island is the site of a primitive DNR campground. Strawberry Island, like other small park islands such as Saddlebag and James islands, has a familiar "dog bone" configuration, with two high, rounded shoulders of land joined by a low, narrow neck—in this case the northern shoulder is considerably larger and higher than the southern one, more like an exclamation point. The island offers a few picnicking and camping sites along with pleasant shoreline scrambles and views of boats parading past in Rosario Strait.

The shores of the main section of the island are so steep that going ashore there is quite difficult. The only landing for small boats is at a sandy cove on the west side of the island between the small southern knob and the remainder of the island. Offshore waters, which are quite deep, have defied attempts to place buoys. Boaters in large craft should anchor in Strawberry Bay and dinghy across to the recreation site.

Strawberry Bay was visited in 1792 by William Broughton of the Vancouver Expedition. Lieutenant Broughton, who first explored the inner channels of the San Juan Islands, anchored his brig *Chatham* here, and was delighted to find great numbers of wild strawberries on shore. Some days later, when Vancouver stopped over in the same spot at Broughton's recommendation, the strawberries were out of season, and his crew had to settle for wild onions. (Be grateful it's not named Onion Bay.)

Cypress Head Recreation Area

Area: 16.5 acres; 4,800 feet of shoreline on Bellingham Channel
Access: Boat
Facilities: 8 campsites, 2 picnic sites, fire rings, mooring buoys, vault
  toilets, *no water* (Designated Cascadia Marine Trail campsite)
Attractions: Boating, paddling, fishing

The tiny peninsula of Cypress Head lies on the easternmost bulge of Cypress Island. The wooded headland, which is joined to its parent island by a low grassy sandspit, has been developed by the DNR as a boat-in recreation area, with picnic facilities and overnight campsites.

This pretty little spot is only 4 nautical miles from the boat launch ramp at Sunset Beach on Fidalgo Island, making it an ideal cruising destination. The long south-facing bay formed by the head is quite shallow and has a rock near the entrance; use care entering. The northern cove, which holds the four mooring buoys, is somewhat deeper. Boats too large to be beached must tie to a buoy or drop a hook. Good anchorages can be found in 20 to 30 feet of water.

The rocky head has five campsites with tables and fireplaces, and two additional day-use sites that are too rocky for spreading a sleeping bag. On a grassy flat on the mainland are three additional campsites. A chain-link fence marks the western boundary of the recreation area.

A rough trail circles the outer edge of Cypress Head, passing vistas gorgeously framed by twisted madrona and juniper. Beaches are rocky; in a few spots it is possible to scramble down the steep, 10-foot-high bank to reach the shore.

Cypress Head Recreation Area also leads to some 3 miles of public tidelands. DNR Beach 211, which is 15,652 feet in total length, including the Cypress Head tidelands, extends north from Cypress Head for about 1 mile and southwest to the middle of the north shore of Deepwater Bay. The western boundary is marked by a row of old pilings. Low tide reveals some nice beach scrambles and a small pocket cove, but at high tide the beach is almost nonexistent—don't get caught at the wrong spot on an incoming tide! All uplands, except for Cypress Head, are private.

Pelican Beach and Eagle Cliff

Area: 220 acres; 7,207 feet of shoreline on Bellingham Channel
Access: Boat
Facilities: 5 campsites, fire rings, picnic tables, picnic shelter, vault toilets, 3 mooring buoys, hiking trails, *no water* (Designated Cascadia Marine Trail campsite)
Attractions: Boating, paddling, fishing, swimming, scuba diving, hiking, beachcombing

The finest parcel of DNR land on Cypress Island is a forested strip spanning the far northern end of the island. On the eastern shore is Pelican Beach, a beautiful little boat-in campground, on the west is the spectacular rocky face of 750-foot-high Eagle Cliff, and between the two is a swath of deep woods holding a few miles of hiking trails for exploration and enchantment.

Pelican Beach has three mooring buoys offshore and five formal campsites just beyond the high-tide level. The gently sloping gravelly shore invites wading (chilly) or sunbathing among the driftwood (warm). At

The sheer face of Eagle Cliff rises above the north end of Cypress Island.

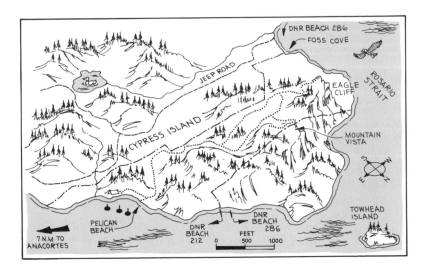

its northern boundary the beach becomes quite rocky. The shore, with its countless little tidepools, can be followed for some distance around the point. However, explorers need to be aware that they can become trapped between an incoming tide and the steep, high bank. Public DNR beaches extend all the way around the north end of the island for 1½ miles to the south side of Foss Cove. South of Pelican Beach public DNR tidelands continue south for ½ mile to Bridge Rock, opposite the Cone Islands.

Leaving the campground, the trail that heads inland and crosses the island rises gradually, but steadily, through open second-growth timber. In ¼ mile a fork is reached. The left leg, signed to Duck Lake, ties into the inland road network for more extensive hiking; from Duck Lake one path leads west to Foss Cove, on the northwest side to the island. The leg to the right, heads to Eagle Cliff, 1¼ miles away. The upper portion of the trail to Eagle Cliff follows a sparsely wooded ridge to the final rocky outcropping of the summit. Look down to Foss Cove on the west side of Cypress Island and out to toylike boats bobbing in Rosario Strait. The masses of Orcas and Blakely islands fill the view to the west. The viewpoint is not a place for toddlers or persons afflicted with vertigo. The Eagle Cliff trail is closed to hikers between February 1 and July 15 to protect a peregrine falcon nesting area.

Cypress Island DNR Beaches

In addition to the public DNR beaches described above at Cypress Head and Pelican Beach, a few other stretches of Cypress Island tidelands are available to the public.

Beach 212A begins at the south side of Eagle Harbor and extends south for 2,118 feet. This very pretty beach has a row of driftwood at the high-tide level and gentles out into a sandy flat at low tide.

Beach 210 encircles the knob at the southeast end of the island, but the shore drops off so steeply that "beach" is virtually nonexistent, even at low tide.

Beach 209 more than makes up for it, however—located on the south side of the island, east of Reef Point, this 1,635-foot-long beach includes a broad sand and gravel tideflat that extends out for some distance at extreme low water.

A final DNR beach, number 287, which is 8,872 feet in length, lies due north of Strawberry Island. Several small caves caused by wave undercutting make this shoreline especially interesting.

Cone Islands State Park (Undeveloped)

Park area: 9.9 acres; 2,500 feet of shoreline on Bellingham Channel
Access: Boat
Facilities: None
Attractions: Scuba diving, paddling, birdwatching

Cone Islands are a cluster of three miniature forested islands and low-tide rocks lying off the northeast shore of Cypress Island. Two of these islands—the largest and southernmost ones—are undeveloped state park lands. Because their steep, rocky shores drop sharply into the water and surrounding kelp beds, most boaters are content to enjoy the is-

The islets and rocks of the Cone Islands are undeveloped state parks.

lands from the distance as they cruise by, although scuba divers sometimes stop and explore from anchored boats. The island walls are so abrupt that going ashore is nearly impossible.

The northernmost of the islands has especially interesting geology, displaying tilted beds of shale along its east side.

Camping is just 1 nautical mile to the northwest at Pelican Beach on Cypress Island. The nearest boat launch ramp is at Washington Park on Fidalgo Island, 5½ nautical miles south.

GUEMES ISLAND

Although separated only by mile-wide Bellingham Channel, neighboring Cypress and Guemes islands are totally different in character. While Cypress Island is steep, rocky, and densely wooded, with deeply notched bays and cliffy shores, Guemes is a rural setting, with wide expanses of flatland and a long, smooth shoreline.

Guemes Island would be just another Anacortes suburb were it not for the ½-mile-wide water barrier of Guemes Channel that serves to keep urban sprawl and industrial boom at arm's length. In the 1960s the island was eyed as a prospective site for an aluminum processing plant; however, the negative reaction of residents sent developers look-

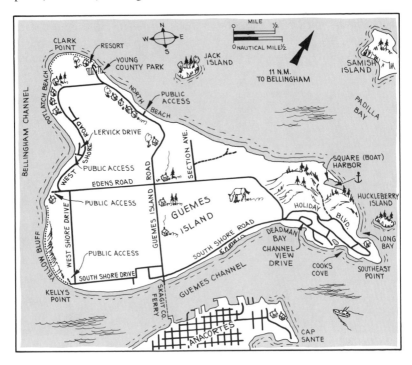

ing elsewhere. The island remains quietly pastoral, providing sanctuary for retirees, artists, farmers, summer vacationers, and Fidalgo Island workers who commute daily from their homes.

The little Skagit County-operated ferry scurries back and forth across the channel like a busy water bug, carrying a few cars on its open deck each trip. The voyage takes about 10 minutes; runs are made half-hourly during morning and evening commute hours, and hourly throughout the rest of the day. The ferry leaves from a terminal in downtown Anacortes at Sixth and I streets.

A ferry has been serving the island since the early 1900s, first carrying horses, wagons, and farm produce. Some horses were so wary of the watery crossing that they had to be blindfolded—not so the Model Ts, however, when they began riding in the 1920s. The first fares were 50 cents for car and driver, 10 cents for milk cans, passengers free. One resident became so incensed when the ferry began charging five cents for foot passengers that from then on he rowed across the channel.

Guemes is ideal bicycling country, with straight and level interior roads that pass by farmlands and orchards, while perimeter roads wind around the shores, with views out to cool sea and distant mist-shrouded islands. The only commercial development is a small resort on the northern tip of the island. There are no boat launch ramps on the island, although hand-carried boats can be put in at several spots.

Guemes Island has a refreshing approach to public use of lands: Here a few beaches are posted as OPEN SPACE. Owners of such lands permit public recreational use as long as such use is compatible with its natural state—in other words, observe posted fire regulations, do not litter, and do not deface or destroy either personal property or natural features. The areas at Kellys Point and Clark Point are presently open space. If their status changes, do not trespass—look elsewhere for recreational land.

Young County Park (Skagit County) and Clark Point

Park area: 11 acres; 500 feet of shoreline on Padilla Bay
Access: Land, paddle-craft
Facilities: Picnic tables, fire grates, Sani-can
Attractions: Picnicking, paddling, clam digging, swimming

A small county park at the north end is Guemes Island's only public recreation site. It faces on a nice driftwood-edged beach and a gradual, gravel tideflat. Tiny Jack Island, ¾ mile due east, is an enticing small-boat destination. Even shallow-draft boats should approach the park with care at minus tide to avoid getting mired on the flat.

To find Young County Park by land, drive north from the ferry landing on Guemes Island Road. The county park is at the road's end in 4½ miles.

The small resort adjacent to the county park has some campsites, RV hookups with water and power, a swimming pool, a few cabins, rental boats, and a store that sells basic groceries and fuel.

Nearly 2 miles of beautiful clean gravel beach wrap around Clark Point to the north, providing terrific views first into Bellingham Bay, then north to Sinclair, Vendovi, and Lummi islands, and finally swinging westward to lovely little Cone Islands and the rumpled mountains of Cypress Island.

To reach the beach, walk north from the resort. As it nears the point, the beach narrows, but it should be passable at all but the highest tides or during heavy wave action. The bank above the beach is steep and heavily wooded, and there is no inland egress, so use care not to get trapped by high water. Open space ends at private property on Potlatch Beach on the eastern side of the point.

Square Harbor, on the east side of Guemes Island, is an ideal anchorage.

North Beach Public Access

On the east side of Guemes Island, facing on a huge tideflat, is a densely settled area of beach-front homes and summer cottages, reminiscent of the south end of Hood Canal. A 40-foot-wide Department of Fish and Wildlife public access to the beach is provided here for clam diggers.

Traveling north on Guemes Island Road, 1½ miles north of Edens Road, watch carefully amid the cottages for a small turnoff on the east side of the road, just south of the house at 427 Guemes Island Road. Hand-carried boats can be launched here, but nearby parking is limited, and property on both sides of the access is private.

Long Bay and Square Harbor (Boat Harbor)

Nearly all the shoreline of Guemes Island is smooth, with long tideflats. The one exception is at the southeast end where slightly mountainous terrain signals steeper underwater walls. Two small bights are located along this shore. The more southerly of these bights, Long Bay, near Southeast Point, offers boaters some anchoring possibilities, although it is quite open.

An even better anchorage is at sublime little Square Harbor, a mile to the north. The 500-yard-wide rocky inlet has space for two or three boats with good protection from all weather except easterlies. It is a handy, secluded spot when nearby Saddlebag Island is filled to overflowing. The bay is easily located by the 100-foot-high sheer, barren cliff immediately to the north. The beach and all uplands on the bay are private.

Kellys Point

On the southwest corner of Guemes Island, at the intersection of South Shore Drive and West Shore Drive, a short road spur continues west to a beautiful gravel and driftwood beach facing Bellingham Channel. The beach can be walked north for more than a mile, beneath the imposing 150-foot scarp of Yellow Bluff. Climbing on the bluff or digging caves can be hazardous, because the bank is composed of soft glacial till and can collapse. Note the numerous holes that birds (probably kingfishers) have burrowed in the hillside.

This is said to be a good beach for finding agates—jasper, carnelian, and aventurine can be collected here as well as numerous other stones, some unique to the area. Many residents have extensive collections of agates gleaned from Guemes Island beaches.

The point is named after the notorious outlaw, Lawrence "Smuggler" Kelly, who had a hideout here in the late 1800s. Kelly brought illegal Chinese aliens into the country from Canada, as well as cargoes of opium and wool, which were heavily taxed at the time.

Guemes Island Road Ends

Two road ends on the west side of Guemes Island provide spots to put in hand-launched boats. Each has parking for a few cars.

Edens Road. From Kellys Point, West Shore Drive heads due north, and in 1½ miles ends at a T intersection with Edens Road. Turn west and in 200 yards, where the main road turns north and becomes West Shore Road, continue straight ahead for another short distance to the dead end at the beach. The beach access is west between adjacent private property.

Lervick Drive. A short side street heads left ¾ mile north of the Edens Road/West Shore Road intersection. In a short distance a large log blocks the road end at the beach, but the street turns north and briefly continues to some private homes. The road end offers a narrow beach access between private property on either side.

SAMISH BAY AND SAMISH ISLAND

Samish Bay, a 2-mile-wide lobe on the southern edge of Bellingham Bay, bares for nearly half its extent during low water. Most boaters avoid its shallow waters; however, it does offer some fine paddling opportunities.

During migratory season Samish Bay is as good as Padilla Bay, to the south, for sighting a variety of waterfowl. Great blue herons from the rookery on Samish Island frequent the flats, and visitors are virtually assured of seeing these large, elegant birds. Flocks of black brant, canvasbacks, and Eurasian widgeons winter here; snowy owls, peregrine falcons, and gyrfalcons may be spotted on shore.

The Samish Bay area was the site of an early utopian settlement. Equality Colony, established near Blanchard on the north edge of the delta,

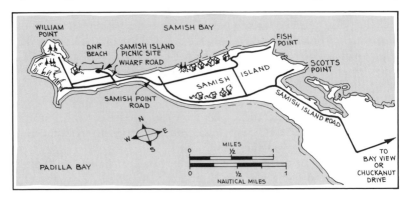

was active from 1898 to 1907. All that remains of the now-disbanded socialist group is a small cemetery. Colony Creek, whose name reflects this early settlement, flows into Samish Bay.

Samish Island Picnic Site

Park area: 0.5 acre; 1,436 feet of shoreline on Samish Bay
Access: Land, paddle-craft
Facilities: 3 picnic tables, vault toilets, *no water*
Attractions: Beachcombing, paddling, scuba diving

When the last land-shaping glaciers withdrew from Puget Sound, Samish Island was two islands. Today it is a peninsula, joined to the mainland by necks of sand. The huge flat delta lands adjoining Samish Island were built up by the Skagit River, which now enters the sound several miles to the south. On the drive through the Samish Flats, watch for the many birds that pause here in their migratory flights; hawks, falcons, eagles, and a variety of passerines frequently can be seen.

To drive to Samish Island, leave I-5 at Exit 231, which is signed to Highway 11 and Chuckanut Drive. After leaving I-5, in 5 miles turn west on Sunset Road, in 1¾ miles at a T intersection, head north on Highway 237. In ¾ mile turn west on Bay View–Edison Road. In 1 mile the road heads south and becomes Samish Island Road. Follow this main road through various turns to Wharf Road, turn north on it, and in ¼ mile reach the picnic site.

The small park with three picnic tables is perched at the top of an 80-foot bank. A short trail followed by a set of stairs descends steeply to the shore. The public beach extends west from the stairs. Low tide reveals a cobble shore and the massive tideflats of Samish Bay, but at high water there is no beach. Views are north to Hale Passage and Eliza and Lummi islands, and across to the rocky cliffs of Chuck-anut Drive. The summit of Mount Baker peeks over the horizon.

Great blue herons nest on Samish Island. (Heidi Mueller photo)

CHAPTER THREE

FIDALGO ISLAND AND PADILLA BAY

Fidalgo seems barely an island at all, lying so close that bridges bind it to the mainland and provide easy access to mainland conveniences. Yet it has an island's advantages of mile upon mile of shoreline, with beaches and bays to suit every purpose, and that sense of unique character that only true physical separation, and not political boundaries, can create.

The island is divided into three distinct sections, or "lobes." The southeastern lobe, bordered on the east by the Swinomish Channel and on the west by Skagit and Similk bays, is almost entirely comprised of the Swinomish Indian Reservation. Waterfront property on the west shore and at Shelter Bay on the southeastern tip is leased by the tribe to non-Indians for homes and vacation cottages. The heavily forested interior is selectively logged.

The long amoebaelike foot of March Point, extending into the tideflats of Fidalgo and Padilla bays, occupies most of the middle section of the

The 100-yard-wide waterway of Swinomish Channel separates Fidalgo Island from the mainland.

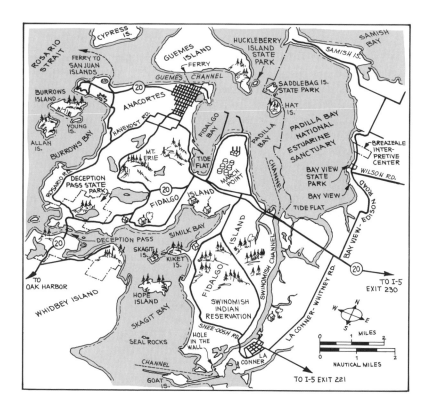

island. Huge storage tanks and oil refineries with billowing smoke stacks and flaming gas vents seem strange bedfellows to the small farms dotting the surrounding lands. Although the refineries, with their pipelines and steady parade of oil tankers, make environmentalists queasy, refinery jobs and the associated economic contribution are generally welcome by Fidalgo Islanders, and the factories have thus far remained environmentally "clean." However, there are those who fear that the refineries herald encroaching industrialism in the environmentally sensitive Skagit Delta and pristine shores of nearby islands.

The western lobe of the island, its largest section, displays the true "San Juan" character, with rugged shorelines, glacier-scrubbed granite domes, and pocket lakes nestled in the folds of forested hills. Here, in its several public parks, visitors can explore beaches and bluffs to their hearts' content and gaze out to the enticing shores of myriad islands.

Fidalgo Island is reached by following Highway 20 west from I-5 Exit 230, just north of Mount Vernon. In 8¼ miles the soaring, 75-foot-high arch of a concrete bridge crosses the Swinomish Channel onto Fidalgo Island. In 4 miles more, at Sharpes Corner at the end of Fidalgo Bay, the highway splits at a Y. Both branches of the Y are still Highway

20. The right leg goes north for 2½ miles more to Anacortes, while the left branch heads southwest, reaching Deception Pass State Park in 6½ miles. A bridge over the Swinomish Channel at La Conner also crosses to Fidalgo Island, connecting with roads up the center and along the west shore of the Indian reservation.

The island can be reached from the south by taking the ferry from Mukilteo to Clinton on Whidbey Island and driving north on Highway 525 (which at mid-island becomes Highway 20) for a distance of 50 miles to the Deception Pass bridge. The ferry from Port Townsend to Keystone on Whidbey Island provides access to the island from the Olympic Peninsula.

Fidalgo Island's two unique waterways, the Swinomish Channel and Deception Pass, serve as boating portals to the San Juan Islands and Canada's Gulf Islands for hordes of pleasure vessels traveling up Saratoga Passage from Puget Sound. The southern entrance to Swinomish Channel is about 50 nautical miles from Shilshole Bay in Seattle, and Deception Pass is 6 nautical miles farther.

PADILLA BAY

Huckleberry Island State Park (Undeveloped)

Park area: 10 acres; 2,900 feet of shoreline on Padilla Bay
Access: Boat
Facilities: None
Attractions: Kayaking, scuba diving

Centered in the channel between the southeast corner of Guemes Island and Saddlebag Island is small, steep-walled Huckleberry Island, an undeveloped piece of state park property. The only accessible shoreline lies in a break in its precipitous shores on the south side of the island. Here a wide gravel beach lies below a high bluff. Water off this beach is less than 2 fathoms deep, and dotted with submerging rocks, so it is not a particularly appealing spot for large boats. However, it does make a nice spot for a lunch break for passing kayakers.

Saddlebag Island Marine State Park

Park area: 23 acres; 6,750 feet of shoreline on Padilla Bay
Access: Boat
Facilities: Campsites, picnic tables, fireplaces, pit toilets, *no water* (Designated Cascadia Marine Trail campsite)
Attractions: Fishing, crabbing, scuba diving, hiking

Conveniently located only 2 nautical miles northeast of Anacortes, near the mouth of Padilla Bay, Saddlebag Island Marine State Park is

Saddlebag Island Marine State Park is a popular stopover for boaters.

heavily used by boaters who drop by for the day to try their hand at crabbing and fishing, and by those on their way to somewhere else who use its coves as handy anchorages. For visitors who take the time to go ashore, the trails that circle the island's grassy bluffs give boaters a chance to steady their sea legs and enjoy bird's-eye views of the activity below: sailboats with bright spinnakers looking like flowers blowing in the wind, fishing boats drifting offshore, and behemoth tankers heading for the oil refinery at March Point. Dot Island, just a clam toss away from Saddle-

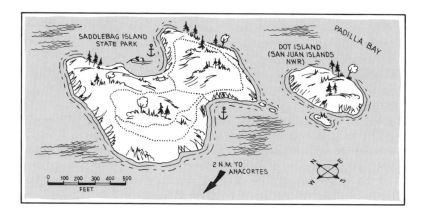

bag, is a bird nesting area and animal refuge of the San Juan Islands National Wildlife Refuge.

Saddlebag Island is cast in the familiar San Juan pattern of two rocky, scrub-covered headlands joined by a low, narrow neck, creating the outline that inspired this island's name. The two coves formed on either side of the landmass face north and south, with the northern one slightly larger and more deeply indented.

The water east of the island is extremely shallow—approach from the west, especially during a minus tide. There are no mooring buoys at the park; however, numerous good anchorages are available. The best are in the northern cove. The southern cove is shallower, with a thick growth of eelgrass, making it difficult for anchors to dig in.

A small camp area is at the head of the northern bay; pit toilets are along the trail that crosses the middle of the island. The southern bay has space for picnicking on the beach. Two Cascadia Marine Trail tent sites are on the south side, above the narrow driftwood-choked beach.

Saddlebag, Dot, and Hat islands are perched on the edge of a huge submarine shelf; to the east is less than a fathom of water, while immediately west the shelf plummets to a depth of 30 to 40 fathoms. The rich variety of marine organisms living on the long flat and in niches of the steep walls of the shelf make this a feeding area for seabirds, fish, crabs, and even the local river otters.

Padilla Bay National Estuarine Sanctuary

Area: 11,600 acres
Access: Land, paddle-craft (limited)
Facilities: (At Breazeale Padilla Bay Interpretive Center, see below)
Attractions: Paddling, fishing, crabbing, birdwatching

Until recently most boaters have looked on Padilla Bay as just a place to hurry through quickly—the huge shoal areas marked on marine charts were enough to give any sea captain nightmares. Now, thanks to the dedicated work of some Skagit County residents, the bay has received recognition as the ecological phenomenon that it is, and more and more people are pausing to learn about and enjoy the estuary.

Padilla Bay lies in a protected pocket between Fidalgo and Guemes islands and the mainland. The north end of the Swinomish Channel is dredged along the western edge of the bay. In 1980 a large section of the bay was established as a National Estuarine Sanctuary, encompassing 11,600 acres of marsh and tidelands stretching along the east side of the bay from the Swinomish Channel to Samish Island. The vegetation, marine creatures, fish, birds, and mammals living in this area are all part of an important ecological system that has been preserved in its natural state for study and for the benefit of future generations.

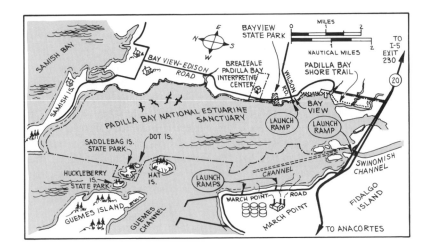

Twice yearly Padilla Bay hosts large populations of black brant. These small geese with a particular palate dine almost exclusively on eelgrass and sea lettuce such as that found in huge beds in the brackish water of the bay. By late October they begin to arrive, pausing to feed on their way to wintering grounds in Baja California. A small number remain to winter in the bay. In early spring the large populations return, flying in long wavering lines, to again refuel on the bay's vegetation before the final leg of their trip to nesting grounds on the Alaska Peninsula.

To reach the sanctuary by land, leave I-5 at Exit 230, just north of Mount Vernon, and follow Highway 20 west 5¼ miles to the intersection of Highway 237, which is signed to the Padilla Bay sanctuary. Follow Highway 237 north for 3 miles and turn west on Wilson Road. In 1½ miles is the small town of Bay View, on the edge of Padilla Bay.

Boat launch ramps can be found at the town of Bay View, at March Point, and at the south end of Padilla Bay, where Highway 20 crosses the Swinomish Channel. Hand-carried boats can also be put in at Bay View State Park.

Padilla Bay Shore Trail

Access: Land
Facilities: Informational displays, picnic tables, benches, Sani-cans
Attractions: Birdwatching, walking, jogging, bicycling

During the late 1800s (and before the days of Environmental Impact Statements), settlers in the Skagit Valley built a network of dikes to hold the saltwater at bay and claim the delta for farmland. A 2¼-mile-long section of these dikes is now officially open as a walking and bicycling path along the edge of Padilla Bay.

The south end of the trail is on one of the branches of Indian Slough, on the Bay View–Edison Road, ¾ mile north of its intersection with Highway 20. There is parking here for a dozen cars on the shoulder. The north end of the Shore Trail is at the southern edge of the town of Bay View; parking is two blocks away on Second Street. Handicapped parking is by the trailhead.

The wide path atop the dike, surfaced with fine crushed gravel, is ideal for jogging or family bicycling. Several interpretive signs along the route tell about the wetland habitat, and the effect of the dikes upon it. The Breazeale Interpretive Center provides a checklist of more than 125 different species of birds that may be spotted here; take binoculars to scan the marshes and bay. Hunting is permitted from the dike, in season.

Bay View Launch Ramp

A short block north of the Wilson Road intersection in Bay View is a state Department of Fish and Wildlife boat launch ramp. The single-lane concrete ramp is usable only at high tide; it ends in a mucky tideflat at low tide. Parking space for a half dozen cars with trailers is adjacent to the ramp.

Bay View State Park

Park area: 25 acres; 1,285 feet of shoreline on Padilla Bay
Access: Land, boat
Facilities: 67 standard campsites, 9 RV sites, 3 primitive campsites, group camp, group day-use area, picnic shelter, picnic tables, fireplaces, drinking water, restrooms, showers, vault toilets, children's play area
Attractions: Camping, picnicking, swimming, fishing, paddling, birdwatching

This state park is on the north edge of the town of Bay View. The overnight camping area is on the east side of the road in stately old-growth timber, and RV sites with power and water hookups are in an open grassy area near the entrance. Some tenting campsites lie around the perimeter of a grassy field, but most are on shady forested loops.

A wooden staircase leads from the picnic area down an embankment to meet the park road, which ducks through a highway underpass and emerges on the west at a large parking lot and broad, sandy beach. This lower, day-use area of the park has picnic tables, fireplaces, and plenty of places to loll in the sun or test the water of the bay.

Kayaks or inflatable boats can be carried the short distance from the parking lot and launched here for exploration of the vast waters of Padilla Bay.

Breazeale Padilla Bay Interpretive Center

Area: 64 acres
Access: Land, paddle-craft (limited)
Facilities: Nature trail, view tower, restrooms, meeting room, interpretive displays
Attractions: Educational displays, hiking, birdwatching

To better appreciate the many forms of life in Padilla Bay, stop at the Breazeale Interpretive Center, which serves as headquarters of the sanctuary.

The center is ½ mile north of Bay View on Bay View–Edison Road, within easy walking distance from Bay View State Park.

While walking or driving to the center, watch for birds. Eagles nest near here, and there is a heron rookery on Samish Island. Hawks are commonly seen foraging above hedgerows.

At the interpretive center, models, illustrated displays, dioramas with preserved animals, saltwater aquarium tanks, and a "hands on" room for young visitors present a fascinating explanation of the marine environment. The center regularly offers programs and other environment-related activities for visitors, schools, and teachers; films are shown at 1:00 P.M. and 4:00 P.M. on Sundays. The center is open Wednesday through Sunday from 10:00 A.M. to 5:00 P.M., and is closed Monday and Tuesday.

North of the building a ¾-mile nature trail loops through the wildlife habitat area. Numbered posts along the route are keyed to a descriptive pamphlet that is available at the center. A second short path leads west from the building to a beach observation deck and a staircase that winds down to the beach. The observation deck is open from April to September; the beach access is open only from July to September; both are closed other times to avoid disturbing nesting and wintering birds. Visitors in small boats may land here to visit the interpretive center when the staircase access is open.

The ideal way to view the bay is by kayak or other small boat at high

Displays at the Breazeale Padilla Bay Interpretive Center fascinate small visitors.

tide, when most of the bay is 6 feet deep or less. Boaters are likely to
sight seals, herons, and a variety of waterfowl. At low tide the bay becomes a mucky flat where even kayaks may become mired. Below, in the
shallow water, is a teeming display of plant and animal life. The best
place to launch hand-carried boats is from the beach at Bay View State
Park. Strong winds can cause problems for small boats.

The eelgrass beds offshore from Bay View State Park and north to
Joe Leary Slough are vital wintering areas for black brants. Avoid this
area from September to November and February to May so the migrating birds are not disturbed.

Swinomish Channel Boat Launch

The easiest boat access to Padilla Bay is from a fine new launch ramp
maintained by Skagit County Parks and Recreation at the north end of
the Swinomish Channel.

To reach the boat launch, leave I-5 at Exit 230 and follow Highway 20
west toward Anacortes. In 8¼ miles, just before the road crosses the
Swinomish Channel bridge, turn right onto the old road that parallels the
north side of the highway. It ends in a large parking lot under the bridge.

The two-lane concrete launch ramp has a float for loading boats. A
donation is requested for use of the ramp. The launch is for day-use
only. A picnic table and latrines are near the head of the ramp.

Tangled high grass and cattail-laden marshes that flank the launch
ramp site provide forage and protective cover for birds such as red-winged
blackbirds. You may want to come here just to birdwatch.

March Point Boat Launch Ramps

Although the heart of March Point is given over to the oil industry,
timid shorebirds still skitter along its shores and rafts of migratory waterfowl still gather in the adjacent bays, providing good birdwatching in
fall and winter from beach or boat.

To reach the shoreline road around March Point from Highway 20,
turn right onto March Point Road, ½ mile after crossing the Swinomish
Channel bridge. The blacktopped road circles the point for about 7
miles, returning to Highway 20 at a junction at the head of Fidalgo Bay.
Stopping places along the road are few.

Two primitive boat launches are found along the east side of the
point. One is near the head of the tideflat; the other is near the end of
March Point. Both ramps are gravel and not well maintained; however,
they are generally usable at high tide. RV camping is permitted in broad
shoulder parking areas at both spots, but there are no toilet facilities or
water. Boats launched here frequently head for Saddlebag Island Marine State Park, 2½ nautical miles north, or to the popular salmon fish-

ing grounds just off nearby Hat Island. The two launch ramps at the very end of March Point are on private property; do not trespass.

Small boats such as kayaks or inflatable rafts can spend a pleasant afternoon along the shoreline and in the waters of huge Padilla Bay. Bay View State Park lies 3 nautical miles to the east on the far shore of the bay. Use caution, for the majority of the bay is less than 2 feet deep at mean lower low water. Watch water depth carefully, or explore on a rising tide so that incoming water can float off boats that become mired.

ANACORTES

When Amos Bowman first arrived at Fidalgo Island in 1876, he came to the conclusion that Ship Harbor, on the northern tip of the island, with its fine deep harbor and strategic location at the entrance to Puget Sound, was perfectly suited for a major seaport. He purchased 186 acres of land, convinced other settlers of the merits of the island, and founded a town, naming it Anacortes after his wife, Anna Curtis Bowman.

All that was needed to assure its future as "The New York of the Pacific Coast" was a railroad to provide connecting land transportation for the impending rush of people and goods. This was a time of feverish financial speculation—five different railway depots were built at locations around the island, each one expected to be the Northwest's connection to the Orient. When the Northern Pacific finally completed its

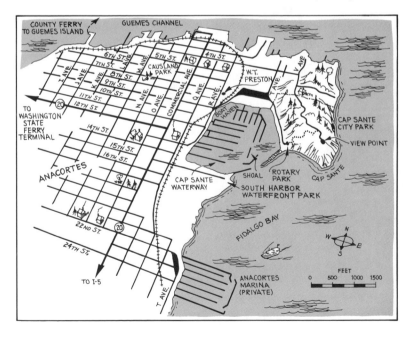

first set of transcontinental rails to western Washington, its terminus, alas, was in Tacoma, not in Anacortes as Bowman had been led to expect. Instead of unloading at the wharf already constructed and awaiting cargoes at Ship Harbor, ships headed up the sound to Commencement Bay. The anticipated boom had fizzled.

The great westward expansion did benefit Anacortes, although in a more modest way than had been hoped. Railroad spurs in due time came down the sound, and canneries, sawmills, shipyards, and other industries brought steady growth to the area. However, nothing inspired the boom that early entrepreneurs had prophesied. Perhaps the failure of those early city fathers eventually became a triumph—reflecting on the industrial sprawl and pollution attendant to Tacoma today, and imagining all of that transplanted to Anacortes, one can only shudder at what this beautiful, fragile area might be if Amos Bowman had fully realized his dream.

Today the city serves as the portal to the San Juan Islands, with its ferries transporting more than 1.5 million visitors and residents to the islands annually, and its marinas chartering boats and offering marine services to thousands more. The Washington State ferry system provides service from Anacortes to Lopez, Shaw, Orcas, and San Juan islands and Sidney, B.C. A second ferry, operated by Skagit County, provides service to Guemes Island from its terminal in downtown Anacortes at Sixth Street and I Avenue.

Private airplanes can land at the municipal airport on the west side of town, 1½ miles from the ferry terminal, or the local air service can be chartered for flights to the San Juan Islands.

Many tourists hurry through the city on their way to distant islands, not realizing that Anacortes itself has beaches, bays, viewpoints, and natural treasures to rival those found on the more remote islands. The city has perhaps the finest parks of any city of similar size in the state, ranging from carefully groomed, pocket-sized Causland Park to

Anacortes from Cap Sante Park, Fidalgo Island

Washington Park, with its rugged bluffs beautified by time and weather.

Anacortes has stores, restaurants, and services to meet every shopping need; most are on Commercial Avenue. The old section of the town, at the north end of Commercial, is a mixture of a few new stores and a number of turn-of-the-century buildings that have been nicely renovated. One remarkable feature for a town of this vintage is the width of the streets. The men who platted the town were so sure of its future as a major city that they planned the streets accordingly. They even envisioned a grand, 200-foot-wide avenue that would run the entire length of Fidalgo Island, from north to south.

To reach Anacortes, leave I-5 at Exit 230, just north of Mount Vernon. Head west on Highway 20. In 12 miles Highway 20 splits, one branch going left to Deception Pass, and the other angling right to Anacortes. The way is well signed. Total distance from the freeway to Anacortes is 15 miles.

Anacortes Marinas

Facilities: Complete boat and crew facilities, fuel, laundromat, restrooms with showers, boat pumpout station, boat launch (hoist), U.S. Customs, boat rentals and charters; **[nearby]:** restaurants and shopping

For tourists arriving at Anacortes in their own boat, or those planning to charter one, marinas are located around the saltwater perimeter of the city at Flounder Bay on the southwest and on the east behind the protective headland of Cap Sante. Marinas on the north side of town, facing on Guemes Channel, have mostly permanent moorages but may have some space for visiting boaters. Some have fuel and boat rentals.

The Port of Anacortes provides moorages and amenities for visiting boaters at its facilities at Cap Sante Boat Haven. A dredged channel leading into Cap Sante Waterway is marked with daybeacons and lights. Do not stray out of the channel, because several submerged rocks lie near the headland. The harbormaster's office is on Dock C, on the west shore.

Guest moorage is available both on the main floats just inside the breakwater and on the north side of the harbor; before tying up here, check in with the harbormaster. The service complex on the north shore has restrooms with showers and the marina laundromat. By foot, to reach the old section of the marina from the newer section, one must mosey around the shore a couple of blocks on a blacktop path. The restaurants and stores of downtown Anacortes are within walking distance.

Anacortes Marina, a large facility behind a piling breakwater on Fidalgo Bay, south of Cap Sante, has no guest facilities.

For a description of the facilities at Skyline Marina, which is on the west side of Anacortes at Flounder Bay, see the section below describing the Burrows Bay area. Public ramps for trailered boats are located at March Point and Sunset Beach in Washington Park.

The *W. T. Preston* and South Harbor Waterfront Park

An interesting highlight of the Anacortes waterfront is the *W. T. Preston,* a historic sternwheeler built in 1929 that for many years worked as a snag boat on Puget Sound rivers and Lake Washington. It was used to tow away tree snags and stray logs that endangered boats. It is now retired and rests on shore, restored as a museum.

The sternwheeler is at the northwest corner of the Cap Sante boat basin, at Seventh Street and R Avenue, just south of the old Anacortes Railroad depot.

The boat is open for viewing Thursday through Sunday from 10:00 A.M. to 4:30 P.M. during summer months, and other times when volunteer staff is available. A self-guided tour of the boat explains the intricacies of the unique paddlewheeler as it leads visitors through the engine room, crew quarters, galley, pilothouse, and decks.

Two small parks with rockeries, picnic tables, and a boardwalk flank the bow and west side of the historic boat. One commemorates lives lost in the sinking of two fishing vessels. A plank deck built on the stern of the *Preston* serves as a performance stage for entertainment events during the summer.

The old Burlington Northern Railroad depot, which is immediately north, has been restored and now serves as a community center. Art galleries in the depot are open afternoons from Tuesday through Sunday.

At the end of Seafarers Way, on the south side of Cap Sante Marina, is South Harbor Waterfront Park. The shallow waters off shore have 10 buoys and a float for day use by boaters. The strip of beach holds picnic tables, restrooms with showers, and a memorial and statue dedicated to seafarers.

Causland Memorial Park

Access: Land
Facilities: Picnic tables
Attractions: Picnicking, museum (nearby)

If the boat crew is ready to mutiny after days of confinement aboard, a stroll and a picnic at Causland Memorial Park may be in order. The Museum of History, just across the street, provides another diversion ashore.

From Cap Sante Waterway, walk west to N Avenue, then north to Eighth Street, an eight-block stroll. The museum is across the street to the west, at Eighth Street and M Avenue.

Causland Memorial Park displays some remarkable rock work.

The one-block park, which has stone walls and a band shell with intricate mosaic patterns, is a small delight—and there are picnic tables to boot! The nearby Museum of History contains mementos of pioneer days on Fidalgo Island (hours are 1:00 to 5:00 P.M., Thursday through Monday).

Cap Sante City Park and Rotary Park

Park area: 40 acres; 15,000 feet of shoreline on Padilla Bay
Access: Land
Facilities: Picnic tables, fire braziers, picnic shelter, trail, water
Attractions: Picnicking, hiking, viewpoint

An imposing rocky headland rising 200 feet above the marinas of Anacortes provides breathtaking views of Fidalgo Island, March Point, Hat and Saddlebag Islands, and Mount Baker reigning over all.

To reach Cap Sante City Park from Anacortes, drive north on Commercial Avenue and turn right on Fourth Street. Continue on Fourth to its end and turn right on V Avenue, following the winding road uphill to a parking lot atop the imposing monolith. A picnic area at Rotary Park at the base of the rock can be reached by turning south off Fourth Street onto T Avenue and following it past private residences to a parking lot at road's end.

The paved path leads along the high bank above the beach and is spotted with benches and picnic tables. Midway to the end of the point, a staircase from the road above descends to the path; a companion staircase leads down the bank to the beach. The path ends at the rock jetty that protects the harbor.

Here is a picnic shelter, picnic tables with fine views of the harbor, and staircases to the beach. A crude trail leads through timber up the hillside to the top of the cape.

Rotary Park is a pleasant hike from the Cap Sante Marina; the top of the headland, with its stunning views, makes a challenging alternate destination. To reach the paved path leading to the park, follow a sidewalk at the east side of the new section of the marina. Total distance by foot from the marina to the top of Cap Sante is about ¼ mile, with an elevation gain of nearly 200 feet.

The rolling grassy hillsides on the west side of the cape can be descended with care, but they are certain to give mothers of small children cardiac arrest, for they seem to drop quite abruptly to the water. The south and east slopes are glacier-polished granite broken by patchy grass. Midway down, a row of iron posts marks the point where "rather steep" becomes "extremely steep" (and dangerous). End your exploration here.

Washington Park

Park area: 220 acres; 40,500 feet of shoreline on Guemes Channel and Rosario Strait
Access: Land, boat
Facilities: 48 campsites, picnic tables, fireplaces, drinking water (at Sunset Beach and in the campground only), restrooms, showers, shelters, playground, boat launch (ramp) (fee)
Attractions: Camping, picnicking, boating, hiking, viewpoints, scuba diving

Undoubtedly the crowning glory of the Anacortes city park system, Washington Park has 220 acres of forest and beach and panoramic viewpoints. In addition to the steady flow of auto-bound sightseers, many others wisely choose to use the park for road walking, jogging, or cycling, traveling slowly enough to fully soak in its beauty.

To reach the park from Anacortes, follow signs on Highway 20 west for 3¼ miles toward the San Juan ferry landing. When the highway turns right and downhill to the ferry terminal, bear left on Sunset Avenue for ¾ mile to the park entrance. A bicycle lane is provided along the left side of the road much of the way.

Immediately to the right of the park entrance is the day-use area of Sunset Beach. Here are picnic shelters, tables on a large grassy area above the beach, and a children's play area. To reach the boat launch area at Sunset Beach, continue past the day-use area for 500 yards and take the next right. An excellent two-lane concrete launch ramp with a boarding float between drops into the bay. The huge parking lot, accommodating about 100 cars and boat trailers, attests to the popularity of this launch site.

For visitors arriving by boat, Sunset Bay is the only possible landing spot within the park. There is no overnight moorage; for long-term stays boats must be beached or anchored out in the bay. Boaters staying at Skyline Marina in Flounder Bay (see Burrows Bay, below) can reach the park by walking the road, a distance of about ¾ mile, to the park entrance.

A few hundred yards beyond the boat launch area is the campground, with pleasant sites inland, separated by timber and undergrowth. The campground is open year-round.

From here the route and mode of transportation are up to the visitor. Pedestrians may choose to walk the loop road from sea-level forest upward to grassy knolls and glacier-scoured rocks 250 feet above the water, or hike the rocky beach from Sunset Bay westward until tide and the steep bluffs of Fidalgo Head force the route inland. The road can be avoided almost entirely by following forest paths near the edge of the bluff from West Beach all the way to the Havekost Memorial. A loop trip is about 3 miles—longer if enticing side trails are explored.

Whether traveling by trail or road, West Beach is an inviting wayside stop. Near Green Point are several single-car pull-offs; picnic tables on the grassy point below have balcony views of boating and ferry traffic in Guemes Channel, with backdrops of Cypress, Guemes, and other more distant islands. A concrete staircase leads from the road just south of Green Point down to West Beach, where waves from Rosario Strait toss driftwood logs onto the narrow bedrock beach. South, beyond Fidalgo Head, a lighthouse situated high on a bluff on Burrows Island can be

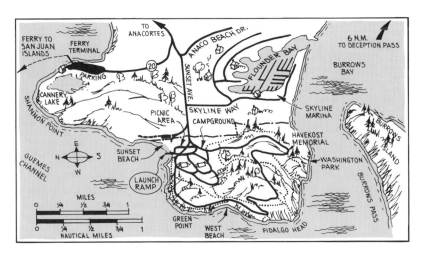

The slopes of Washington Park overlook Burrows Bay.

seen. This side of the park is a favorite with scuba divers experienced enough to handle the strong current and deep water.

Uprising cliffs of Fidalgo Head prevent a complete beach circuit of the park; however, the shoreline on the south side can be reached by carefully descending the steep grassy slopes from the road viewpoints above. The bluffs drop off abruptly, so there are no beaches, but the tawny grass sprinkled with wildflowers, the weathered trees, and the briny view more than compensate.

As the road makes its final loop before heading back down to the park entrance, a viewpoint features a small marble monument to T. H. Havekost, who bequeathed 8 acres of land to the city for this park. Havekost was a pioneer industrialist and land speculator on Fidalgo Island in the late 1800s. He purchased land anticipating, like many others, that Burrows Bay would be the terminus of the new railroad. Following his initial donation, the city of Anacortes acquired additional lands over a period of time; the park now exceeds 200 acres.

BURROWS BAY

Skyline Marina

Facilities: Fuel, groceries, marine supplies, marine repairs, yacht brokers and charters, boat storage, moorage, groceries, ice, fishing supplies, boat pumpout station, boat launch (slings), restaurant

This commercial marina on Fidalgo Island is a favorite stopover for pleasure boaters who are traveling through Deception Pass. Skyline

Marina lies within Flounder Bay, a dredged harbor on the north side of Burrows Bay. The Anacortes city center is 4 miles away; however, the marina can meet most boating needs in the vicinity.

The entrance to the harbor is at the east end of the protective jetty. The channel is marked with lights and daybeacons on pilings. To secure overnight moorage, stop at the fuel dock and check in with the harbormaster. Hand-carried boats can be put in at the jetty for exploration of Burrows Bay and its islands.

To reach the marina from downtown Anacortes, head west from Commercial Avenue on 12th Street. In 4 miles turn left (south) on Skyline Way, which leads to the marina.

Burrows and Allan Islands

Lifting greenly forested shoulders from the waters of Burrows Bay, Burrows and Allan islands may seem to be everyone's dream of an island hideaway; however, the very rugged nature that gives the islands their beauty, coupled with the lack of water, has served to limit settlement.

Spanish explorers, viewing their fortresslike slopes, named them *Las Dos Islas Morrows*—"Two Islands of the Forts." Mountainous Burrows Island, rising abruptly to a height of 650 feet, is often admired from promontories in Washington Park. Against the massive island backdrop, boats in the channel below seem almost to be toys.

Boaters attempting to run between Young and Burrows islands should be wary of a large rock that lies in the middle of the channel. A rocky shelf extends out from the south side of Allan Island; use care approaching this shore.

Small bays around the two islands serve as pleasant fair-weather lunch stops; however, all shorelands are private, except for the western point of Burrows Island.

Burrows Island State Park (Undeveloped)

Park area: 329 acres, 8,670 feet of shoreline on Rosario Strait
Access: Boat
Facilities: None
Attractions: Beachcombing, kayaking, boating

When the Coast Guard automated all of its light stations, property at Burrows Island Light became surplus and was acquired, along with some adjoining property, by the state parks. Ultimate use of the former Coast Guard facilities is still unresolved; proposed plans include a marine park, or a Cascadia Marine Trail hostel for kayakers. For now, the undeveloped park is open to public access.

Because of occasional heavy weather, placing mooring buoys in the slight cove just north of the lighthouse is impractical, but during calm weather small boats can be landed in the cove for onshore picnics or exploration.

A stairway leads up the bluff. Overnight camping is permitted; however, there is no water.

SWINOMISH CHANNEL AND LA CONNER

Fidalgo makes the grade to island status by virtue of the Swinomish Channel, a 10-mile-long waterway that separates it from the Skagit mainland. The slough, 100 yards wide for most of its length, is dredged throughout to a depth of 12 feet and both entrances are well marked with navigational devices for the use of commercial and recreational boaters seeking to avoid the turbulent waters of Deception Pass.

A trip on the channel is reminiscent of European canal boating, cruising slowly by farms, homes, and a village, waving cheerily to people on shore and to fellow boaters. It is a unique experience for Northwesterners. On the west shore of the canal, immediately across from La Conner, are boat docks and a fish cannery of the Swinomish tribe.

While the run through the channel is fun in a large boat, it can be enchanting in a small one, with side trips up narrow, meandering sloughs and eye-to-eye encounters with great blue herons, ducks, and other marsh birds. During the winter many of the birds common to the Skagit Wildlife Recreation Area a few miles to the south—whistling swans, snow geese, black brant, gulls, ducks, and terns—may also be seen here from the water or from roads and trails along the levees.

When approaching the Swinomish Channel from either end, even small boats should have on hand a navigational chart and follow it closely; only the marked channel is dredged and all the surrounding area is tideflat, where in places even a kayak can run aground. Do not be tempted to cut the corner into innocent-looking water, but follow the channel clear out to its end, or you may spend a tide change on the mudflat.

Travel at a no-wake speed in the canal—La Conner has a strict law against boats throwing wakes. Stay on the starboard side; there is ample room for two good-sized boats to pass, unless one is a "road hog" and insists on taking the half right down the middle. On rare occasions a raft of logs under tow may be encountered in the channel. Don't panic. There is room if you pass cautiously.

The southern entrance, known as Hole in the Wall, is a dogleg run between the 100-foot vertical walls of two rock knobs. A lovely spot, but no fun in a fog. From here the canal straightens out to gently flow through Skagit flatland edged by levees.

Because the waterway connects two large bodies of saltwater (Skagit Bay on the south and Padilla Bay on the north), water flows inward at both ends of the channel during a flood tide and outward during the ebb. The precise location of the transition is hard to predict; however,

Many floats in La Conner are open to visiting boaters.

general knowledge of the forecasted tides can be useful to boaters in small craft. Tidal current in the channel can exceed 2 knots.

The rock jetty that stretches between Goat and McGlinn islands and runs west from Goat Island for 1,000 yards was built to divert the flow of the North Fork of the Skagit River and prevent it from filling the Swinomish Channel with silt. Near McGlinn Island a narrow break in the jetty was designed to allow migrating salmon to get back to the Skagit River if they had mistakenly turned into the channel. The fishway is dry at low tide, but at mid to high tide the narrow slot can be used by kayakers to go between the two channels.

La Conner

Access: Land, boat
Facilities: Restaurants, lodging, shops, galleries, restrooms
Attractions: Fishing, bicycling, museum, historic sightseeing

Located a mile north of Hole in the Wall, the southern entrance to Swinomish Channel, La Conner is the quintessential little seaside tourist village, with waterfront businesses built on pilings edging the canal. Founded in 1867, it was a center of commerce during the time of steamboat traffic on Puget Sound; many of the town's buildings are listed in the National Register of Historic Places. Today it is an artists' colony and tourist center with interesting shops, restaurants, museums, and historic sites. Favorite browsing places are antiques stores, art galleries,

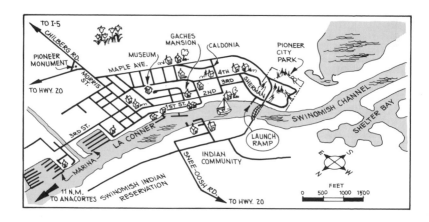

and crafts shops. Town merchants can provide maps of the numerous tourist attractions.

To reach La Conner by car, take Exit 221 from I-5. The route is clearly signed. La Conner can also be reached via Swinomish Channel. A number of floats along the La Conner waterfront offer temporary moorage to boaters stopping by to shop or dine in town. Some permit overnight moorage (for a fee).

The most elegant landmark in La Conner is the fully restored, 22-room Gaches Mansion. The home, which was built in 1891, is a registered National Historic Place. It is open for tours Friday through Sunday from 1:00 to 5:00 P.M. from April through October, and Saturday and Sunday from 1:00 to 4:00 P.M. in the winter. A small admission fee is charged.

The Fireman's Museum in the 600 block of First Street in downtown La Conner will delight young visitors as they peer through the windows at its three retired fire engines. One engine is a relatively "modern" 1930s model, while the others, a horse-drawn hose cart and a steam pumper, were built in 1850.

At the south end of First Street, where a totem pole stands in front a building, a small wooden pavilion protects an old Indian shovel-nosed Skagit River canoe. A signboard here tells of canoe construction, the various styles of Indian canoes, and relates historical tales involving early day experiences with canoe travel in the area.

The Tillinghast Seed House, at the corner of Morris and Maple on the east side of town, has a small garden-oriented museum and offers fascinating shopping amid the tulip bulbs and turnip seeds.

Dramatically arching over the Swinomish Channel at the south end of La Conner is the orange-painted "Rainbow Bridge." From some viewpoints, the design award-winning bridge picturesquely frames the rustic town clinging to the shore, with the icy crown of Mount Baker rising above. From other vistas, it frames husky fishing boats moored in the quietly flowing waterway.

The rich, flat delta land between I-5 and La Conner is favorite bicycling country, offering views of farms and, in spring, vast fields of brilliant tulips. A public restroom in the middle of town on First Street offers welcome relief to touring cyclists.

In late winter and early spring the docks along the Swinomish Channel are frequently lined with fishermen jigging for tasty little surf smelt. The sport is so popular here that the city annually schedules a smelt derby the first Saturday of February, with usually around 3,000 people participating.

Skagit County Historical Museum

Perched on a small hill above La Conner, the Skagit County Historical Museum has one of the best viewpoints in town, with a breathtaking vista of the pale specter of Mount Baker and green and brown Skagit farmlands. When tulips blossom, the valley is transformed into a tapestry of riotous color.

The museum is located at 501 Fourth Street; to walk to the museum from downtown La Conner, look for a signed stairway on First Street, next to a bank.

The museum's excellent displays cover a broad range of Skagit Valley life, including a moonshine still that operated during the time of prohibition, a gas-operated light from an early lighthouse, a collection of baskets, spears, and other Native American artifacts, and a wide array of household items from pioneer life. Don't miss the "calf weaner"—a muzzle with 2-inch metal spikes guaranteed to make any mama cow keep her hungry offspring at a distance. Youngsters will enjoy interactive displays where they can try on pioneer clothing, operate a telephone switchboard, or guess at the practical function of obscure household and farm utensils.

Museum hours are Tuesday through Sunday, 11:00 A.M. to 5:00 P.M. A modest admission fee is charged.

La Conner Marina

Facilities: Complete boat and crew facilities, laundromat, boat pumpout station, boat launch (slings), boat charters, bait, ice, tackle, fishing pier, bicycle rentals

Just north of town, the La Conner Marina, operated by the Port of Skagit Valley, has overnight berths with full facilities for boat and crew. The 500-slip marina occupies two large dredged yacht basins.

Guest moorages are on the two outside floats on the south basin of the marina and on the long outside float on the north basin. Tying up on the channel side of these floats can be difficult due to current in the channel and boat traffic, and these moorages can also be uncomfortable at night due to excessive rocking, but they are fine for a short stay.

Fishing is permitted from the outer docks of the marina. The angled floats that lead to the guest moorage on the north basin are a particularly popular spot.

A number of businesses near the marina provide most boating necessities, and downtown shopping is just a few blocks walk away. Bicycles can be rented from a store at the head of the dock on the north marina basin. At the northeast end of the north marina basin is a dual sling hoist launch facility. Boats up to 27 feet in length can be whisked from their trailers and deposited in the moorage basin 25 feet below.

To reach the boat launch, continue on North Third Street past the south basin, then turn east then north on South Pearle Jensen Way. The spur to the launch area is reached ¼ mile after this road turns north.

A large commercial RV park east of the marina has nicely landscaped, level campsites with trailer hookups. The park's facilities include a grocery store and an indoor swimming pool.

Pioneer City Park

Access: Land, boat
Facilities: Boat launch (ramp), picnic shelters, pit toilets, picnic tables, drinking water
Attractions: Picnicking, viewpoint

At the eastern end of La Conner's Rainbow Bridge is a combination city park and public boat ramp.

To reach the launch ramp, follow Chilberg Road into La Conner. Just past the Pioneer Monument at the outskirts of town, turn south onto Maple Avenue, then west onto Caldonia, south on Second, and finally west on Sherman to the waterfront. A parking area for a dozen cars and trailers is at the head of the concrete-surfaced ramp and its boarding float. The park section of the area lies on the embankment above the ramp. It can be reached by the trail that leaves from the edge of the parking lot.

The more developed section of the park can be reached by car by following Fourth south, where it winds steeply uphill to dead-end at a parking area with a picnic shelter, a few tables, and pit toilets.

To reach the main area of the park from La Conner, follow Caldonia Street east to Maple Avenue, and turn south and follow the road uphill and west as it climbs toward the Swinomish Channel bridge. The main area of the park is located at the end of a signed side road that branches south just before the road crosses the bridge.

Here are picnic tables, a kitchen shelter, and a picnic shelter. Through

Harvesting tulips near La Conner

the trees, boat traffic can be seen in the channel below. Trails lead to the bridge; walk across for wide-open views of the Swinomish Channel, La Conner, and Mount Baker rising majestically to the north.

Goat Island

The old World War I forts of Casey, Flagler, and Worden are well known to anyone who has done a bit of traveling around Puget Sound, but what about Fort Whitman? It did exist, and right here on Goat Island on the south side of the Swinomish Channel. The fortification was built as part of the system protecting the Northwest's inland waters from enemy attack and was in service from 1911 until 1944.

The island can be accessed only by boat. The best access is at the rock beach on the north side, next to the old dock.

From here a trail climbs west to the old, overgrown battery emplacements on the western end of the island. The four 6-inch disappearing guns located at Battery Harrison guarded Deception Pass and Saratoga Passage. The fort also had a mine-control center similar to the one that can be seen at Middle Point in Manchester State Park, but there is no evidence that mines were ever planted in the passage.

Goat Island is now part of the Department of Fish and Wildlife's Skagit Wildlife Recreation Area. Hawks and eagles nest in the tall firs; use care when exploring, especially in spring. Camping is not permitted.

CHAPTER FOUR

SKAGIT DELTA AND CAMANO ISLAND

DELTA FLATLANDS

Not long ago, as such things are measured, when the last of the land-gouging ice sheets melted, Puget Sound lapped against the rugged Cascade foothills, and mountain streams tumbling down precipitous slopes emptied directly into tidal waters. After the last glaciation, it took 13,000 years for the constant wearing-down of streams and rivers to build up more than 100,000 acres of rich Skagit flatland stretching from the base of the Cascades to its present boundary on Puget Sound. The growth continues at a reported rate of 100 million tons of sediment deposited each year, and in time, although certainly not for many generations to come, Fidalgo, Camano, and Whidbey islands will be solidly bound to the mainland.

The Skagit Delta is a prime bird-watching area for both waterfowl and land birds.

The two rivers that meander through the Skagit Delta, the Skagit and the Stillaguamish, terminate at an estuary that edges Skagit Bay and Port Susan.

Boaters passing by wisely stay well to the west, in the channel that follows the Whidbey Island shoreline. Although it is not generally

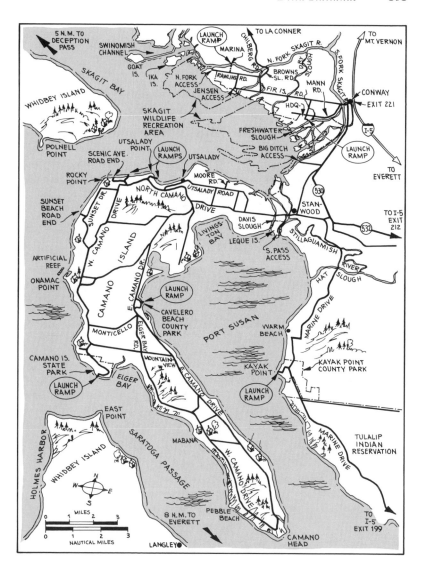

thought of as a cruising-boat destination, it is possible to approach the tidelands from the west in a shallow-draft boat at mid to high tide. A cautious approach from the water side can be the best way to observe the enormous flocks of snow geese and other waterfowl that winter in the estuary. Channels lead along the north side of Camano Island into West Pass, and also north into Tom Moore and Boom sloughs. Consult a navigation chart and proceed with care.

The tidelands west of Browns Slough are good for clam digging.

Skagit Wildlife Recreation Area

Area: 12,700 acres
Access: Land, boat
Facilities: Hiking trails, information center, restrooms, boat launch (ramp)
Attractions: Birdwatching, paddling, clam digging, hiking, fishing

The Skagit Wildlife Recreation Area (WRA) covers a major portion of the shoreline from Camano Island north to the Swinomish Channel. Here the state Department of Fish and Wildlife has preserved a natural habitat that supports a wide variety of birds, fish, and small mammals. The tidelands, sloughs, and adjoining fields of the estuary are a major stop on the Pacific Flyway for migratory birds. Hunting and fishing are permitted in season, but the area is also heavily used by observers who come to hike along the dikes or boat in the channels to simply enjoy the wildlife and scenery.

The most spectacular attraction of the area is the 25,000 to 30,000 snow geese and some 100 whistling swans that winter here. The best time for viewing the flocks is from the end of hunting season in December through April. In spring the snow geese depart for breeding grounds on Wrangell Island, north of Siberia. Any time of year one is assured of seeing birds of one species or another: brightly feathered ducks bobbing placidly on coves and sloughs; gangly great blue herons on stiltlike legs wading in tideflats; hawks, owls, and even bald eagles, soaring over fields; or meadowlarks, wrens, and other songbirds flitting in dense hedgerows. Over 175 species of birds have been observed here as well as river otter, rabbit, muskrat, beaver, skunk, and raccoon. Anglers land Dolly Varden, steelhead, and several species of salmon.

A network of sloughs meanders through the Skagit WRA.

The inner edge of the Skagit WRA is bordered by private farmland. Birds feeding in pastures and fields can sometimes be seen from the roads, but for best viewing and for boat put-ins, drive to the area's road-end access points. To reach the WRA headquarters, leave I-5 at Exit 221 to Conway and drive west on Fir Island Road. Immediately after crossing the Skagit River, an intersection is marked Mann Road—do not take this turn, but continue west another mile to the intersection with Wylie Road, marked by a PUBLIC HUNTING sign. Turn left here and continue south to road's end at the WRA headquarters. A boat launch into Freshwater Slough is at the left end of the T intersection, immediately east of park headquarters.

Hand-carried boats can easily be put in north of Stanwood at Big Ditch access. Boats launched southwest of the tide gate can follow the ditch out into meandering channels at the south end of Skagit Bay. If they are put in northeast of the gate, the narrow ditch leads north nearly 3 miles to Milltown. An access point ¼ mile north of Milltown can be used to launch hand-carried boats into Tom Moore Slough, for trips southwest into Skagit Bay. The southernmost access is at Leque Island west of Stanwood (see Leque Island, below).

The other recreation access points, North Fork and Jensen, may entail a very long, soggy carry to reach navigable water. At the north section of the WRA, a commercial resort and marina on the North Fork of the Skagit River, just off Rawlins Road, has a launch ramp as well as boat rentals and supplies, RV camping, and a few cabins; canoes and kayaks can be put in for a fee.

Personnel at the WRA headquarters can give advice regarding boating in the estuary. Mid to high tide is necessary to navigate many of the channels. Improper planning can result in becoming stranded in the muck and having to get out and wade. In the river channels, the current can be quite strong. It is possible to become disoriented in the reedy marshes if it is foggy or if low overcast covers the mountains; carry a map and compass.

Land-bound visitors can also walk trails along the dikes or wander for miles on the tideflats. Rubber boots are a good idea.

Leque Island and South Pass Access

Leque Island lies at the mouth of the Stillaguamish River, between the mainland and Camano Island.

A road that skirts the southeast shore of the island provides water access to marshes at the south end of the Skagit WRA. To reach it, leave I-5 at Exit 212 and follow Highway 532 to Stanwood. Drive west from Stanwood on Highway 532 onto Camano Island. Immediately after crossing the bridge over West Pass, a side road to the south, Eide Road, heads back toward the channel, paralleling the bridge abutments. At the channel a short road stub goes straight ahead to the water. The dirt ramp here is suitable for launching hand-carried boats—trailers may become mired in the mud. Parking space for a couple of cars is under the bridge. Eide Road continues south, paralleling the dike. During hunting season the Department of Fish and Wildlife releases pheasants here, and the area is used extensively by hunters. At other times wander freely on the south end of Leque Island and on to the tideflats at the end of Port Susan. Eide Road is gated a mile south of the bridge; in the vicinity of the gate, parking is extremely limited.

CAMANO ISLAND

Although Whidbey and Camano are joined together politically to form Island County, the two islands are quite different in character. Unlike Whidbey, which is three times larger, Camano Island has no towns or major businesses—there are just a few grocery stores and gas stations near centers of population. Many of the homes concentrated along the shoreline are owned by retirees or summer residents.

The island was logged between the 1850s and the 1880s to supply local mills and ship builders, and to meet demands of a thriving trade in export of lumber products to worldwide markets. Relatively little of the second-growth forest that now covers much of the island has been cleared for farming or agriculture.

Because it lies in the protection of Whidbey Island, Camano has fewer wind-buffeted beaches, but the western shore does suffer some of the severe weather off Saratoga Passage and the island's shallow bights offer little shelter for boaters.

Camano and Whidbey islands were more closely allied in early times when boats were the major mode of transportation and Saratoga Passage was seen as a water link, not a barrier between them. Today it is not possible to travel directly between the two islands except by private pleasure boat. By car, Camano Island can only be reached via Highway 532, which you can take from I-5 exit 212 west through Stanwood to a low bridge over West Pass at the north end of the island.

Utsalady Point County Park (Island County) and Launch Ramp

Access: Land
Facilities: Picnic tables, picnic shelter, Sani-can; **[nearby]:** boat launch (ramp)
Attractions: Picnicking, boating, historical marker

Utsalady Point marks the northwest tip of Camano Island. Here a small day-use park provides a grassy, shaded spot on a 100-foot-high bluff overlooking Saratoga Passage. A bas-relief carving on a large wooden panel at the park pictures the point in its early days; brass plates relate the history of Utsalady.

The lazy little bay with its swath of beach homes is a far cry from the industrial center it was during the 1870s. At that time Utsalady had a population of 147, and the shores of the bay boasted a large sawmill and a major shipwright that operated for over 30 years. A number of the steamers of the fabled Mosquito Fleet that plied Puget Sound were built here.

To reach the park and ramp, drive west on North Camano Drive, which climbs steeply as it rounds the bay. On the far side of the bay, turn right at a sign reading UTSALADY POINT. At a Y in a few hundred feet, the left fork, Shore Drive, soon passes the park. The right-hand fork drops steeply downhill for ¼ mile to a 50-foot strip of beach on the west side of Utsalady Bay that holds a single-lane concrete ramp. There is parking nearby for three or four cars with trailers; do not park along the road.

Saratoga Passage Beach Accesses

Maple Grove Launch Ramp. Just around Utsalady Point and 1 mile to the west is a public launch ramp. To reach it, turn off North Camano Drive onto Maple Grove Road, ¼ mile west of the Utsalady Point Road intersection. As it reaches the water at the community of Maple Grove in ½ mile, a short side road leads to the 100-foot-wide stretch of undeveloped beach between a dense collection of shoreside residences. Here is a single-lane concrete launch ramp, a Sani-can, and parking for eight or 10 cars and trailers. From the water the launch ramp is about halfway between Utsalady Point and Rocky Point.

Scenic Avenue Road End. From the Maple Grove launch ramp, Maple Grove Road continues west and in ½ mile dead-ends at the intersection with Scenic Avenue. The block-long gravel road end of Scenic Avenue is also a public beach access between private lands. There is no launch ramp here and very little parking space—only a place to reach the water and possibly put in a kayak.

Sunset Beach Road End. Driving from the north, 1 mile south of Utsalady Point, turn off West Camano Drive onto Sunset Drive and follow it for 2¾ miles to its intersection with Blackburn and High roads. Turn west on High Road, and at its end in about a block is a low-bank beach access suitable for launching hand-carried boats.

Onamac Point

Midway along the western shore of Camano Island, the meager sandspit of Onamac Point thrusts outward into Saratoga Passage. Immediately north of the point a pair of lighted buoys mark an artificial reef placed by the state Department of Fish and Wildlife for the benefit of fish and fishermen. Crags and crannies of the broken concrete reef provide habitat for lingcod, rockfish, and other bottom species. The protected waters of Saratoga Passage are favored by small-boat fishermen; many troll for winter blackmouth and spring chinook salmon in the area between Polnell Point on Whidbey Island and Camano Island's Rocky Point.

Although it sounds quite exotic, Onamac Point is not some ancient Native American word meaning something such as "place where giant fish leap out of the water"—it is merely Camano spelled backwards. The name Camano, by the way, comes from Francisco de Eliza, an early Spanish explorer of the region, who named the island for one of his buddies back in Spain.

Camano Island State Park

Park area: 134 acres; 6,700 feet of shoreline on Saratoga Passage and Elger Bay
Access: Land, boat
Facilities: 87 campsites, group camp, picnic tables, picnic shelters, fireplaces, restrooms, drinking water, nature trail, hiking trails, boat launch (ramp) (Designated Cascadia Marine Trail campsite)
Attractions: Camping, picnicking, boating, hiking, swimming

What is perhaps the finest beach on all of Saratoga Passage is, astonishingly, not in an exclusive real estate development but in a magnificent state park where all can enjoy it. The park stretches for more than a mile along the Camano Island shoreline, incorporating both superb upland forests and gently flaring, wave-swept beach.

The land route to the park is well signed, and the island is small enough and major roads are few enough that it is difficult to miss the

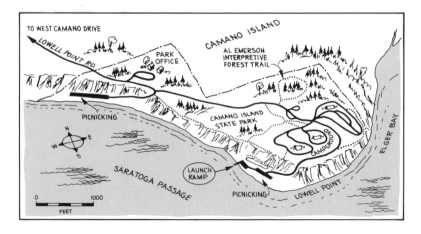

Camano Island State Park is a great place for all kinds of water sports.

way. From Utsalady, drive south on West Camano Drive about 10 miles south from Utsalady. At a major intersection, Lowell Point Road branches off to the southwest; follow it to the park entrance in ¾ mile.

Immediately inside the park entrance the road forks; the branch to the right swings downhill to the day-use area at North Beach. Picnic tables and fireplaces are stretched along a grassy embankment 30 feet above the beach. Stairs drop down to the beach, and a ¾-mile bluff-top trail leads south to Lowell Point.

The left fork of the park road passes an interpretive forest trail, the group camp, and two campground loops. All upland park campsites are away from the bluff in timber; none have views of the water. The road loops steeply downhill to the beach and parking lot at Lowell Point, where Cascadia Marine Trail campsites, reserved for kayakers, are found south of the day-use area.

At the far north end of this beach area are a three-lane, surfaced launch ramp and a large parking lot for vehicles with trailers. There is no boarding float; a bit of wading may be necessary to launch and load boats.

Below a silvery collar of driftwood, the beach slides gently outward— fine swimming or wading for souls brave enough to test the chilly water of Saratoga Passage. A salt lagoon separates the marshy beach and the bluff; by summer the beach-side marsh dries enough to host games of Frisbee or one o'cat. In late May buttercups and wild roses bloom here in profusion.

Hiking trails climb the steep 150-foot glacial-till bluff and wander along the bluff top. Rough-hewn benches along the way provide spots to pause and enjoy eagle's-eye views down to boating traffic in Saratoga Passage, out to Whidbey Island, and far beyond to crystal Olympic peaks.

PORT SUSAN

Most boaters hurry by on the main highway of Saratoga Passage, rarely lingering to enjoy the detour into the quiet waters of Port Susan. The 11-mile-long inlet leads only to a long, shallow tideflat and limited shoreside marine facilities, but it is a pleasant out-of-the-way corner, well worth a visit. The cove offers some anchorages along the northwest shore in 10 fathoms; beware of shoals that rise up abruptly 2 miles from the head of the bay and the extensive mudflat that lies along the north-east shore.

Cavelero Beach County Park (Island County)

Park area: 0.6 acre; 300 feet of shoreline on Port Susan
Access: Land, water
Facilities: Picnic tables, Sani-can, boat launch (ramp)
Attractions: Wading, picnicking, paddling

The east shore access in this little park gives boaters and beach lovers a chance to sample Port Susan waters.

To reach the park by land, turn onto East Camano Drive from Highway 532 and drive south for 5½ miles. Turn east onto Cavelero Road and in ¼ mile turn left onto a narrow, steep, single-lane road that drops down to the park.

The boat launch road is dirt, leading down to a concrete ramp at the water level. The narrow access road, the primitive condition of the ramp, and the shallow outfall preclude launching large boats. At low tide, launching of any but hand-carried boats may be impossible.

Park facilities consist of a half dozen picnic tables and a Sani-can; however, the pretty beach needs no embellishments. Mount Baker and Whitehorse and Three Fingers mountains line the horizon to the east. The park is a favorite in summer with families who bring toddlers to dabble in the shallow, sun-warmed water.

Kayak Point County Park (Snohomish County)

Park area: 670 acres; 3,300 feet of shoreline on Port Susan
Access: Land, boat
Facilities: 34 campsites, picnic tables, fireplaces, 15 picnic shelters, restrooms, drinking water, boat launch (ramp), float, fishing pier, hiking trails, Cascadia Marine Trail campsite, 9 yurts
Attractions: Camping, picnicking, boating, paddling, fishing, crabbing, scuba diving, swimming, hiking

In summer the sun-warmed waters of shallow Port Susan find the perfect complement in the wide beaches of Kayak Point, along its east shore. On hot summer days the park becomes a northern version of Seattle's Golden Gardens, with mobs of swimmers, sunbathers, picnickers, and sand-encrusted kids. But even in chilly weather the park has a lot to offer visitors. Hiking trails lace the upland woods between the beach and Marine Drive. Ten picnic shelters and a yurt village line the shore at the north end of the park; half of the shelters can be reserved.

Cod, perch, flounder, or (with luck) salmon can be caught from the 300-foot-long fishing pier that juts into Port Susan, and crab pots or star traps strategically lowered may result in Dungeness or red rock crab. At the end of the pier is a short float for loading boats; a single-lane launch ramp is immediately north of the pier. Boaters should leave or approach the area with caution, watching for swimmers and scuba divers in the water.

The weak current in the bay makes this a popular spot for beginning scuba divers who may find crabs, nudibranchs, moon snails, and orange sea anemones on the smooth bottom. Divers should stay well away from the pier and launch ramp where there are fishing lines and boat props.

By land the park can be reached by leaving I-5 at Exit 199, turning north in ½ mile on a road signed to Tulalip and following this arterial, Marine Drive, all the way to the park—a total distance of 14 miles. At one time the point was occupied by a resort that loaned kayaks to its guests, thus the name of the area. The resort is long gone, but the joy of paddling around the placid bay remains.

The fishing pier at Kayak Point County Park

Above: *North Beach provides stunning views up to the Deception Pass Bridge.*
Right: *Starfish and other marine invertebrates may be found on Deception Pass beaches.*
Below: *Mama duck takes her brood for a spin around Cranberry Lake.*

CHAPTER FIVE

DECEPTION PASS STATE PARK

Park area: 3,599 acres (including Heart Lake area); 77,000 feet of saltwater shoreline on the Strait of Juan de Fuca and Samish Bay, 28,200 feet of freshwater shoreline on Cranberry, Pass, Campbell, and Heart lakes

Access: Land, boat

Facilities: 246 standard campsites, 5 primitive campsites, group camp, picnic sites, picnic shelters, restrooms, bathhouse, docks, floats, buoys, boat launches (ramps), swimming area, fishing piers, interpretive trail, 27½ miles of hiking trails, underwater park, Environmental Learning Center

Attractions: Camping, hiking, boating, bicycling, paddling, swimming (fresh- and saltwater), scuba and free diving, beachcombing, birdwatching, sand dunes, tidepools, fishing (fresh- and saltwater), sightseeing, viewpoints

With its generous samplings of all the treasures created when land meets sea, Deception Pass serves as a perfect introduction to the San Juan and North Sound islands. Here are quiet virgin forests; coves, bays, and wave-tossed beaches holding treasures from the sea; awesome rock escarpments; grassy bluffs festooned with twisted "bonsai" trees and bright meadow flowers; deer, seals, otters, eagles, and bizarre marine life; and lakes hosting trout and waterfowl—all to be enjoyed by motorist, bicyclist, pedestrian, or boater. These attractions are not unnoticed, however, and the park is swamped by sightseers and recreation-seekers on weekends and holidays. An estimated 1.5 million people visit the park annually.

Although Deception Pass is separated from the San Juan Islands by bureaucratic boundaries, it has a strong geologic and historic kinship with that region. The same strata of Late Jurassic igneous rock that underlies Turtleback Mountain on Orcas Island forms the enclosing granite walls of Deception Pass. The Pleistocene glacier that rasped its way across Orcas, San Juan, and Lopez islands 15,000 years ago also

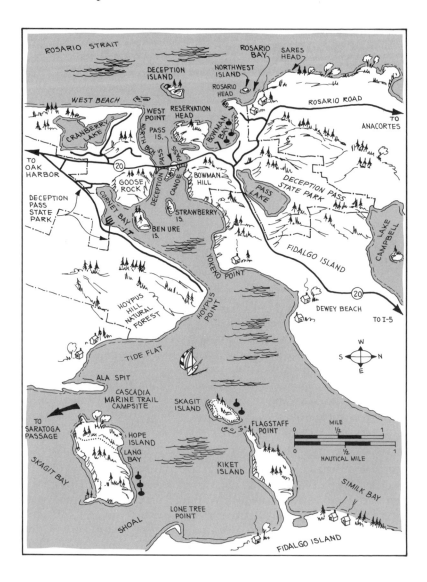

gouged out the bays and channels of Deception Pass and smoothed the brows of Bowman Hill and Goose Rock. The first Spanish explorers who charted the islands noted the relationship of these islands and their network of waterways and designated the entire area as the "San Juan Archipelago."

So captivating are the physical beauties of the park that many visitors never realize that the area is equally interesting historically. Pioneer life of the Deception Pass area was colorful, sometimes even lurid—replete with tales of hardy settlers who tamed the land and of some equally hardy smugglers, cutthroats, and pirates who sought greater fortune, or perhaps just greater adventure.

During the late 1800s a portion of the land within the present park was designated as a military reservation for the coastal defense of the region. At the end of World War I, local residents began a movement to have the area, already a favorite picnicking, camping, and rhododendron-viewing spot, officially designated as a park. In 1921, 1,746 acres were dedicated as Deception Pass State Park.

At the outbreak of World War II, some of the land was temporarily requisitioned back from the park by the U.S. government. Three 3-inch guns brought from Fort Casey, on Whidbey Island, were set up at North Beach and Reservation Head and a searchlight was installed at West Point. Some concrete pads from these emplacements are still to be seen in the park.

Since the dedication of the original tract of land, additional property has been purchased, donated, or transferred from the Department of Natural Resources to the jurisdiction of the park from other state agencies and private citizens, so that the present acreage is slightly less than 3,600 acres, encompassing six entire islands, parts of Whidbey and Fidalgo islands, two lakes, and one ocean (as one park brochure describes it).

Deception Pass State Park can be reached by ferry from Mukilteo to Columbia Beach on the southeast tip of Whidbey Island, then by car or bicycle along Highway 525 (which becomes Highway 20) the length of the island to its northern end, a distance of 50 miles. To approach Deception Pass from the north, avoiding the occasionally crowded (although always scenic) ferry ride, leave I-5 at Exit 230, just north of Mount Vernon, and follow Highway 20 east. Signs direct the way to the park, 18 miles from the freeway.

Deception Pass lies just east of the confluence of the Strait of Juan de Fuca and Rosario Strait. Mariners approaching from the south often duck behind the shelter of Whidbey Island and run Saratoga Passage and Skagit Bay northward to reach the pass. Trailered boats can be launched at ramps at Cornet Bay and Bowman Bay within the park.

DECEPTION PASS AREA

One cannot fail to be impressed by the drama of Deception Pass, whether viewing it as a land-bound tourist from the heights of the 182-foot-high bridge or experiencing it as a skipper attempting a first white-knuckle run through the narrow passageway. Measured against the timelessness of granite and the power of the boiling tidal current, man's great structural achievement of concrete and steel seems fragile indeed.

The entrance to the waterway was charted by early Spaniards, but it

The Deception Pass Bridge is stunningly dramatic, whether viewed from above or from the water.

was British sea captain George Vancouver who first explored it in 1792. Vancouver named it to express his feeling of deception, for he originally thought the pass was the mouth of a large bay indenting the peninsula that is now known to be Whidbey Island. Before the days of engines, large sailing ships, unable to maneuver in its confines, avoided the pass, choosing instead to sail southward along the outside shore of the island. Captain Thomas Coupe, who settled near Penn Cove in 1852, was the first man to brave the pass in a square rigger. Coupe, a mariner noted for his exceptional courage and skill, challenged the pass under full sail in his three-masted bark the *Success*.

The rock-walled main channel of Deception Pass itself is scarcely 500 feet across, and Canoe Pass, on the north, is a claustrophobic 50 feet wide at its narrowest point, with a sharp dogleg along the way. It is, however, the current pouring through the channels and its associated churning eddies that are the concern of most skippers, for it reaches a velocity of up to 8 knots as the granite spigot of the pass performs its twice-daily task of filling, then draining, then refilling Skagit Bay. Very experienced kayakers use the pass as an area to practice running strong currents.

Skippers are advised to consult local tidal current tables and enter the pass during slack water, when the velocity of the current is at its minimum. Although fast boats do make the trip through the channel at other times, boating skill and knowledge of the local waters is advisable. High-powered boats should stay well away from other boats in the waterway so their wake does not cause the less-powerful vessels additional problems.

Deception Pass Bridge

The Deception Pass Bridge, which was begun in 1934 and completed the following year, spans the gulf between Fidalgo and Whidbey islands, utilizing little Pass Island for its central pillars. Nearly 30 years of effort in state and national government were needed to bring the bridge into being.

The bridge is part of Highway 20, reached from the north via Anacortes and from the south via Whidbey Island. Parking areas at either end of the bridge enable sightseers to leave their cars and walk along the span for a view of the pass.

As early as 1907 the land link to Whidbey Island was urged in order to support the military garrison at Fort Casey and as an assistance to agricultural growth on Whidbey Island. Blueprints were prepared, but time and again hopes were dashed as the government failed to appropriate funds for the project.

Finally, in 1933, the bridge appeared about to receive approval in the state legislature; Skagit and Island counties earmarked $150,000 in local funds and work began on the approaches to the span. However, once more the state legislature balked, and it was not until the following year, after some fast footwork by local politicians, that the money was finally approved, along with some matching funds from the federal Public Works Administration. In August the excavation of solid rock for the first pier of the bridge was begun.

A highline with four-ton capacity was rigged to Pass Island to transport the derrick for structural steel work, water lines were laid from Cranberry and Pass lakes for mixing the concrete, and a month was spent building an aggregate bunker and a cement warehouse. Month after month the steel fretwork grew against the sky until in July 1935, slightly less than a year from the beginning of the first excavation, the cantilevered spans stretching outward from Fidalgo, Pass, and Whidbey islands were ready to be joined. Steelworkers clambering on the bridge under the hot summer sun were unable to align the sections; however, in the cool of the following morning when the metal had contracted enough to allow proper matching of the diagonals, the final joining was completed. Deception Pass was bridged!

Pass (Canoe) Island

Parking areas at either end of the bridge and on Pass Island (which is sometimes known as Canoe Island) allow sightseers to leave their cars and walk along the span for a view of the pass that Captain George Vancouver never enjoyed.

Trails eastward from the middle parking area traverse the rocky meadowland of grass, sedges, wildflowers, and gnarled, weather-twisted trees. The wildflower diversity on the island was once famous, but heavy visitor traffic has tramped most to oblivion. Please treat any remaining plants and flowers with care—take photos, not blossoms. Use extreme care and keep a tight hand on small children because the bluffs drop off steeply into the churning water. At the far eastern tip the slope gentles enough to enable hikers to reach the water's edge.

A magnificent display of underwater life on the walls of Goose Rock and around Pass Island rewards venturesome scuba divers; however, the treacherous tidal current makes this an area only for experts.

Prison Camp

Looking from the east end of Pass Island north to the cliff wall of Fidalgo Island, a gaping cave and an outfall of rock debris can be seen. This is the remainder of a rock quarry that was operated in conjunction with a state prison camp, through Walla Walla State Penitentiary, from 1909 to 1914. A large wooden rock crusher was built below the quarry, stretching down the cliff to the water's edge. Rock dug from the quarry was put into the crusher, then mechanically sorted into bins, and eventually loaded via chutes onto barges that were brought into Canoe Pass.

The penal colony was located on a small bay due north of the eastern end of Pass Island. Up to 40 prisoners at a time lived in the stockade; service buildings and homes of the prison guards were nearby. Only scant evidence of the colony remains—a round cistern, some bricks, and scattered tiles, all nearly covered by brush. Park rangers discourage hikers from climbing on the cliffs in the quarry's vicinity because they are extremely dangerous. Be content to view it from the water or Pass Island.

Strawberry Island

Perhaps Strawberry is the perfect island; its 3 acres are just enough to assure visitors a measure of solitude in the middle of a busy freeway, while its mossy granite slopes are an insular rock garden bedecked with wind-shredded junipers, sedums, and wild strawberries. To this add the crowning touch: a stupendous view into the jaws of Deception Pass.

Salmon fishermen sometimes anchor offshore, but the island itself is accessible only to kayaks and other boats small enough to be drawn up on the rocky beaches. Skill and experience in boat handling are necessary to reach the island. Landing is easiest on the south and east sides, where the slopes flare more gently into the water. Small boats should approach on a rising tide, when the flow will push the craft eastward into quieter water, rather than draw it into the pass, less than ½ mile away.

Although the island is part of the state park, there are no camping amenities on shore. Please take any trash back home with you and leave the island as pretty as when you arrived.

The view east from Deception Pass Bridge. Pass Island is in the left foreground, Strawberry Island on the right.

Cornet Bay

Access: Land, boat
Facilities [at the state park]: Dock with float, offshore floats, boat launch (ramps), picnic tables, fireplaces, drinking water, restrooms, showers; **[at the marina]:** dock with floats, boat launch (hoist), diesel, gas, groceries, snack bar, laundromat, restrooms, showers
Attractions: Fishing, boating, paddling, bicycling, scuba diving, hiking, beachcombing, clam digging

Just a watery mile east of Deception Pass, Cornet Bay is a placid refuge from the often-turbulent waters of the pass. For boaters heading east to cruise the quiet of Skagit Bay, or those waiting for slack tide to enable them to run the pass, Cornet Bay offers both launching for trailered boats and mooring facilities for larger ones that arrive by water.

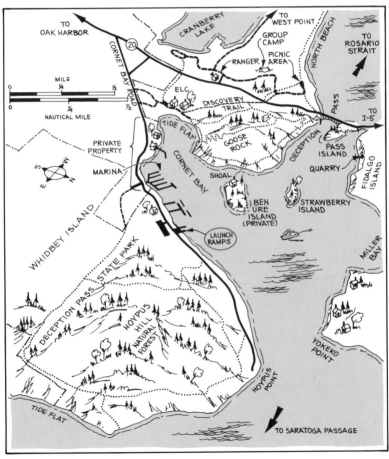

To reach Cornet Bay by land, drive south across the Deception Pass bridge (Highway 20) onto Whidbey Island and past the park headquarters at the state park entrance. About 1 mile south of the bridge, turn east onto Cornet Bay Road. The state park marine facilities are reached in 1¼ miles.

A wide grass strip along the beach of Cornet Bay is dotted with picnic tables and fire braziers. The park dock drops to a 250-foot-long float. Two more 50-foot floats are anchored to offshore pilings, parallel to the inshore float. A dock and float to the west are restricted to use by state park service boats.

Four boat launch ramps, with two loading piers between, drop into the bay. Parking is in a nearby lot or in a larger area across the road to the south. A commercially operated marina that is slightly farther into the bay has fuel, a float with overnight moorages, a launching lift, and supplies.

Privately owned Ben Ure Island, lying in the mouth of Cornet Bay, was named for an Anacortes businessman-turned-smuggler who lived there with his Native American wife during the late 1800s. The story goes that when planning to be away on a "business" trip, Ure would instruct his wife to build an evening campfire on the northern tip of the island. If Revenue agents were lying in wait in Cornet Bay, she would signal her husband by standing in front of the fire to block the light. If all was clear she sat to the side and its beacon would guide him home. Today a navigational light is located near the spot where Ben Ure's wife maintained her navigational aid.

Boaters unfamiliar with the area should not attempt to enter Cornet Bay on the west side of Ben Ure Island as a shoal extends westward from the island.

Traffic is generally light on Cornet Bay Road, making it an excellent bicycle detour. The blacktopped run is downhill or level all the way to road's end at Hoypus Point, with a 100-foot climb back to the Highway 20 intersection on the return.

The Environmental Learning Center and Goose Rock

Facilities: Trails, beach; [available for use by reservation]: cabins, kitchen, dining hall, infirmary, recreation hall, swimming pool, playing fields, campfire circle
Attractions: Hiking, group activities

The state park's Environmental Learning Center on Coronet Bay provides a base of operations for visiting environmental-education groups. Camp facilities, located at the head of Cornet Bay, are reached via the turnoff road to the ELC, ½ mile east of the Highway 20/Cornet Bay

Road intersection. Towering nearly 500 feet above Cornet Bay, Goose Rock is a small echo of Mount Erie to the north on Fidalgo Island, with its glacier-scoured northern slope reflecting the southbound course of an ancient ice field, and its near-vertical south face, to the lee of the glacier, exhibiting little evidence of such wearing.

Trails on the rock interweave, merge, and sometimes end abruptly. Most lead to spectacular views. Trailheads are at the ELC or North Beach parking lot. The Discovery Trail, which runs from the ELC to Highway 20, has numbered stations that identify flora and unique geological features along the way. A wide choice of other side paths and alternate destinations permits an interesting variety of trips and scenery. Total distance for an average loop hike is about 3½ miles.

Low tide bares acres of eelgrass-coated mudflat in Cornet Bay—a marked contrast to the wave-scrubbed beaches on the west side of the park. Muck about and examine the variety of tiny marine life that inhabits the intertidal zone. The ½-mile section of property to the east, between the ELC and state park dock, is privately owned, so do not trespass.

Hoypus Point

Cornet Bay Road continues northeast from Cornet Bay along the shore to Hoypus Point, passing a gated side road and a borrow pit that are starting points for the 3½-mile hike that loops around Hoypus Hill. The hill has been designated as Natural Forest Area, which means it is open to foot travel only—bicycles and horses are prohibited. Four hundred acres on the south of the hill were acquired from the DNR to preserve one of the last vestiges of lowland old-growth fir forest in the region. There are no trails in this acreage, and plans are to designate it a Natural Preserve Area, with no entry permitted except for research studies.

The road drive is scenic enough, with glimpses through a fringe of trees and brush of boating traffic in the channel; however, walking the beach provides a more pleasant activity, with unobstructed views of Mount Erie due north and Mount Baker rising above Similk Bay to the northwest. The beach is narrow, but is passable during all but the highest tide. When high water forces the route inland, the low bank can easily be scrambled and the road walked for a distance. Hoypus Point, at road's end, is reached in slightly over a mile.

From 1912 until the Deception Pass bridge was completed in 1935, a ferry operated between here and Dewey Beach, linking Whidbey and Fidalgo islands. A concrete bulkhead, remnants of the old ferry landing, can still be seen at the road end at Hoypus Point. Old newspaper accounts tell of the crowded ferry conditions on Sundays (even then!), when carloads of tourists made springtime excursions to the park to picnic and to view the pink masses of wild rhododendrons. Although the ferry has long since ceased operating, the flowers are still a spring attraction.

Beyond the point the walking is even better, with a broader beach and views across the channel. In about a mile the park boundary is reached; the tideflat continues on for yet another mile to Ala Spit, a Cascadia Marine Trail campsite. The trip from Cornet Bay to the park boundary and back is about 4 miles.

Hope and Skagit Islands

Area: Hope Island, 166 acres; Skagit Island, 21 acres
Facilities: Mooring buoys, picnic tables, fireplaces, pit toilet, *no water*
Attractions: Camping, picnicking, fishing, canoeing, crabbing, clam
    digging, scuba diving, beachcombing

Stretched across the middle of the channel between Whidbey and Fidalgo islands, Hope Island heralds the end of Skagit Bay and the beginning of Similk Bay. Hope and its smaller neighbor, Skagit Island, are undeveloped parts of the state park.

On the north side of Hope Island is the meager indentation of Lang Bay. Three mooring buoys are stretched along the shore to the east. Ashore, a few picnic tables with fire grates can be found in clearings above the beach; drinking water is not available. A trail that cuts across the island can be followed from the campground to the south shore. During moderate to low tides, the beach can be walked for a mile or more from Lang Bay around the east end of the island to a magnificent sand and driftwood beach on the south. Incoming tide can trap unwary hikers on any of three beaches.

Hope Island is currently being considered for designation as a Natural Preserve Area, because the site was traditionally used by the Samish tribe. If the state Parks and Recreation Commission approves this designation, no public access will be permitted on the island.

Less than a mile to the north, Skagit Island is a much smaller version of Hope Island, duplicating its open, grassy bluffs on the southwest side and thick forest on the remainder. A 6-foot rocky bank circles the island, except on the northwest side where a shoal reaches out to Kiket Island. Two

Walking the beach at Hope Island

buoys off the northeast shore provide a place to hang a boat while din-ghy-exploring nearby shallow waters, or while waiting to go through the pass. Shore adventurers can hike the trail that rings the island along the top of the embankment. On the northeast end of the island are two primitive campsites. Raccoons, porcupines, crows, and other scavengers often scatter trash; to minimize the problem take your garbage home with you.

The waters around the islands west to Hoypus Point and north to the shallows of Similk Bay offer splendid small-boat excursions; how-ever, the tidal current is quite strong in some areas and a paddle-pro-pelled or underpowered craft may find itself going in a different direction than intended. Use care, watch for tide rips, and stay well away from large, moving boats.

Skagit Island is said to have been a hideout for smugglers and all sorts of ruffians on the run from justice at the turn of the century. Its strategic location, at the bend of the channel with views into Deception Pass and up-channel into Skagit Bay, made any stealthy approach by law boats quite difficult.

Deadman and Little Deadman Islands

Two tiny islands that sit on the fringe of the low-tide mud banks of Skagit Bay, about 1½ miles southeast of Hope Island, are undeveloped state park property. Deadman and Little Deadman islands are shown as Tonkon Islands on some charts. Their names come from the Native practice of interring the dead in canoes fastened to high branches of trees on the islands.

These two islands lie in such shallow water, 0 to 6 feet at mean lower low water, that they can only safely be visited by kayaks or other shal-low-draft craft. There are no shoreside facilities on either island, and camping and fires are prohibited.

Bowman and Rosario Bays

Access: Land, boat
Facilities: 24 campsites (on Bowman Bay), picnic tables, fireplaces, drinking water, picnic shelters, kitchens, restrooms, showers, boat launch (ramp), dock with float, mooring buoys, CCC Interpretive Center, fishing pier, underwater park, children's playground
Attractions: Camping, picnicking, boating, paddling, hiking, fishing, scuba diving, hiking, tidepools, windsurfing

Yet another facet of this diverse park: here rounded bays facing away from the swirling current of the pass enable sea life to grow in profusion on rocks and beaches. Offshore, salmon runs attract commercial and sport fishermen.

Bowman (Reservation) Bay

Some nautical charts still designate Bowman Bay as Reservation Bay, a holdover from World War I when a military reservation was located here. Local residents, agreeing with the U.S. Geological Survey, prefer the name of Bowman Bay, honoring the Fidalgo Island pioneer who had a summer cabin on the shore.

Bowman Bay is reached by car by following the signs at the intersection of Highway 20 at the west end of Pass Lake. The road, which may be closed in winter, drops sharply downhill to a large open flat at the head of the bay. The campground is located in timber on the northern edge of the bay. A single-lane concrete ramp between the campground and a long pier is the only launching facility for boats in this section of the park.

The bay offers some anchorages for boaters, although care must be used on entering because numerous rocks foul the entrance. Five mooring buoys in the bay provide tie-ups for visiting boaters. The long sta-

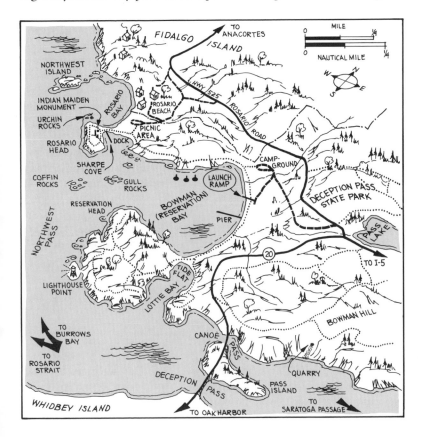

tionary pier in the bay is the remains of a defunct fish hatchery. While the pier is a fine place from which to fish, it is unsatisfactory for mooring boats because the vertical pilings are widely spaced, and the dock level is so high above the water that disembarking is impossible.

Although much smaller than Bowman Bay, Sharpe Cove to the north, tucked behind Rosario Head, is usually a better spot for a layover. The park maintains a small dock with a float on the cove, and there is space for several good anchorages.

The CCC Interpretive Center

The strong, road-edging guardrails of rock and logs, sturdy stone-walled restrooms and kitchen shelters, and rustic cedar and cedar-shake picnic shelters that the state park boasts are all products of the Depression-era Civilian Conservation Corps. The CCC was one of the most popular New Deal programs instituted by President Franklin D. Roosevelt to break the country free of the effects of the Great Depression. Over 300,000 unemployed young men flooded into selection offices during the summer of 1933. They were enrolled in the Corps and sent on minimum six-month tours of duty to camps scattered across the nation where they worked on projects to conserve natural resources. They erected and managed their own camps and then constructed trails to fire lookouts, fought forest fires, felled snags, planted trees, and built parks. The men, led by regular and reserve Army officers, were trained in basic educational and job skills to equip them to find work once they left the Corps. A number of Washington's older state parks owe their facilities to the CCC.

At Bowman Bay, between the campground and the boat launch area a rock-walled building that was built by these men now houses displays telling the story of the CCC. Panels describe the CCC and camp life, display cases contain photos and memorabilia from the camps, and in a video program a veteran of the Deception Pass CCC Camp tells of his experiences. The volunteer-staffed center is open Thursday through Monday during summer months, or at other times by appointment.

Reservation Head

The path south along the shore of Bowman Bay leads to hiking trails that traverse Reservation Head and a smaller, unnamed headland lying east of Lottie Bay.

Climbing high on exposed, grassy bluffs, the trails offer views into Deception Pass, across to Cranberry Lake, and out to the inviting blue-green islands of the San Juans. Shallow Lottie Bay separates the two cliffy headlands. Long ago Bowman and Lottie bays were joined as a continuous waterway; over the years, wave action built the sand neck linking Reservation Head to Fidalgo Island that created the two bays. At extreme low tide, Lottie Bay is nearly drained, and the interesting sea life on its muddy bottom is exposed.

Rosario Bay

The state park shares this choice bay with a university marine research facility and a number of private homes.

To reach the beach, turn north from Highway 20 at Pass Lake onto Rosario Road (Highway 525). In about a mile signs direct motorists to Rosario Beach. Follow the road to the state park.

The spacious picnic area faces on Rosario Bay and Sharpe Cove. Restrooms have outside showers for rinsing saltwater from swimmers and scuba divers. Trails from the picnic area lead upward to the modest heights of Rosario Head or around Sharpe Cove and on to Bowman Bay. Lanky firs along the trail extend horizontally out over the water, supported by but a few roots. Possibly the next storm will see their demise, or perhaps they will still be stubbornly clinging there when your grandchildren hike the trail.

The underwater park is legendary among divers and marine biologists for its extravaganza of sea life. Beneath the water is a rococo world of flamboyant anemones, sea pens, nudibranchs, sponges, and a large concentration of purple and green sea urchins. The rocks lying just off Rosario Head are well named as Urchin Rocks. The bay itself is suitable for snorkelers and divers with beginning skill; greater experience is needed to venture out of the bay into deeper, swifter water. At low water, tidepools give land-bound sightseers a glimpse of what lies beneath the water. This is a marine preserve; the taking or destruction of any marine life is prohibited.

The territory from Deception Pass eastward belonged to the Samish tribe, who harvested the vast runs of salmon that swarmed through the channels. The pass obviously impressed early Native Americans as much as it does

A monument at Rosario Head commemorates a Native American legend.

people today, for it is mentioned in several of their legends. One tells of an Indian princess named Ko-kwal-alwoot who lived at Deception Pass and who became the bride of the king of the fishes, going to live with him in his underwater kingdom. Her long, flowing hair, turned green from its long exposure to water, can still be seen drifting in the current, although some people see it only as seaweed.

A monument representing this legend has been placed near the beach on Rosario Head. The 24-foot cedar log, carved in the traditional style of the Samish Indians, shows Ko-kwal-alwoot on one side as an Indian maiden and on the other as the sea spirit she became.

Northwest Island

Northwest Island, ½ mile northwest of the Rosario Beach picnic area, is yet another of the park's small undeveloped islands. The grassy, 1-acre rock is visited mainly by gulls and scuba divers. Although it lies temptingly close, divers are advised to take a boat to the island rather than attempt to swim the distance, because the tidal current is very strong.

CRANBERRY LAKE VICINITY

Access: Land
Facilities: 221 campsites (at Cranberry Lake), bicycle campground, picnic tables, fireplaces, drinking water, picnic shelters, kitchens, restrooms, bathhouse, showers, swimming beach, boat launch (ramp on Cranberry Lake), fishing dock, playground
Attractions: Camping, picnicking, boating, paddling, fishing, hiking, beachcombing, swimming

The Cranberry Lake entrance to Deception Pass State Park is on the west side of Highway 20, slightly less than ¾ mile south of the Deception Pass bridge. At the entrance, two intersections direct visitors first north to the North Beach picnic area, then west to the campground and West Point or south to the Cranberry Lake picnic area. At the second intersection is the trailhead for a ¼-mile nature walk and a large display board detailing park information.

This is one of the best bicycling areas in the park, with smooth and level roads first wending through cool forest, then edging the lakeshore. Tent sites for late-arriving bicyclists are usually available at Cranberry Lake Campground, even if the campground is filled with car campers.

North Beach

Whether seen from the forest trail that traverses it or from the water's edge, North Beach is one of the most popular areas in the park. A trailhead can be found on the outside loop of the lower Cranberry Lake Campground, or by heading east on any of several well-beaten paths from the West Point parking lot. The nearly mile-long curve of the beach is broken by three rocky headlands. The most prominent of these, Gun Point, was the location of 3-inch rapid-fire cannons that guarded the pass during World War II.

At low tide the beach is easily walked from West Point to the base of the vertical cliffs below the Deception Pass Bridge. Higher tides force the route inland at times for scrambles over the rocky bluffs or a retreat to the trail higher up in the forest. From the North Beach picnic area the trail continues east beneath the bridge and on to Goose Rock. East of Gun Point hikers enjoy ant's eye views of the bridge and, at slack tide, the parade of boats through the pass.

The picnic area lies at the end of the first spur road inside the park entrance. From a parking lot in ¾ mile, a path leads across a rustic wooden bridge over a marsh to the sandy beach area with a picnic shelter, picnic tables, and fire braziers.

On the south side of the road leading to the North Beach picnic area is a 64-person group camp. This popular camp area in a wooded setting is available by reservation only.

Cranberry Lake

Had the ancient glacier that carved Deception Pass tried a little harder and dug a mere 50 feet deeper, Cornet Bay would have reached through to Rosario Strait, Goose Rock would have been an island, and Cran-

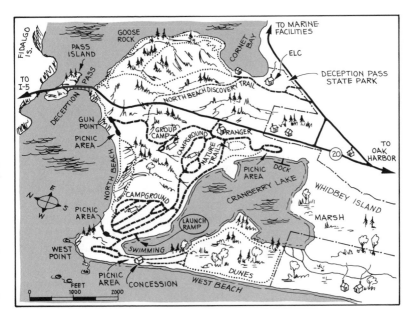

Cranberry Lake is ideal for swimming, paddling, and small boat sailing.

berry Lake never would have come into being. As it was, a neck of land remained, joining Goose Rock to the glacial outfall of Whidbey Island and forming the Cranberry Lake area merely as a shallow saltwater inlet of the sea. Over the centuries, wind and waves sweeping in from the Strait of Juan de Fuca built a sandbar that eventually joined to the rocks of West Point, forming a lagoon similar to those found in other places on the island. However, instead of the brackish seawater entrapped in other lagoons, here an underground spring filled the shallow depression and changed the environment from salt to freshwater marsh, with cattails, willows, skunk cabbages, lily pads, muskrats, beavers, river otters, ducks, and fish.

Cranberry Lake is only about 10 to 20 feet deep throughout, with its deepest point a 40-foot "hole" near the north shore. It continues to be filled in with sediment; the closing-in of the lake margins is quite evident in photos taken over a period of years. In perhaps just a few hundred years the lake will be completely filled in and overgrown with vegetation.

The lake, which is stocked with trout, is inviting for either fishing or quiet-water paddling; boats with gasoline motors are not permitted.

Muskeg bogs on the southwest can only be reached by water; there the observant may spot beaver and muskrat lodges at the edge of the marsh. A gravel boat launch ramp is on the north shore of the lake between the campground entrance and the day-use area. Lightweight boats can be put in from the picnic area by carrying them the short distance from the parking lot to the water.

On the southeast corner of the lake is a large picnic area in grass studded with shade-providing trees. Paths lead from the parking lot down to a long fishing dock that parallels the shoreline. The massive CCC-built kitchen shelter above the dock is located on the site of an old Native American longhouse; apparently the early members of the Samish tribe enjoyed the spot in the past as much as visitors do today.

West Point and West Beach

Contained in this small area is probably the greatest diversity of environment within the park: forest, lake, cattail bogs, rocky headland, ocean surf, and one of the finest sand beaches and dunelands on Puget Sound, all enhanced by views back to Mount Erie and out across the Strait of Juan de Fuca to snowy Olympic peaks. The downside of its attractions, however, is seen on sunny spring and summer weekends or on holidays when the area draws Coney Island-sized crowds, and park rangers become traffic cops attempting to handle the throngs.

On hot summer days, visitors can bathe in the supervised swimming area on the northwest beach of bathwater-warm Cranberry Lake or dash across the sandbar for a bracing dip in the frigid sound. Picnic tables along the beach face on either the lake or the sound. Prospective clam diggers will find slim pickings on West Beach—waves sweeping in from the strait constantly shift the sand, making it an impossible environment for sea life. The beauty of the shore lies in its pristine, unbroken sweep, and in the dunes that back it. A blacktop path leads into the dunes, which are now anchored by vegetation. Several picnic tables are along the path; a small wooden balcony provides an overview of the marsh.

In winter, when storm winds howl in from the ocean, sending waves crashing against the rocks at West Point, hardy souls who savor the excitement of marine pyrotechnics will enjoy a visit to West Beach. Such storms are literally breathtaking; at times they are so severe it is impossible to stand against the force of the wind. Post-storm beachcombing may yield driftwood, agates, interesting flotsam, and seafoam to play in.

Deception Island

Lying less than ½ mile northwest of West Point, rugged Deception Island is a far outpost of the state park. Eastern approaches to the island are shallow and rock-riddled and the current can be strong; boaters should use great care. Immediately to the west, the underwater shelf drops off quickly, making for excellent fishing and scuba diving just offshore.

Small boats may be beached on any of several rocky coves; the largest bay on the northwest side of the island is probably the easiest.

Due to its difficult access and limited use, the island has not been developed by the park and has no onshore amenities.

PASS LAKE AND HEART LAKE AREAS

Pass Lake

Access: Land
Facilities: Boat launch (ramp on Pass Lake)
Attractions: Fishing (freshwater), paddling

Water holds its own special fascination, whether as ocean swells surging through narrow rocky channels, as placid waves lapping on sandy beaches, or in brackish marshes choked with cattails. Here the state park offers 100 acres of crystal-clear lake water for trout fishing or still-water canoeing.

Pass Lake lies at the junction of Highway 20 and Rosario Road (Highway 525). A gravel public boat ramp and parking lot adjoin the intersection. Some pull-offs where the road parallels the lakeshore provide spots to put in portable boats or to park and have a waterfront picnic.

The trout-stocked lake is open to fly fishing during fishing season; gasoline motors are not permitted. A favorite means of fishing the lake is with a float tube and waders. Canoeists find paddling the length of the lake and along the brushy shoreline to be idyllic. Deer, muskrat,

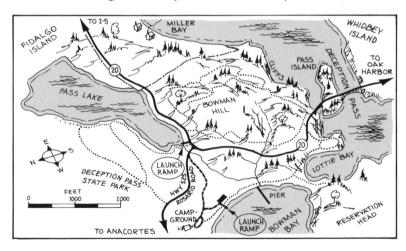

skunk, fox, and other small wild animals may be seen on shore, especially at dusk. In winter migratory ducks stop to rest on the lake, floating together in convivial rafts. A boot-path wanders along the northwest shore of the lake, and connects to other primitive trails through the woods that reach Rosario Road ¼ mile west of Highway 20.

Bowman Hill, south of the lake, is a densely wooded, undeveloped section of the park. About 2 miles of unimproved trails loop over and around the hill, leading to stunning panoramas from bald viewpoints. The trails are recommended only for hikers experienced in route finding. The south slope of Bowman Hill is extremely cliffy; hikers are warned to stay well away from the edge. Trails begin at the pullout just north of the bridge.

Shoreline trees reflect in the quiet water of Heart Lake.

Heart Lake

Access: Land
Facilities: Boat launch (ramp), vault toilets
Attractions: Boating, fishing (freshwater), hiking

Heart Lake was transferred from the state DNR to the Parks and Recreation Commissioner in 1981 as part of Deception Pass State Park. Since it was disjointed from the remainder of the park, the property was transferred to the City of Anacortes in 2001.

The boggy shoreline is a critical wetlands environment. Marsh birds twitter and scold in the cattails; a sudden splash of water gives evidence of a hungry trout—or perhaps only a frog.

The land surrounding the 66-acre lake, now designated as a Natural Forest Area, is restricted to foot traffic only. The only public access to the lake is on its east side, off Heart Lake Road, 3 miles south of Anacortes. A poorly marked turnoff leads to a broad parking lot above a single-lane concrete launch ramp on the east side of the lake. Foot trails leave the parking area for circuits around the lake. The area is open for day-use only; its only amenities are a pair of vault toilets. The 66-acre lake, a favorite with anglers, is stocked with rainbow trout. The lake also serves as a backup water supply for the city of Anacortes.

CHAPTER SIX

WHIDBEY ISLAND

Early sea captains, seeking shelter from Puget Sound storms, found refuge for their vessels and crews behind Whidbey Island. They were so fond of this long, sheltering arm that upon retirement many of them, along with their men, settled on the friendly island. Thomas Coupe, the most well-known of these seamen, had the town of Coupeville named after him.

The island was given its name by British sea captain George Vancouver during his voyage of discovery. In May 1792 Vancouver, along with his lieutenant, Peter Puget, explored the southern channels of what was to become Puget Sound. The examination of the South Sound completed, Vancouver turned his attention to the maze of waterways lying to the north. On May 31, Vancouver anchored in Possession Sound, just off Gedney Island, and dispatched Ship's Master Joseph Whidbey to explore the two branches of the waterway leading to the north. After a brief examination of the waterway to the east, Whidbey explored the western one along the shores of a long island, as far north as Deception Pass. Vancouver named these two channels Port Susan and Port Gardner. The name of Port Susan remains today, but Port Gardner later came to be known as Saratoga Passage; only the small bay by Everett is now Port Gardner.

As he continued his exploration up Admiralty Inlet, Vancouver discovered that Deception Pass, which he had thought to be a bay, was a passageway that connected to the long channel that Whidbey had explored earlier, and therefore the landmass was an island. He honored Whidbey by naming the island after him.

Vancouver and Whidbey had noted the friendly, peaceful nature of the Skagit Indians living on the island. Although these natives warred with their enemies, the Haida Indians from Canada, their early contacts with white settlers were usually amicable. One of the Skagit chiefs, Snatelum, invited a French Catholic missionary from Fort Nisqually to visit the island. In 1840 Father Blanchet visited the island, conducted a mass baptism, and established a mission.

Thomas Glasgow is credited with being the first European to settle on Whidbey Island. He traveled to the island by canoe in 1848 and selected a homestead site on a windswept prairie near the west shore of the island. The Native Americans were beginning to have second thoughts about intrusions by the white men, and the threatening attitude of the natives caused Mr. Glasgow to depart quickly, leaving his crops of wheat and potatoes behind. In October 1850 Colonel Issac N. Ebey filed the first land claim on the island—on exactly the same fertile prairie that Glasgow had left.

The central section of Whidbey Island is markedly historic, with pioneer relics around nearly every bend of the road. Eight separate vicinities, commemorating over 100 years of rural settlement and coastal defense, are included in Ebey's Landing National Historical Reserve.

The northern part of the island has a distinctive Dutch flavor, with Dutch names on some streets and businesses, a Holland festival in the spring, and even a replica of a windmill in the Oak Harbor city park. Back in 1894 a Whidbey Island land company made a concerted effort to attract Dutch settlers to the island, touting the rich farmland and temperate climate, quite similar to their homeland. More than 200 Hollanders came to Whidbey Island, some who had previously immigrated to the Midwest and others who came directly from the old country. Most settled on the northern end. The farming skills of these

The wharf at Coupeville is a Penn Cove landmark.

industrious people turned much of the rich soil, and even some of the poorer, into productive farmland.

A second industry, the military, has also left its mark on the island. Admiralty Head was the site of Fort Casey, one of the World War I forts that guarded Puget Sound. Although the Army post at Fort Casey is closed and the site is currently a state park, the military influence is now felt in the form of the huge U.S. Navy air base on the north end of the island. Military planes are so commonplace that a jet screaming overhead attracts less attention than the presence of a soaring bald eagle. Navy personnel, civilian employees, and their families account for nearly half of Whidbey Island's population. Quite a number of these, like the sea captains of yore, have settled permanently on the island after being mustered out of the service.

This 45-mile-long ribbon of an island averages a mere 3 miles in width. From some vantage points it is possible to see at one time both bodies of water that flank it—Saratoga Passage on the east and the Strait of Juan de Fuca or Admiralty Inlet on the west. Whidbey holds the

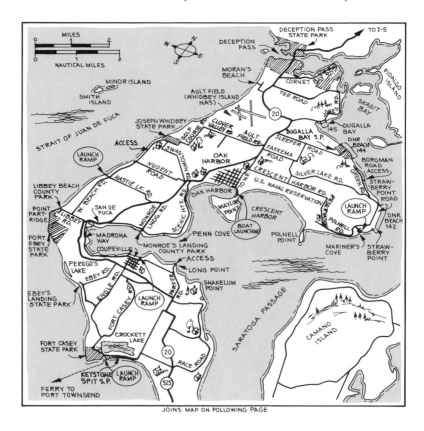

JOINS MAP ON FOLLOWING PAGE

honor of being the longest island in the United States; for many years New York's Long Island was considered to be the longest, but in 1985 the U.S. Supreme Court, ruling in a boundary dispute case, determined that Long Island is actually a peninsula.

The western edge of the island is frequently buffeted by winds and heavy seas sweeping in from the strait. Boaters will find no protection along the long, smooth windward shoreline or in its few broad, open bays. Whidbey's leeward eastern shore is deeply indented by several

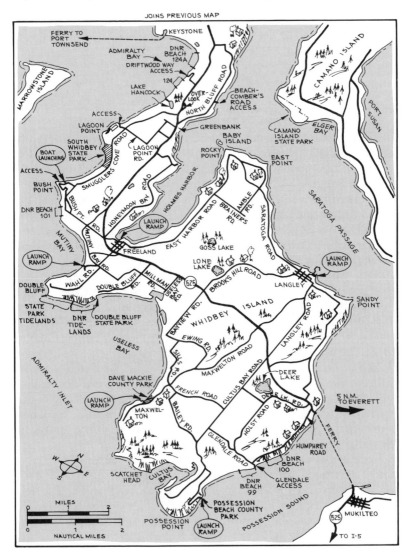

snug coves, providing welcome protection in foul weather. Much of the island's population and its few small towns are concentrated along this eastern side.

Access to Whidbey Island is by the Highway 20 bridge at Deception Pass at the north end of the island or, at the southern end, by ferry from Mukilteo on the mainland to Clinton. To reach the ferry, leave I-5 at Exit 189 and follow signs for 2½ miles to the terminal at Mukilteo. One main thoroughfare traverses the length of Whidbey Island—state Highway 20 from the northern end becomes Highway 525 in the southern part of the island. Midway on the island, at Keystone, a second ferry gives access to and from the Olympic Peninsula via Port Townsend.

STRAIT OF JUAN DE FUCA

Smith and Minor Islands

The extreme eastern end of the Strait of Juan de Fuca is marked by the navigational lights on Smith and Minor islands, which serve as an important landmark for boats traveling between Puget Sound and the San Juan Islands.

The two islands lie 4 nautical miles off the northwest shore of Whidbey Island. At low tide Smith joins the much smaller Minor Island. West of Smith Island a large kelp bed that extends for 1½ miles and a rock that bares at extreme low tides are boating hazards. Smith and Minor islands are designated as a National Wildlife Refuge in order to protect nesting seabirds. Minor Island is a major breeding site for harbor seals.

In the mid-1800s Smith Island, along with points on Cape Flattery, New Dungeness, and Admiralty Head, was noted as a critical navigational point and was selected as a site for a Coast Guard light. Construction on the Smith Island light began in 1857 and it was first lit in October 1858. The beacon was manned continuously until it was automated in 1976. Life on this remote rock was hardly exciting. Generally two men, with their families, were assigned to Smith Island. When not tending the lights they raised food in their garden or hunted the rabbits that overran the island. When seas were calm they could row their small boat 8 miles to the closest civilization—Richardson, the tiny general store on the southern tip of Lopez Island.

Battering by wind and waves from the strait has caused extreme erosion of the island—sometimes as much as 5 feet in a single year. In 1860 the island was about 50 acres in size; today it is less than 15. The light was originally located on a frame building, but erosion endangered the old structure, necessitating the relocation of the light on a tower farther inland. Some of the buildings were so badly undercut by erosion they collapsed into the sea.

Joseph Whidbey State Park

Park area: 112 acres; 3,100 feet of shoreline on the Strait of Juan de Fuca
Access: Land, boat
Facilities: Picnic tables, fireplaces, picnic shelter, pit toilets, Cascadia
    Marine Trail campsite, *no water*
Attractions: Picnicking, beachcombing, birdwatching

One of the most glorious beaches on Whidbey Island lies just south of the Naval Air Station. Here the state acquired from the Navy a section of land and turned it into a popular day-use park. The park has a dozen or so picnic tables on a grassy bench and paths leading down to the beach; other picnic tables are sequestered in the trees. At the lower beach-side area are about a half dozen more picnic sites, a picnic shelter, and a grassy playfield. Waves toss driftwood onto the long sandy beach. Smith and Minor islands can be seen directly offshore, 4 miles away.

Trails through the beach grass just above the driftwood line follow the beach north out of the park property and continue for more than a mile to the Navy's Rocky Point Picnic Area. Just before leaving the park the beach-side trail passes an inland marsh area—an excellent spot for birdwatching. Beach homes of Swantown delineate the southern end of the park. A second access to the park is on the south, immediately next to the first residence. Here is a graveled parking space for a few cars and a trail that leads directly to the beach.

To reach Joseph Whidbey State Park, take Highway 20 south out of Oak Harbor. Just outside of town at a major intersection, turn right onto Swantown Road and follow it for 3 miles to its intersection with West Beach Road; the park entrance is immediately to the right. If traveling from the north, just after passing the Navy base, turn west off Highway 20 onto Ault Field Road, which becomes Clover Valley Road in 2¼ miles, then successively transforms into Golf Course Road and Crosby Road before reaching the park.

Driftwood on the beach at Joseph Whidbey State Park makes a grand teeter-totter.

Point Partridge Launch Ramp

At the intersection of West Beach Road and Hastie Lake Road,

2¼ miles north of Libbey Road, is a parking lot sandwiched between private homes. Near the south end of this parking lot, a single-lane, concrete boat launch ramp leads to a cobble and boulder beach.

The paved lot, protected by a boulder-and-concrete bulkhead, has space for a half dozen boats with trailers. A park bench at the head of the launch ramp offers grand vistas of pleasure boats at play in the Strait of Juan de Fuca.

Launching at any of the ramps on this side of the island can be difficult. The access may be choked by sand, logs, or debris; winds off the strait frequently cause additional problems, and launching of large or heavy boats is difficult.

Libbey Beach County Park (Island County)

Park area: 3 acres; 300 feet of shoreline on the Strait of Juan de Fuca
Access: Land, paddle-craft
Facilities: Picnic tables, fireplaces, picnic shelter, pit toilets, *no water*
Attractions: Beachcombing, picnicking, boating

A very small county park just north of Point Partridge gives access to some wild and wonderful beach walks below the steep eroded cliffs on the west side of the island.

To reach it, turn off Highway 20 onto Libbey Road and follow it 1½ miles to its end at the loop road in the park.

Picnic tables in a grassy pocket away from the beach are well protected from wind, but do not provide a view of the water. A badly eroded and barricaded former launch ramp attests to the hard life launch ramps have on this side of the island. Beach walks south around the point lead to connecting trails from Fort Ebey State Park, ½ mile away. To the north lie 6 magnificent miles of public tidelands beneath 200-foot-high sandy bluffs. Use care not to become trapped by incoming tides.

Fort Ebey State Park

Park area: 644 acres; 11,000 feet of saltwater shoreline on Admiralty Inlet, 1,000 feet of freshwater shoreline on Lake Pondilla
Access: Land
Facilities: 53 campsites, bicycle campground, 3 primitive sites, picnic tables, fireplaces, drinking water, restrooms, 3 miles of hiking trails, Cascadia Marine Trail campsite
Attractions: Historical display, hiking, beachcombing, surfboarding, paragliding, parafoiling, viewpoints, fishing (freshwater)

As you stand on the heights above the Strait of Juan de Fuca you'll find it easy to see why the Army chose this site for a fort to protect the inland waters. From here, there is a vast panorama out to Point Wilson

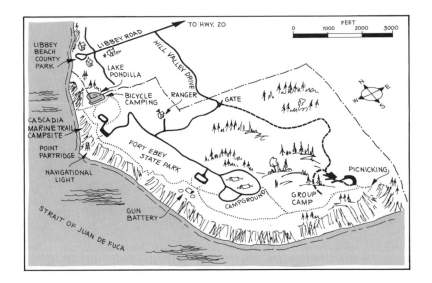

and Port Townsend, south down Admiralty Inlet, and north to Vancouver Island and the San Juans. This park does not have as fine a display of old military equipment as does Fort Casey to the south, but there is enough to keep inquisitive youngsters busy for a day and the campground is much nicer.

Fort Ebey State Park is reached from Highway 20 by driving west on Libbey Road. One mile from Highway 20, turn south onto Hill Valley Drive and follow the signs to the park. Near the ranger's residence the road splits at a T intersection. By following the road to the north, you reach trails and picnic tables. The trail begins near the restrooms, heads north along the top of the grassy bluff, passes picnic tables, and finally descends the bluff to the sandy, gently sloping beach. A wide, bay-head beach holds a layer of silvered driftwood.

More picnic sites are found at another roadside parking area at the bend just before the road's end. A short trail leads from here to the Point Partridge navigation light, then south along the bluff to the gun battery site.

A short trail from the north parking lot goes to Lake Pondilla, which has a bicycle camping area on its shores. Drinking water is available at the south end of the lake, but campers must hike the short distance back up the hill to use the restrooms. Bass fishing is rumored to be good in the 3½-acre pond.

The southern section of the park, at the other end of the T intersection, has the gun battery and the campground. This coast artillery fort was established in 1942, a world war later than Fort Casey. Fort Ebey was manned during World War II, but was surplused soon after its end.

Looking south from Fort Ebey State Park to Point Partridge

The smaller, more modern Navy guns placed here were designed as backup for the large guns on the emplacements built farther out on the Strait of Juan de Fuca at Point Flattery, Point Angeles, and Striped Peak west of Port Angeles.

There are no guns remaining, but youngsters enjoy prowling through the old battery shell rooms, spotting room, plotting room, and switchboard room, or climbing a metal ladder down a concrete shaft to a fire-control center located lower on the bluff, overlooking the strait. From the fire-control center observers directed the fire of the two 6-inch guns located in the battery. Picnic sites on the grassy bluff just north of the battery have excellent views across Admiralty Inlet to the snow-clad peaks of the Olympic Range. Trails from the emplacements continue south to Point Partridge, ¾ mile away.

Campsites with picnic tables and fireplaces are along two forested loops at the end of the road. None have RV hookups. Rhododendron bushes scattered throughout the timber promise a blaze of beauty in the spring.

A gated road heading south near the state park entrance ends at a former DNR Recreation Site that has been incorporated into the state park. The mile-long gravel road is a popular bicycle tour. At road's end picnic tables, each on its own terraced log-edged platform, give picnickers "balcony views." Just past the picnic area the trail breaks out onto a grassy windswept slope 150 feet above the water. Wide views encompass Perego's Lake, a saltwater lagoon at the end of a sweeping crescent of beach. Across Admiralty Inlet are Marrowstone Island and Port Townsend, and north of it Protection Island and Discovery Bay.

The old trail that diagonaled down the soft, glacial-till bluff to the beach has become eroded and unsafe; it may be replaced in the future if funding becomes available. A trail atop the bluff leads back to the campground at Fort Ebey State Park.

SKAGIT BAY AND NORTH SARATOGA PASSAGE

DNR Beaches 142, 144, and 145

Three sections of Department of Natural Resources public tidelands are located along the northeast shore of Whidbey Island.

At the very tip of Strawberry Point is DNR Beach 142, a 4,800-foot strip of tidelands accessible only by boat. There is good clam digging here during low tides, and good beach walking beneath towering bluffs anytime tides permit.

Farther north, as the bluffs begin to temper near Dugalla Bay, DNR Beach 144 offers 4,800 feet of shoreline as well as access to several acres of Dugalla Bay State Park uplands. This beach may also be reached by land. Turn off Highway 20 onto Sleeper Road and follow it 2½ miles to a gate at the park boundary (and a de facto garbage pit where slobs have been dumping their trash). Hike the single-lane dirt road beyond the gate to a Y, take the right fork, and hike ¼ mile to another Y. Here take the left fork and in ¼ mile the road ends; a trail continues downhill to a steep bluff and then descends to Beach 144. The beach is a broad mudflat at minus tides, and virtually non-existent at high tide.

Near the head of Dugalla Bay, along the north shore, DNR Beach 145 is an 800-foot-wide chunk of rocky tideflat below steep, wooded headlands. Although the uplands are private, the beach is easily reached from the dike at the end of the bay. About 3¾ miles south of Deception Pass State Park, turn east off Highway 20 onto Jones Road. In 1 mile head south on Dike Road to reach the dike at the head of the bay in 200 yards. For beach-goers, the beach itself has little appeal, and the shore east of the dike dries to a ¼-mile-long mudflat at low tides. Birds, however, love it. Birdwatchers will spot herons, shorebirds, and wintering waterfowl. Hedgerows and brush along the dike harbor a variety of passerines.

Strawberry Point Boat Launch

An obscure, unmarked, but nevertheless public boat ramp on Strawberry Point gives access to Skagit Bay and several nice DNR beaches.

To reach the ramp from Oak Harbor, head north out of town on the road that follows the boundary of the Navy base, 70th Northeast. Turn east onto Crescent Harbor Road, following the blacktop road along the north edge of the reservation. In 3½ miles the road turns south and becomes Reservation Road. In another 1½ miles, as the road turns east, it becomes Polnell Road. In 2 miles is an intersection; Polnell Road becomes Strawberry Road, and the road that forms a T intersection to the east is Mariner's Beach Drive. Turn onto it into the Mariner's Beach subdivision and follow the road downhill for ½ mile to a small parking area above a one-lane concrete launch ramp.

A single park bench graces the grass area above the ramp, sandwiched between two private homes. Parking in the vicinity is minimal. All surrounding property, as well as the dredged lagoon housing a small yacht club, is private. Boaters can explore the shoreline north along Strawberry Point and on to Dugalla Bay.

Oak Harbor

Whidbey Island's largest town, Oak Harbor, strongly feels the effects of the nearby naval air base. The town does not have the "quaint" aura that Langley and Coupeville have—most of the stores are modern, and the main highway is lined with fast-food restaurants, car dealerships, and service stations. Despite the jets streaking overhead, life here is still relatively sedate, with both townfolk and tourists on hand to take part in its "Holland Happening" festival the last week of April and its "Old Fashioned Fourth of July."

Instead of cluttering the waterfront with high-priced restaurants and privileged businesses, Oak Harbor has devoted most of its shoreline to parks, ranging from the tidy little picnic area overlooking the marina to the multi-use City Beach Park on the west end of the shore. These parks provide a nice setting for visitors approaching the city by water.

Oak Harbor lies on Saratoga Passage near the north end of Whidbey Island. To reach it by land from the Clinton ferry terminal, drive north on Highway 525, which becomes Highway 20 mid-island. From the north, follow Highway 20 over the Deception Pass bridge and continue south.

Oak Harbor Marina

Facilities: Complete boat and crew facilities, boat launch (ramp and hoist), boat rentals and charters, boat pumpout station, tidal grid, picnic tables, children's play equipment, shopping (nearby)

Oak Harbor offers the best marine facilities on Saratoga Passage. In fact, the city-operated marina ranks with the best to be found anywhere on Washington's inland waters. The harbor itself is a 1½-mile-long curving arm tucked behind Maylor Point.

Navigational markers on the dogleg channel leading into the marina should be followed scrupulously; shoals lie immediately outside the dredged channel, and several rocks lurk just off the end of the point.

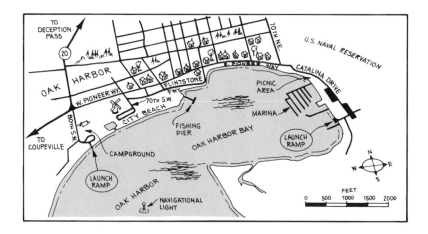

Behind a unique floating breakwater protecting the marina are transient moorage slips for more than 36 boats. Part of the breakwater's wave-canceling design includes a series of 18-foot-square concrete floats on the outboard side of the walkway. For the slips behind, these make an excellent "front porch" for picnicking or sunbathing. A key card, obtained at the marina office, is necessary to open the main gate and restroom doors after hours.

A very nice little park on shore has picnic tables, a barbecue pit, and a view of downtown Oak Harbor. The boat launching area is immediately to the south. Here a former Navy seaplane ramp has been converted into a four-lane ramp, with an adjoining float for loading. An additional pier with float has overnight space for a dozen boats. A lonely picnic table is perched in a small grass plot at the head of the ramps.

The Oak Harbor marina is about ½ mile from downtown stores; taxi service is available. The town offers a full range of services and boating supplies.

Oak Harbor Marina

Oak Harbor City Parks

Park area: 30 acres; 2,100 feet of shoreline on Oak Harbor
Access: Land, boat
Facilities: RV campground, picnic tables, fireplaces, drinking water, restrooms, tennis courts, basketball court, children's play equipment, wading pool, swimming beach (saltwater lagoon), boat launch (ramp), fishing pier with float
Attractions: Camping, picnicking, fishing, paddling, swimming, field sports

The shoreline on the west side of the city is devoted to City Beach, a large, multi-use park. The park has two entrances; the one at the south end of 70th Southwest Street leads to the day-use area; the second road farther west, 80th Southwest Street, goes to the RV campground. A single-lane concrete boat launch ramp is on a loop at the end of the latter road, just past the campground. Ample parking for cars and trailers is nearby. Because the park faces on a long tideflat, the ramp may not be usable during moderate to low tides.

The centerpiece of the park is a full-sized replica of a windmill, paying homage to the city's Dutch heritage. Near it are a saltwater lagoon swimming beach (lifeguard on duty in the summer), a wading pool, and a wide assortment of play paraphernalia. Views from the park are down the length of Saratoga Passage.

A second city park is east of City Beach, at the end of Flintstone Freeway, the street that parallels the shore. The park includes a small grassy waterfront area with park benches, picnic tables, two picnic shelters, restrooms, a fishing pier, and fish-cleaning stations. The pier has a short float with space for approximately four boats. Because water surrounding the pier is shoal, it is recommended only for shallow-draft boats, and even they should approach with care.

Penn Cove

The eastern shore of Whidbey Island bends around two major bays— Holmes Harbor on the south and Penn Cove on the north. Penn Cove runs westerly from Saratoga Passage for 3½ miles. A ½-mile-long sandspit extends north from Snakelum Point, the southernmost point at the entrance to the cove. Boaters entering the bay from the south should stay well outside the buoy marking the end of the spit.

At the turn of the century a syndicate had plans to dig canals through the island at points where the land was constricted to a mere mile in width. One canal would have gone from Penn Cove through to West Beach, in the vicinity of Libbey Road. The second canal would have been built from the northeast shore of Holmes Harbor through to Lake

Hancock. It was reasoned that shipping traffic would take advantage of the canals as a shortcut between the Strait of Juan de Fuca and the growing port of Everett. The canals, of course, were never dug, and one can only imagine what Whidbey Island would be today if the plans had come into being.

The island is still wrestling with commercialism—the latest venture is mussel-raising farms on Penn Cove. Seed mussels are attached to ropes suspended from floats or rafts, where they grow in the nutrient-filled water. After two years the bivalves are harvested and shipped to restaurants and lucky gourmets throughout the U.S. Most of the floats lie along the side of the cove, between Coupeville and the head of the bay, and do not present a navigational hazard.

A scenic drive or bicycle route follows the shoreline of Penn Cove, with views of the cove, Saratoga Passage, and Skagit Bay. Follow the shore south out of Oak Harbor on Scenic Heights Road. About ¾ mile south of Oak Harbor, a portion of Scenic Heights road along the bluff has slipped away, necessitating an inland detour via Balda and Miller roads, before Scenic Heights can be rejoined. At the junction with Monroe Landing Road, Scenic Heights Road becomes Penn Cove Road. At San de Fuca turn right (north) on Main Street to reach Highway 20. Follow Highway 20 southwest for ½ mile, and then turn left onto Madrona Way and follow it into Coupeville. As the road nears Coupeville the broad view is lost, and there are only brief glimpses through the trees of Penn Cove and the mussel floats.

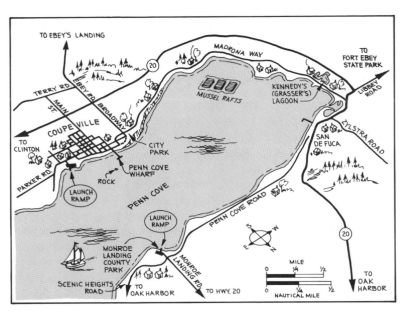

Monroe Landing County Park (Island County)

Park area: 0.5 acre; on Penn Cove
Access: Land, boat
Facilities: Boat launch (ramp), interpretive displays, *no water*
Attractions: Boating, beachcombing, historical site

This undeveloped park on the north shore of Penn Cove gives access to some of the cove's shoreline. Monroe Landing County Park is 2 miles east of the community of San de Fuca at the intersection of Penn Cove Road, Scenic Heights Road, and Monroe Landing Road.

Here is a parking lot, a single-lane concrete launch ramp, some pretty beach, and an interpretive display. A larger gravel lot for parking boat trailers is located on the other side of Scenic Heights Road.

Monroe Landing is one of the eight sites in Ebey's Landing National Historical Reserve. Ship's Master Joseph Whidbey found a large village of Indians here in 1792, while he was conducting explorations for George Vancouver. The park's interpretive tells of the Skwdab subgroup of the Skagit tribe, who had numerous villages around Penn Cove, Oak Harbor, Dugalla Bay, and the lower Skagit River. A potlatch house stood here until about 1910. Indian canoe races and athletic competitions took place on Penn Cove each summer through the 1930s.

Coupeville

Coupeville is in many ways the essence of Whidbey Island—at times salty, at times rural, but always conscious of its pioneer heritage. The town is one of the sites in Ebey's Landing National Historical Preserve. It was the earliest town on the island; a number of homes bear signs telling the date they were built and the name of their original owner. The residence of Thomas Coupe, the sea captain who founded the town, dates back to 1852.

By land, Coupeville is reached by turning off Highway 20 at the signed intersection and following the road ½ mile into town. It can also be reached via the scenic route from Oak Harbor (see Penn Cove, above). By boat it is 23 nautical miles from Port Gardner in Everett and 18 miles from Deception Pass.

All of the interesting old store-front buildings are along either side of Northeast Front Street. Many of these stores now house antique shops, arts and crafts galleries, and other businesses catering to tourists. A guide Historical Society Museum (see below). During the summer the museum conducts guided tours past these historic houses and businesses.

After exploring the town, take time for a picnic in the city park located on a high grassy bluff immediately west of the Port of Coupeville wharf. The park has picnic tables, a picnic shelter, restrooms, children's play equipment, tennis courts, a bandstand, and wide views out over Penn

Imagine eating your morning Cheerios in a kitchen like this one at the Island County Historical Society Museum.

Cove. There is no access to the shore down the steep embankment; walk a blocked-off road down the hill for beach access near the wharf.

Island County Historical Society Museum

Facilities: historical displays, bookstore, gift shop

The historical museum in Coupeville is well worth a visit for its insights into Whidbey Island life from early Native American times through pioneer days.

The beautifully carved wooden doors at the entry hint at the treasure trove the building holds. Fascinating, well-presented displays tell of such things as the ships and sea captains that sailed out of Whidbey Island ports and show models of early day vessels that plied north Puget Sound. The culture and craft techniques of local Native American tribes are depicted; a miniature diorama dramatizes Captain Vancouver's encounter with the local tribe. Rooms and nooks are outfitted as a late-1800s school room, a pioneer cabin, and a shipping office on the Coupeville Wharf. Displays change regularly.

The museum also houses a collection of historic artifacts that have been donated by island residents, and a reference library for researchers of local history. Adjacent to the museum is Alexander's Blockhouse, which was built to protect Penn Cove residents during the brief 1855–1856 Indian Wars, but was never used.

In summer the museum building is open from 11:00 A.M. to 5:00 P.M. weekdays, and from 10:00 A.M. to 5:00 P.M. weekends. Winter hours are 11:00 A.M. to 5:00 P.M. Friday through Monday. It is located on

Alexander Street between Front Street and Ninth, immediately uphill from the Port of Coupeville wharf.

Port of Coupeville Wharf and Captain Thomas Coupe Park

Facilities [at the wharf]: fuel (gas only), deli and gift shop, kayak rentals, restaurants and shopping (nearby); **[at the park]:** boat launch (ramp), RV pumpout station, restrooms

Focal point of Coupeville is the long Port of Coupeville wharf that stretches into Penn Cove. Overnight moorage is available on a float off the head of the wharf; gas is available at the red, barnlike building on the end of the wharf.

There is only 5 to 9 feet of water under the float at a zero tide, so deep-draft boats are better advised to anchor offshore within dinghy distance of the float. Boaters should be wary of a large submerged rock that lies 300 yards northeast of the wharf.

A public launch ramp is located in a small park on the east side of town at the corner of Northeast Ninth and North Otis Street. The single-lane concrete launch ramp has a finger pier alongside. Be warned that the float is aground at low water. The large parking lot has space for a number of cars with trailers. At the entrance to the parking lot is an RV sewage disposal dump.

ADMIRALTY INLET

Ebey's Landing National Historical Reserve

Colonel Isaac Ebey certainly did not intend to make history in quite the way he did—by being decapitated by some surly Canadian Indians. Ebey was already assured a place in Washington history as the first permanent settler on Whidbey Island and as a political leader. As it was, this very leadership quality brought him to the attention of the Indians who, in August 1857, were looking for some kind of white "chief" on whom they could avenge the untimely demise of one of their chiefs a year earlier near Port Gamble.

The beach section of the late Colonel Ebey's homestead is now a state park; the upland portion of the farm as well as the cemetery where he is buried are a part of Ebey's Landing National Historical Reserve. The purpose of Ebey's Landing National Historical Reserve is to "preserve and protect a rural community that provides an unbroken historic record from the 19th-century exploration and settlement in Puget Sound to the present time." The historical reserve is comprised of 17,000 acres on central Whidbey Island, about 90 percent of which is privately owned.

Included are the town of Coupeville; Fort Casey, Ebey's Landing, and Fort Ebey state parks; state DNR's Rhododendron Park; Sunnyside Cemetery; Ebey's Prairie; Grasser's Hill and Lagoon (in the San de Fuca vicinity); Monroe's Landing; Smith Prairie (south of Snakelum Point); and Crockett and Perego's lakes. Located in the reserve are three block-houses dating from the 1850s as well as dozens of other structures that are related to the history of central Whidbey Island.

Ebey's Landing State Park

Park area: 45.8 acres; 6,120 feet of shoreline on Admiralty Inlet
Access: Land, boat
Facilities: Hiking trails, vault toilets, *no water*
Attractions: Historical displays, hiking, beachcombing

Ebey's Prairie and the adjacent state park can be reached by land by turning south off Highway 20 onto Terry Road, which becomes Ebey Road in ½ mile; follow the signed route. The road travels through the finest farmland on all of Whidbey Island—a green and gold prairie that has seen human habitation for around 12,000 years. Land at Ebey's Prairie is owned by the National Park Service, but it is leased for agricul-ture, assuring that its traditional use will remain unchanged.

Sunnyside Cemetery, which lies on a slight hill above the prairie, offers a panoramic view of the plain. To reach it, turn northwest off Ebey Road onto Cook Road and proceed ½ mile to the intersection of Cook, Cemetery, and Sherman roads. For headstone history stroll through the cemetery; Colonel Ebey is buried here, as well as a number of early pioneers. The James Davis blockhouse, dating from the 1855 Indian uprising, is also located here.

The Ebey's Prairie Trail to the state park starts from the west end of Cemetery Road at an overlook. Three display panels found here de-scribe geological history of the prairie and farming of the central Whidbey

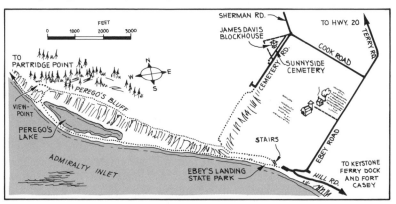

The historic James Davis blockhouse at Sunnyside Cemetery

prairies by Indians, and later by settlers. The trail drops downhill to a private road paralleling Cemetery Road, follows it west to its end near uphill residences, swings upslope to a fence line below woods, then follows it southwest. Watch for hawks and eagles soaring above. Sights and sounds fill the senses: jagged peaks of the Olympic Range piercing the horizon, the ghostly white cone of Mount Baker at your back, the muted booming of waves breaking on the long curve of beach. Near the edge of the bluff the trail intersects the path rising from Ebey's Landing.

Ebey Road continues on from Cook Road toward the beach; at the end of a sharp turn is a parking lot at the state park. A kiosk holds historical displays; other information panels identify points on the horizon and silhouettes of typical vessels spotted offshore. A trail gradually ascends the 200-foot wind-blown bluff, which is Nature Conservancy property, and gives glorious views out over Admiralty Inlet and the tawny beach below. The path then descends to the north end of Perego's Lake, a saltwater lagoon named for a recluse who once lived on the bluff above. From here continue on by trail to Partridge Point or walk the beach back to the parking lot. The trip around the end of the lagoon and back is about 3½ miles.

Fort Casey State Park

Park area: 137.5 acres; 4,000 feet of shoreline on Admiralty Inlet
Access: Land, boat
Facilities: 35 standard campsites, 3 primitive campsites, picnic tables, fire grates, restrooms, showers, drinking water, lighthouse, interpretive center, hiking trails, interpretive signs, boat launch (ramp), underwater park
Attractions: Historical displays, scuba diving, hiking, beachcombing, clam digging, fishing

The kids will have so much fun they will never suspect they are getting a history lesson! Here are dozens of darkened corridors to explore, masses of concrete parapets to scramble over, and acres of bluff and beach to roam.

Do not miss the searchlight emplacements below the rim of the bluff and the switchboard building to the east that controlled electrical power to the emplacements; take along a flashlight to aid your investigations. Use care in exploring the fortifications. Do not allow youngsters to become rowdy, and keep a tight hand on the younger ones. Falls from the bunkers and bluffs have caused serious injuries and even fatalities.

Fortification was not the initial governmental use of Admiralty Head. A lighthouse reservation was acquired here in 1858, and the first light, which stood west of the present emplacements, was shown in 1861. When Admiralty Head was chosen as one of three sites for primary defense of Puget Sound, the lighthouse was moved to its present position. In the 1920s it was determined to be obsolete and the beacon was removed in 1927. During World War II the lighthouse building was used as a training center and kennel for the dogs of the military K-9 Corps, much to its detriment. It was finally refurbished and converted to an interpretive center when the fort became a state park.

The first gun emplacements at Fort Casey were completed in 1899. Over the following years more batteries were added, until by 1907 the fort complement included 10 batteries with 19 guns ranging in size from 3-inch to 10-inch, 16 12-inch mortars, and a garrison of over 200 men. The most lethal of the armaments were the seven 10-inch guns

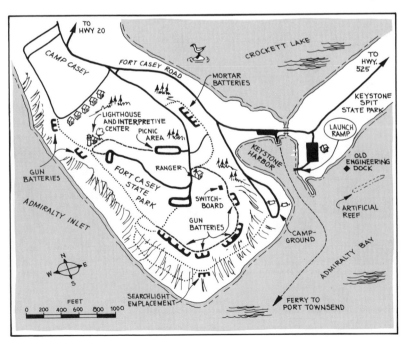

mounted on disappearing carriages that withdrew behind a thick protective wall after each round was fired. The batteries at Fort Casey, along with those at Fort Worden near Port Townsend and Fort Flagler on Marrowstone Island, formed a "Triangle of Fire" designed to guard Puget Sound and the vital Navy shipyards at Bremerton.

In 1917, when the U.S. entered World War I, the fort was placed on 24-hour alert and activities expanded to provide training for harbor defense companies headed for Europe. At the end of the war the fort was placed on caretaker status and then used as a training center by the National Guard, Reserve Officers Training Corps, and Citizen's Military Training Corps. Some of the guns had been removed during the war for use on the European front. By 1933 all the remaining original armaments were taken to be melted down; however, a few new antiaircraft batteries were placed in recognition of that new style of warfare.

With the outbreak of World War II the fort again served as a training site, and for five years after the war was a satellite camp for engineering troops stationed at Fort Worden. The property was eventually surplused, and in 1956 was acquired by Washington State Parks.

Fort Casey's emplacements, which are the best preserved in the state, include four guns in place; the two 3-inch rapid-fire and two 10-inch disappearing carriage guns were procured from Fort Wint in the Philippines in 1968 for display here. Several information boards explain the history of coastal fortification. The interpretive center in the lighthouse exhibits some of the ammunition used in the guns and other informative displays. The lighthouse tower can be climbed for views of the huge

The lighthouse at Fort Casey now serves as an interpretive center.

water highway that the fort guarded. The interpretive center is open from 10:00 A.M. to 4:00 P.M., Thursday through Sunday.

After curiosity with the Army fortification is satisfied, there are still a beach and several miles of trails to wander. Footpaths lace the bluff below and around the gun batteries. Reach the shore from the campground or from the northernmost battery; this can be the start for a 5-mile beach walk beneath the wildest bluffs on the island, all the way north to Point Partridge.

The picnic area is in trees on the hillside above the emplacements. The old wooden barracks, passed on the way into the park, are now a part of Camp Casey, a Seattle Pacific University facility used to house school and youth groups that schedule educational camps here. On the east side of the park, below the bluff, is the overnight camping area. The campsites lie in rather cramped quarters on a beach formed by material dredged from the Keystone channel. Due to the popularity of the park, the 35 sites are usually claimed by midday in the summer. Reservations are not accepted. A trail leads from the end of the campground up the bluff to the emplacements, or the road can be walked to the upper portion of the park.

On the east shore of Keystone Harbor, behind a piling breakwater, are the two concrete ramps of the state park boat launch, separated by a loading float. This is one of the best launch ramps on the island, with a good drop-off and excellent protection by breakwater and rock jetty. Launching can be difficult during the comings and goings of the Keystone–Port Townsend ferry.

The state park's offerings do not end at the water line. Keystone's rock jetty and pilings of the old Army quartermaster dock immediately to the east are now an underwater state park. This marine habitat is the most popular diving spot on Whidbey Island for both snorkeling and scuba diving. Underwater is a kaleidoscope of sea life—lacy white sea anemones, brilliant purple plume worms, swarms of kelp greenlings, shy octopus hiding in dark niches, rockfish, and large lingcod. Because this is a protected sanctuary, many of the fish are quite tame and can easily be approached.

To reach Fort Casey State Park from the north turn south off Highway 20 onto Engle Road at the pedestrian overpass in Coupeville and follow signs to the Keystone Ferry. From the south, turn west at the point where Highway 525 joins Highway 20 and follow signs.

Boaters in craft that can be beached can land along the shore and scramble up the trails to the fort. However, the beaches are narrow and drop off sharply, so a careful eye must be kept on the incoming tide. Floats at Keystone are intended for loading while launching boats. Anchoring offshore is not recommended.

Scuba divers leave the water at Keystone Spit. In the distance are the remains of Fort Casey's old engineering wharf.

Keystone Spit State Park (Undeveloped)

Park area: 274 acres; 6,810 feet of saltwater shoreline on Admiralty Bay, 7,000 feet of freshwater shoreline on Crockett Lake
Access: Land, boat
Facilities: None
Attractions: Picnicking, beachcombing, birdwatching, surf fishing, kite flying, windsurfing, scuba diving, interpretation

Keystone Spit, located just east of Fort Casey, has several of its own attractions, as well as being the terminal for the Port Townsend ferry.

Highway 20 runs the length of the spit, between the beach and Crockett Lake. A couple of small parking areas along the south side of this road are public accesses.

Crockett Lake, the 250-acre marsh formed by the sandbar at Keystone, is a prime birdwatching area, especially during migratory season. Look for hawks and passerines around the edges of the lake, and herons and transient waterfowl in the water. The saltwater side of the sandbar is good for birdwatching too, as well as beachcombing. The two shores, one freshwater and one saltwater, are open for day use.

Keystone Spit was originally a part of the Fort Casey Military Reservation. Fire control techniques of the day required triangulation points spaced as far apart as possible; an observation tower located on Keystone Spit was the easternmost fire control station for the fort's main batteries. The area nearest the Keystone ferry landing was the site of the Army engineer camp used during the construction of the fort. Moldering offshore ruins were once the end of a pier where construction supplies and equipment were offloaded. In 1988 Washington State Parks acquired all of Keystone Spit, running for 1½ miles west of the ferry landing between Crockett Lake and Admiralty Bay.

Driftwood County Park (Island County)

Park area: 0.2 acre; 500 feet of saltwater shoreline on Admiralty Inlet
Access: Land
Facilities: Picnic tables, fire braziers
Attractions: Picnicking, beachcombing, kite flying, birdwatching

This small, austere park lies just east of Keystone Spit State Park, where Keystone Road (Highway 20) makes a sharp bend to the west and parallels the spit. A pair of picnic tables alongside the gravel parking lot overlook Admiralty Bay; stop for a snack, let sea breezes ruffle your hair, and watch offshore for maritime traffic.

DNR Beaches 124A and 124

Two public DNR beaches stretch beneath steep cliffs on Admiralty Bay south of Keystone. Beach 124A is a 4,200-foot strip south of the Admiral's Cove subdivision. Beach 124, which is 2,400 feet long, lies a mile farther south. Neither of these beaches have land access; they must be reached by boat. The public beach is below the mean high water level.

Lake Hancock

Still considered part of the Whidbey Island Naval Air Station reservation, and occasionally used for training of helicopter crews, Lake Hancock has led a colorful past.

A roadside pull-off from Highway 525, ½ mile north of Greenbank, tells of the history of the lake.

The lake was once a freshwater marsh protected from the onslaught of waves from the strait by a sandbar. Native Americans harvested a potatolike root called *wapato*, wild cranberries, and wild carrots from its boggy shores, and early settlers grew oats, hay, and corn on the surrounding fertile land. Over time the protective sandbar was breached by storms, and the lake was transformed into a brackish saltwater marsh. An amazing variety of salt- and freshwater plant species took possession of ecological niches in which they alone could survive—often only 1 or 2 feet from an entirely foreign plant community.

In 1940 the Navy established an aerial target range at the lake, and wave-upon-wave of military aircraft used the lake as their target for practice bombing. The target practice on Lake Hancock ceased in the 1960s. Because tons of practice ordnance has been dropped on the lake, and despite recovery efforts, there is still the possibility of dangerous explosives in the area; it remains under Navy control and is closed to public access. Now undisturbed by humans, the marsh, transition zone, and forest habit are a haven for a varied population ranging from marine invertebrates to migratory seabirds, small mammals, songbirds, hawks, and eagles.

South Whidbey State Park

Park area: 85 acres; 4,500 feet of shoreline on Admiralty Inlet
Access: Land, paddle-craft
Facilities: 54 standard campsites, 6 primitive sites, group camp, group day-use area, picnic tables, fireplaces, picnic shelter, restrooms, showers, trailer dump station, drinking water, amphitheater, trails
Attractions: Camping, picnicking, fishing, clam digging, beachcombing, hiking, crabbing, birdwatching

Here are both greenly forested uplands and open, wave-washed beach in what is probably the prettiest park on all of Whidbey Island. The forest is wonderful old Douglas-fir and massive western red cedar, with a thick layer of undergrowth. Trails are edged by ferns, red elderberry, salmonberry, and a goodly amount of stinging nettles (don't stray off the trail!). The shore is gently sloping sand, giving way to cobbles and rocks at the low-tide level. At high tide the strip of exposed beach is quite narrow. A northerly breeze sweeping down from the Strait of Juan de Fuca cools the shoreline much of the time.

Trails lead from the campground and parking area down the high bank to the beach. Another trail loops through the dense forest in the southern section of the park, giving quiet-stepping hikers a chance to

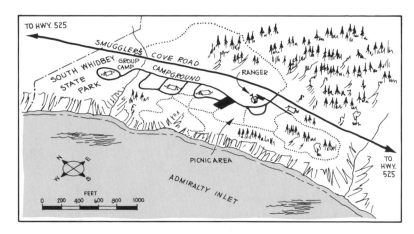

Sunshine and sand at South Whidbey Island State Park

spot deer, raccoons, pileated woodpeckers, and other little critters. A 255-acre section of the park, lying on the east side of Smuggler's Cove Road, includes a stand of old-growth forest, with some giant Douglas-firs and red cedars over 250 years old. A 1½-mile trail starts immediately across the road from the park entrance.

To reach the park from the north, turn off Highway 525 just south of Lake Hancock onto Smugglers Cove Road and follow it for 4½ miles to the park. From the south, 9 miles from Clinton turn west off Highway 525 onto Bush Point Road, which eventually joins Smugglers Cove Road and goes north to the park, a distance of 6 miles from the highway intersection. The state park can be visited by boat, but because the shore is unprotected, anchoring offshore is difficult except during calm weather.

Bush Point

Bush Point has a mixture of small attractions. On the north side of the point are a restaurant and a commercial marina on Main Street, the only such facility on this side of Whidbey Island. The marina has boat rentals, fuel, a grocery store, sling launching, and the usual marine amenities, although it has no moorage. A lot offering overnight RV parking (no hookups) is located next to the store.

The small marina can be reached by turning west off Smugglers Cove Road on either Scurlock Road or Spyglass Road, either of which intersects Main Street. A narrow road-end access that offers, at best, a boat hand-carry to the water is near the end of the point. From the south end of Main Street, turn west on Sandpiper Road, and in ½ mile arrive at the public access, flanked by private property. Parking in the vicinity is limited.

Boats launched here can reach DNR Beach 101, a public beach 1 mile to the south. This 1,650-foot section of beach lies beneath bluffs just north of Mutiny Bay. Use care in small boats because the tide can be very strong in this area.

Mutiny Bay Launch Ramp

Why Mutiny Bay? The stories vary—one tale is that British sailors jumped ship here to become settlers; another story claims that local Native Americans serving as crew on a ship carrying whiskey mutinied here and seized the cargo. Although the name is intriguing, the bay is not much—just a slight inward curving of the shoreline, as bays along this side of Whidbey Island are inclined to be. The only public area on Mutiny Bay is the launch ramp at the end of Robinson Road.

To reach it, drive east out of Freeland on the Bush Point Road, and turn south at the intersection of Mutiny Bay Road. In 2 miles turn southwest onto Robinson Road.

On the north side of the road is a gravel and grass lot with parking space for a dozen cars with trailers. The single-lane concrete ramp is straight ahead, between private homes. This ramp, like others on this side of the island, is subject to considerable wave action, and the access may be choked by sand or debris. Watch for mergansers swimming offshore. This adaptable duck usually breeds and nests in a freshwater habit, but often takes to the sea for the summer.

Double Bluff State Park Tidelands

Access: Land, boat
Facilities: Sani-can, stairs to beach
Attractions: Beachcombing, swimming, paddling, clam digging

The beach area on Useless Bay along the shore north of Double Bluff is owned by the state Parks Commission, but is undeveloped except for the blacktopped parking lot at the end of the road. One could certainly argue that nature has done all the development necessary on this shore, and any further refinement by man would be sacrilegious. This is just the place for the serious beach fanatic, with acres of sand for wandering at low tide and piles of driftwood providing private little niches for an afternoon of daydreaming. Rustling beach grass, slapping waves, and the plaintive cries of seabirds create a salty symphony.

To reach the park by land, 9¼ miles from Clinton turn south off Highway 525 onto Double Bluff Road and follow it for 2 miles to its end. To the east of the road are rows of homes snuggled against the beach; to the west, beyond a fence and a concrete bulkhead, lies the park beach.

A sandbar in the long, shallow tideflat traps shallow ponds of water at low tide for toddlers to dabble bare toes. At the far end of the beach is a glacial-till bluff—at 367 feet one of the tallest and sheerest precipices on the island. The beach can be walked west all the way around the point to the homes of Mutiny Bay.

Sailors call this Useless Bay because its widespread arms offer scant protection against wind and waves, and the shallow bottom reaches out to grab unwary keels. For kayakers, though, when the weather is calm the bay offers interesting exploration along its shores and south around the corner to Cultus Bay. Here are two bays, side by side, with identical names (albeit in different languages)—Cultus is the Chinook jargon word meaning "useless." Most of Cultus Bay dries at low tide, except for a dredged basin, and becomes useless, even for canoes.

A heron searches for fishy tidbits at Double Bluff State Park.

Dave Mackie County Park (Island County)

Park area: 4 acres; 400 feet of shoreline on Admiralty Inlet
Access: Land, boat
Facilities: Picnic tables, picnic shelters, fireplaces, restrooms, drinking water, children's play area, baseball field, boat launch (ramp)
Attractions: Boating, paddling, swimming, clam digging

With its baseball diamond and bleachers, Dave Mackie County Park is obviously a facility meant for the use of residents, not necessarily tourists. But residents (who know a nice beach when they see one) probably won't object to an outlander or two dropping by to share it.

The park is at Maxwelton on the extreme south end of Useless Bay. To drive to it, turn south off Highway 525 onto Maxwelton Road and follow it for 5 miles to the community. Maxwelton is a collection of homes strung along the beach on either side of the road.

Dave Mackie County Park lies on a low grassy bank above the bay; a boulder bulkhead lines the high-water level. Two roads reach into the park—the one on the south leads to the one-lane concrete boat launch ramp. Mooring buoys offshore are private. Because the ramp faces on a long tideflat, launching is possible only at moderate to high tide, and with boats that are small enough to be at least partially carried or dragged. There is no loading float.

Water flowing over the gently sloping bottom warms to temperatures bearable for wading and swimming. Picnic tables along the bank offer lunchtime views of the beach and boating activity as well as impressive views across Useless Bay to the rapidly rising cliffs at Double Bluff.

SOUTH SARATOGA PASSAGE AND POSSESSION SOUND

Holmes Harbor

The largest cove on Whidbey Island, Holmes Harbor runs southward off Saratoga Passage, penetrating the shoreline for over 5 miles. There are no public docks or moorages on the bay; the only public facilities are the launch ramp and park at Freeland, the small town at the head of the bay. Holmes Harbor is large enough that boaters can spend a full day here—fishermen trying the traditional "hot spots," sailors enjoying long tacks across the mile-wide bay, and pleasure cruisers drifting along the scenic shoreline.

Anchorages can be found in the bay along the northwest shore by Greenbank. The head of the bay offers good holding ground for a hook in a mud bottom at 17 fathoms; however, there is little protection here

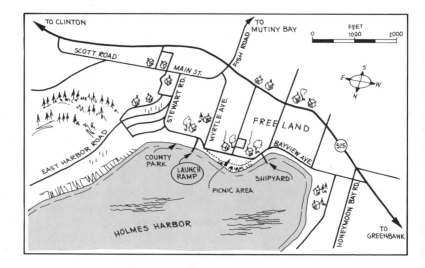

from either northerly or southerly blows because the land at the head of the bay is very low.

Freeland County Park (Island County)

Park area: 7 acres; 1,500 feet of shoreline on Holmes Harbor
Access: Land, boat
Facilities: Picnic tables, picnic shelter, fireplaces, children's play area, restrooms, drinking water, trail, boat launch (ramp)
Attractions: Beachcombing, clam digging, picnicking, hiking

After its 5-mile flow southward, Holmes Harbor peters out in a mudflat at the village of Freeland. Freeland, one of several utopian co-operative communities founded on Puget Sound around the turn of the century, was established in 1900 by a group of defectors from Equality, a socialist colony south of Bellingham on Samish Bay.

The small county park at the head of the bay has a launch ramp—a single-lane concrete affair next to the park restroom. Do not mistakenly try to use the ramp to the west by the shipyard; that one is private. Launching or landing at moderate to low tide or with large trailered boats may be difficult, due to the gentle slope of the tideflat.

The day-use park itself has a nice beach and facilities for picnicking or playing. On a slight knoll to the west are a picnic shelter and a woodland trail that can be jogged or sauntered, depending on whether your interest is fitness or relaxation.

The community lies midway down Whidbey Island, on the east side of Highway 20. Turn north on any of several marked roads and follow them downhill to the bay. The Freeland shopping center, which sits on the hillside ½ mile above the harbor, has grocery, marine supplies, and other stores, service stations, a laundromat, and cafes.

Langley

The town of Langley is in itself a good reason to visit Whidbey Island. The term "quaint" might well have been coined just to describe this small village by the sea. Although local merchants do like to capitalize on it, the town's particular aura is authentic—most of the weathered little store-front shops have been soaking up history along with the salt air for nearly 100 years. For shopping addicts the town is pure heaven, with marvelous little art galleries, crafts shops, antique stores, bookstores, and, when you need a rest, numerous purveyors of refreshments.

Langley was a product of the railroad hysteria that infected so much of Puget Sound during the late 1800s. Jacob Anthes, a Whidbey Island settler, reasoned that the arrival of the railroad on Puget Sound would mean increased steamer traffic as the fleet of boats carried goods up Saratoga Passage and the Swinomish Channel to Bellingham and points north. These steamers would need cordwood to keep their boilers fired. Anthes convinced a Seattle judge, J. W. Langley, to join him in purchasing land on the south end of Whidbey Island and establishing a town that would provide firewood for the steamers and be a trading post for island residents.

The town flourished for a time, but in 1894 the Great Northern Railway completed its line to Bellingham, and steamer traffic on Saratoga Passage virtually stopped. The result was devastating—settlers went bankrupt and left the island, and Langley became a near-ghost town. As Whidbey Island has become increasingly settled and developed over the years, Langley has benefited, but it has never reached the boom proportions that Anthes and Judge Langley anticipated.

To reach Langley from the Clinton–Mukilteo ferry terminal, follow Highway 525 out of town. In 3 miles turn north on Langley Road and follow it for 3 more miles into town.

Langley Marina and Phil Simon Park

Facilities: Guest moorage, gas, groceries, ice, bait, tackle, marine supplies and repairs, boat launch (ramp and hoist), fishing pier, restrooms, showers, picnic table, fireplace

Langley faces directly on Saratoga Passage, without the benefit of any kind of natural land protection. The marina on Wharf Street at the east end of the town once had a meager little guest float that bobbed and rolled with every swell off the channel. Finally the old wharf and the guest float were removed, and in 1986 were replaced with a dandy little yacht basin behind a sturdy breakwater.

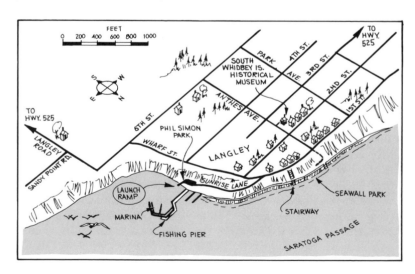

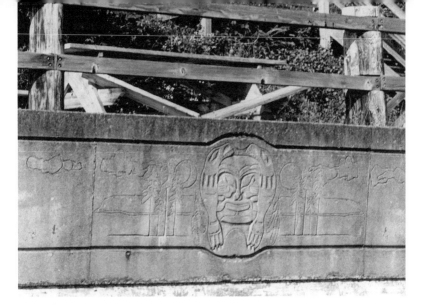
Bas-relief designs decorate Langley's Seawall Park.

Here there are slips for visiting boats as well as additional permanent berths. The moorages are quite short and narrow; boats over 30 feet long may be difficult to get into them. A long fishing pier with cleaning stations and rod holders follows the outside of the breakwater.

On shore, immediately east of the yacht basin, is Phil Simon Park, which has a single-lane concrete boat launching ramp. Parking space for several cars with trailers is adjacent, as is a small picnic area and restrooms. The commercial marina to the west has fuel, sling launching, and marine supplies and repairs. Boaters arriving at the yacht basin will find the town's shopping and dining district is just a block up the hill.

Seawall Park

Park area: 1 acre; 1,000 feet of shoreline on Saratoga Passage
Access: Land, boat
Facilities: Picnic tables
Attractions: Beach walking, viewpoint

The two-block-long business district of Langley sits above the water on a 100-foot embankment. The town has made the most of its beachfront by turning it into a pretty little park. Seawall Park, as it is called, is a 30-foot-wide grassy swath between a concrete bulkhead and the blackberry-covered embankment.

Picnic tables in the park provide vistas of boat traffic in Saratoga Passage and of the impressive bluffs of Camano Head, immediately across the channel. Bas-relief Northwest Indian designs decorate the bulkhead, and two sets of concrete steps breach the wall, giving access to the gravel beach below. From above, near the east end of the shopping district, the park can be reached by a long set of stairs at an overlook. A charming bronze statue of a boy and his dog shares the viewpoint. A second access to the beach leaves from a steep blacktopped path at the intersection of First Street and Anthes Avenue.

South Whidbey Island Historical Museum

The South Whidbey Island Historical Museum is located at 312 Second Street, just west of the corner of Anthes Avenue and Second Street. This old building was once the living quarters for a crew of loggers that cut wood to supply the steamers—the same ones Jacob Anthes had hoped would bring prosperity to Langley.

The museum features period memorabilia: an old-time kitchen, tools, clothing, photographs, furniture from the Anthes family, Native American artifacts, and much more. It is open Saturdays and Sundays, 1:00 to 4:00 P.M., and at other times by appointment.

Columbia Beach (Clinton)

Facilities: Fishing pier, float, stores, restaurants, fuel (service station)

To most people arriving at Whidbey Island via the Mukilteo ferry, Clinton is just a blur as they leave the ferry and whiz by headed for points north. Slow down a bit and you will find the town has several places of interest. Immediately north of the ferry landing is the Clinton Recreational Pier, a combination fishing pier and boat dock. The elevated platform is a nice place to observe ferry and boating activity or watch other people catching fish.

The float below has space for four or five small boats; it may be pulled out during stormy winter months. Parking is at the top of the hill in the ferry parking lot, ¼ mile south of Highway 525 on Humphrey Road. The town of Clinton has a few stores; more are scattered along Highway 525.

Possession Beach County Park (Island County)

Park area: 2 acres; 1,500 feet of saltwater shoreline on Possession Sound
Access: Land, boat
Facilities: Picnic tables, restrooms, boat launch (ramp), interpretive displays
Attractions: Picnicking, beachcombing, birdwatching, boating, clam digging

Possession Beach County Park, near the south end of Whidbey Island, not only offers a public boat launch ramp into waters renowned for their salmon and bottomfish catches, it also represents a valiant at-

Raccoon tracks on the beach at Possession Point tell a tale of nighttime visitors.

tempt to retain a rare and ecologically precious barrier beach berm and saltwater marsh environment.

The beach-front berm, formed by erosion and northward drift from bluffs at Possession Point, encloses a saltwater tidal lagoon and marsh that alternately drains and fills with the tide, and is fed by freshwater from uphill streams. Beach grasses and a scattering of wildflowers anchor the soil of the berm. The richly varied habitat, ranging from beach to forest, hosts dozens of species of birds and mammals. Great blue herons and eagles fish offshore waters, songbirds call from marsh thickets, and at dusk deer and raccoons drift down to the beach from the forest.

The day-use park is located off Possession Road, 1¾ miles south of its junction with Cultus Bay Road. This intersection is 6 miles south of the Cultus Bay Road intersection with Highway 525.

The boat launch ramp is two-lane gravel, with a boarding float. Artificial reefs at nearby Gedney Island and Possession Point provide a protected habitat for bottomfish such as lingcod and true cod—an alternative fishing challenge to the area's plentiful salmon.

Possession Point

Two public beaches on the extreme south end of Whidbey Island can be reached by hand-carried boats put in the water at Clinton or at a

Glendale road end just north of the intersection of Glendale and Humphrey roads. The nearest boat launches are at Mukilteo, at Possession Beach Waterfront Park, or at Dave Mackie County Park.

DNR Beach 100 is a 2,550-foot-long strip beneath bluffs ½ mile north of Glendale. Beach 99 is 1,160 feet of tidelands just north of the beach homes at Possession Point. The public lands are only the area below mean high water. Dungeness and red rock crabs can be caught in the area.

An artificial reef, marked by buoys, has been placed just off Possession Point as an aid to fishing in the area. It lies west of the lighted bell buoy that marks shoals at the south end of the point.

WHIDBEY ISLAND ROAD ENDS

Nearly a dozen road ends give access to beaches and water around the island. Typically these are 50-foot-wide strips of shoreline flanked by a host of PRIVATE PROPERTY, NO TRESPASSING! signs; parking nearby is usually minimal. All accesses provide a place to put in a hand-carried boat or kayak for exploration of nearby shores. Public use of adjoining shoreline is dependent entirely on the goodwill of the property owners and the good manners of the visitors.

Moran's Beach. This day-use parking area, immediately north of the Naval Air Station, faces on the Strait of Juan de Fuca overlooking Smith and Minor islands, and the south ends of Lopez and San Juan islands. To reach it, turn west off Highway 20 at Banta Road, 3 miles south of Deception Pass. In ¼ mile turn north on Murran Road, and in another ¼ mile head west on Powell Road. The beach access lies at the road end in another ¼ mile. A broad sandy beach lies below the parking area.

West Beach Road. Headed south from Swantown and the southern entrance to Joseph Whidbey State Park, West Beach Road parallels the shore. In about a mile from Swantown, just before the road heads up-hill, park in pull-offs on the west side of the road near an overgrown house foundation. Walk the beach southward below towering bluffs (with due caution for tide levels).

Driftwood Way. Three miles north of Greenbank, turn off Highway 525 onto Ledgewood Beach Drive, which ends at a T intersection with Fircrest Avenue in ½ mile. Turn north on Fircrest, and in ½ mile head west on Seward Way, which winds downhill to the south. Midway down the hillside, in ¼ mile, turn northwest onto Driftwood Lane. In 200 yards, where the road drops to water level, a parking area sits just above the beach on the west side of the road. Stairs lead down to a gently sloping sand and gravel beach.

Lagoon Point. Two public beach accesses break the barricade of private homes at Lagoon Point on Admiralty Inlet, north of South Whidbey

Island State Park. To reach the first, just south of the intersection of Smugglers Cove and Lagoon roads, turn west off Smugglers Cove Road onto Mountain View Road. The road drops down steep bluffs; at the beach it forks into Seashore Road and Shell Avenue. Just west of this intersection is a public access sandwiched between private residences. Public beach extends 274 feet south and 160 feet north of this access. All the remaining waterfront and lagoon in the area is private.

A second public access on the south side of the lagoon can be reached by turning south off Mountain View Road onto Bayview Avenue. This road drops sharply downhill to the beach level and becomes Salmon Street as it turns west. A public access can be found at the end of Salmon Street near its intersection with Oceanside Drive.

Borgman Road. Take 70th Northeast Street north out of Oak Harbor, then turn east on Crescent Harbor Road. In 2 miles turn north on Taylor Road, and in another ¼ mile east on Silver Lake Road. Continue east for 3½ miles to an intersection where Silver Lake, Strawberry Point, and Green roads meet. Head northwest on Green Road for ¼ mile, then northeast on Borgman Road for ¼ mile to a road end at the beach, an old launch ramp site. Property on both sides of the road is private, and parking is limited. The slender access overlooks Skagit Bay, the south entrance to the Swinomish Channel, Goat Island, and, in the distance, Mount Baker.

Long Point. At a sharp bend in Highway 20, 2½ miles east of Coupeville, turn north onto Parker Road. In 1¼ miles head northeast on Portal Place, which ends at a T intersection with Marine Drive in 200 yards. Follow Marine Drive northwest for ½ mile to a road end above the beach at Long Point. The broad gravel beach, tapering down to sand at low tide, overlooks Penn Cove and the high bank of Blower's Bluff across the bay. Property on either side of the road end is private.

Beachcomber's Road. At Greenbank head northeast from Highway 20 onto North Bluff Road. In 2¼ miles turn east on Neon Drive, which ends at a T intersection with Crane Landing Drive in a little over a block. Here head north, then twist downhill to the beach on Saratoga Passage. To the south is the Beachcombers Community Club (private); to the north is a road end above a deteriorating piling bulkhead.

Glendale. At the top of the hill above the ferry landing at Columbia Beach in Clinton, turn south on Humphrey Road. In 3 miles reach Glendale, on Possession Sound. Just north of the intersection with Glendale Road, a short gravel spur between two residences gives access to a cobble beach. Parking in the vicinity is limited.

CHAPTER SEVEN

ADMIRALTY INLET

At Admiralty Inlet the waters of Puget Sound and Hood Canal flow together for the final 20-mile leg of the journey to the Strait of Juan de Fuca. It was here, at Foulweather Bluff, on May 10, 1792, that George Vancouver paused, contemplating whether either of these two channels

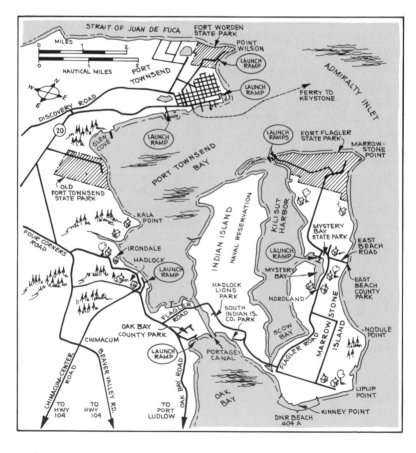

led to the hoped-for Northwest Passage across the top of the continent. It was here also that Vancouver discovered the "joys" of Northwest weather, and named the bluff accordingly.

Admiralty Inlet flows between Whidbey Island and the northeast edge of the Olympic Peninsula. The 3½-mile-wide channel is unobstructed throughout; the only hazards are severe tide rips off Foulweather Bluff that occur when the merging ebbs from Hood Canal and Puget Sound meet with a strong north or northwest wind. In calm weather, boats cutting close to the bluff should watch for rocks that lie 100 yards north of the highest part of the promontory.

OAK BAY AND PORTAGE (PORT TOWNSEND) CANAL

To Puget Sound boaters used to expansive channels, the narrow chute of Portage Canal is an interesting diversion, as well as a quick route between Hood Canal and Port Townsend. The channel is known locally as Portage Canal, although some nautical charts show it as Port Townsend Canal. The south end of the ¾-mile-long channel opens into Oak Bay; public parks lie along both sides of this end of the canal.

The dredged canal has a controlling depth of 14 feet, and the fixed bridge that crosses to Indian Island has a vertical clearance of 58 feet. Both ends are marked with lights. Tides can run up to 3 knots in the channel; tide rips that form at either end, depending on the direction of the current, can cause small boats some concern. Liplip Point, at the southeast end of Marrowstone Island, is a Chinook Indian word meaning "boiling water"— take warning!

In early days the two islands were joined to the Quimper Peninsula by a low neck of land known as the Chimacum Portage. Pressure from commercial shippers in Port Townsend for a protected shortcut up the sound resulted in the dredging of the canal between the Quimper Peninsula and Indian Island in 1913. Island residents were forced to use private boats, and

Sailing on Oak Bay

later a ferry, to reach the mainland. It wasn't until 1952 that a bridge finally linked the islands to the mainland.

Oak Bay County Park (Jefferson County)

Park area: 31 acres; 1,840 feet of shoreline on Oak Bay
Access: Land, boat
Facilities: 68 campsites, picnic tables, fireplaces, restrooms, children's play equipment, boat launch (ramp)
Attractions: Camping, picnicking, fishing, clam digging, crabbing, boating, swimming, scuba diving, beachcombing, paddling

Oak Bay County Park is divided into two sections: one campground sits on the bluff above a lagoon, the other lies on a strip of land between the lagoon and the south entrance to Port Townsend Canal.

To reach the park from the Hood Canal Bridge and Highway 104, take any major road headed north and follow signs to Hadlock. From Hadlock turn south on Oak Bay Road. The roads leading to the park are ½ mile south of the turnoff for the Indian and Marrowstone islands bridge. Here one road, Cleveland Street, heads north and in ¼ mile passes the entrance to the upper section of the park. The second road, Portage Way, starts from the same spot as Cleveland, but drops northeast down the hill to reach the lower section of the park in ¼ mile.

The lower portion of the park, which is on the west shore of Oak Bay, encompasses a rock jetty and a gravel and sand beach that extends all the way north to the bridge. Campsites are stretched along the southern arm of the beach between Oak Bay and a saltwater lagoon. This

Rock jetties and sandy beaches at lower Oak Bay County Park are great places for fishing and clam digging.

section of the campground is best suited for self-contained RVs, because there is no water. The single-lane boat launch ramp at the end of the road through the campground is usable, but is not in the best of condition. The area is excellent for fishing and clam digging.

Geoducks can be dug here at extreme low tide. Once the siphon neck is spotted above the sand, begin excavating, but be prepared to move a small mountain of mud because the body of the clam may be as much as 4 feet down. It cannot move away, although it may seem to as it retracts its enormous siphon. Do not pull on the neck—it will break off and you will lose your prize and the clam will die. The best allies when going for a geoduck are a number of energetic children who love digging in the mud.

The upper section of the park consists of two campground loops on the bluff overlooking the lagoon and the lower campground. One of the loops has power hookups for RVs. Children's play equipment is located in the center of the outer loop. There is no direct beach access from this part of the park.

Indian and Marrowstone Islands

To drive to an island may seem to be a contradiction in terms, but people around Puget Sound are used to such a paradox. Here are not one but two nice little islands that are easily reached by road. Unfortunately most of Indian Island is an off-limits naval ammunition storage depot, so it can only be enjoyed from a distance or from the two parks on its south end that front on Oak Bay and Portage Canal.

The islands are reached by land from the Hood Canal Bridge and Highway 104 by turning north on any of several roads that stretch the length of the Quimper Peninsula. Signs direct you to Marrowstone Island and Fort Flagler State Park. Flagler Road crosses the bridge that joins the islands to the mainland. Chain-link fences on Indian Island prevent any casual straying onto restricted property.

Marrowstone Island is primarily devoted to family homes, small farms, and the large state park that encompasses its northern end. Some beach homes along Kilisut Harbor are owned by summer residents and retirees. The main concentration of homes is mid-island at the community of Nordland, where the only business is a combination gas station and grocery store.

For many years Marrowstone Island was famous for its annual production of thousands of premium turkeys, a business that began in 1924 and boomed until the 1940s, when the rising cost of feed made it unprofitable. When Fort Flagler was reactivated during World War II and the Army planned to commence with practice firings of their guns, alarmed farmers informed the commanding officer that the fort would have to put its war on hold until incubating turkey eggs hatched, because the vibrations would disturb the delicate embryos. Thereafter the Army notified the farmers far in advance of practices so the turkey eggs could be incubated accordingly.

The western shore of Marrowstone Island is well protected by its neighboring island and the Olympic Peninsula. The windward shore is frequently buffeted by heavy weather from Admiralty Inlet. Severe tide rips can occur off Marrowstone Point and at Kinney Point at the south end of the island, especially when the wind and tide are moving in opposite directions. Boats heading out of Port Townsend Bay can run into trouble when they round Marrowstone Point and are suddenly confronted by southerly winds howling down the sound.

Hadlock Lions Park (Lloyd L. Good Memorial Park)

Park area: 2.5 acres; on Oak Bay
Access: Land, paddle-craft
Facilities: Picnic tables, picnic shelter, fireplace, hiking trail, *no water, no restrooms*
Attractions: Picnicking, clam digging, beach walking, hiking

This park on a grassy hillside on Indian Island is a convenient spot for watching activity in Portage Canal and Oak Bay. Facilities are few, but the view is grand.

The park entrance is to the right of Flagler Road, shortly after crossing the Portage Canal bridge onto Indian Island.

At the top of the slope, 50 feet above the water, are the parking lot and a picnic shelter next to an old orchard. After polishing off the fried chicken and potato salad, wander down to the beach, where Hadlock Lions Park joins South Indian Island County Park property. From here enjoy beach walks south to the jetty at the end of the canal or clear around the corner to the picnic area at the county park, ½ mile away. South Indian Island Trail runs along the wooded bluff between the two parks. The trailhead is on the east side of the picnic area.

South Indian Island County Park (Jefferson County)

Park area: 54 acres; 11,350 feet of shoreline on Oak Bay
Access: Land, boat
Facilities: Picnic tables, fireplace, latrines, *no water*
Attractions: Picnicking, fishing, paddling, clam digging, crabbing, swimming, scuba diving, beachcombing

This park is a companion to lower Oak Bay Park, which it faces across the bay. It has minimum facilities; its great attractions lie in its beautiful salt marsh and its 2-mile-long stretch of smooth, gravelly beach.

To reach the park turn east off Oak Bay Road on the road signed to Fort Flagler, which crosses the bridge over Portage Canal. About ½ mile from the bridge (½ mile beyond Hadlock Lions Park) is a side road to the south signed to Jefferson County Park. A single-lane gravel road drops steeply down to the water. Midway down the bluff is the east end of the South Indian Island Trail running from Hadlock Lions Park.

A few picnic tables are scattered about a grassy area near the lagoon. Beach walks go north all the way to the bridge, with an interesting side trip out onto the rock jetty; beyond the bridge, Navy property begins. South, the shore can be walked to the sandspit that joins Indian and Marrowstone islands. At low tide dig for clams and geoducks in the beaches facing on Oak Bay.

Jetty fishing on Oak Bay

DNR Beach 404A

At Kinney Point, on the extreme south end of Marrowstone Island, is DNR Beach 404A. The public area includes a 3,900-foot section of beach that wraps around the point and adjacent uplands.

However, there is no access to the property from above; it can only be reached by boat—or by walking politely across private beaches east of the county park, if landowners will tolerate it. If approaching the point by boat, be wary of tide rips.

East Beach County Park (Jefferson County)

Park area: 1 acre; 100 feet of shoreline on Admiralty Inlet
Access: Land, boat
Facilities: Picnic shelter with tables, fireplace, Sani-can
Attractions: Picnicking, boating, fishing, clam digging

A small county park in mid-Marrowstone Island provides a nice access to the Admiralty Inlet shores. Because most of the mobs head north to Fort Flagler, there is a good chance of finding privacy here, along with gorgeous views across to Whidbey Island, Mount Baker, and the Cascades.

From land, drive north on Flagler Road, and ½ mile north of Nordland turn east on East Beach Road. The park is reached in ¼ mile.

A pretty stone and log shelter holding picnic tables and a fireplace provides protection from winds off Admiralty Inlet. The park is on the only stretch of low-bank waterfront on the east side of the island. The wide, tapering beach, cobble above mid-tide levels and sand below, holds some promise of clams at low tide, or at least a good time romping in the waves.

Kilisut Harbor

Indian and Marrowstone islands are separated by a long waterway that is almost a channel rather than a harbor. Before the digging of Portage Canal, boats sometimes avoided heavy weather in Admiralty Inlet by traveling up Kilisut Harbor and at high tide crossing the sandspit that ran between Indian and Marrowstone islands. Today the islands are joined together at the south by a dirt causeway over which Flagler Road runs. A ¾-mile-long sandspit reaches out from Marrowstone Island to guard the northern end of the harbor.

Entrance to the winding channel is at the far west end of the spit, by Indian Island. Follow navigational markers carefully; the S-curve channel is dredged to a depth of 5 feet at mean low water, and in some places shoal water lurks immediately outside the marked channel. Use care approaching the harbor entrance from the north and consult navigational charts, because a submerged pile lies north of the west end of the sandspit.

Once the channel is cleared inside Kilisut Harbor, good anchorages can be found in 4 to 6 fathoms of water. Stay well away from the shore of Indian Island.

The 5-mile-long inlet was originally known as Scow Bay, and the pair of islands were the Scow Peninsula. Today it has its more lyrical Klallam Indian name of Kilisut, meaning "protected waters"; only the far southern end of the harbor is now called Scow Bay.

Kilisut Harbor and the waters surrounding Indian and Marrowstone islands are ideal for small-boat exploration, with numerous put-ins for dinghies, kayaks, and canoes. A circumnavigation of Indian Island is about a 12-mile trip, with a variety of adventures ranging from the quiet water of the harbor to the busy highway of Portage Canal. Boats can easily be carried across the causeway and sandbar at the south end of Kilisut Harbor. Plan the trip so the direction of the tidal current is favorable in the canal, and watch for tide rips. Do not go on shore at Indian Island except at the parks on its south end.

A quiet moorage at Mystery Bay State Park

Mystery Bay State Park

Park area: 10 acres; 685 feet of shoreline on Kilisut Harbor
Access: Land, boat
Facilities: Picnic tables, fire brazier, vault toilets, chemical toilet dump, marine sewage pumpout station, fishing pier with float, 7 mooring buoys, boat launch (ramp), water
Attractions: Picnicking, boating, paddling, fishing, crabbing, clam digging

Halfway down Kilisut Harbor, past a scattering of beach homes, is Mystery Bay. The small recreation area on the north shore, near the entrance to the curving bay, is an outpost of Fort Flagler State Park. The onshore portion of the park is day-use only, but the boating facilities invite overnight moorage.

The pier that extends from shore has a 550-foot float at its end; additional tie-ups are on seven mooring buoys, and there is plenty of space to spare for dropping a hook. The only hazards in the bay are two submerged concrete blocks that lie 20 to 30 feet off the east end of the float.

The park's single-lane boat launch ramp is west of the pier. Picnic tables on shore have a nice view of the Olympic Mountains rising behind Indian Island and of bird life in the bay. The Navy manages Indian Island as a wildlife refuge, and herons, cormorants, and a wide variety of ducks and shorebirds are commonly seen along the beaches.

If nautical legs are aching to be stretched, take a ¾-mile stroll across the narrow island to East Beach County Park. Walk south from the park on Flagler Road and then east on East Beach Road. Quiet walkers may be rewarded by seeing deer—if not, cows and other local wildlife are assured. The windswept beach of East Beach County Park is a marked contrast to the calm shores of Kilisut Harbor.

Fort Flagler State Park

Park area: 783 acres; 19,100 feet of shoreline on Kilisut Harbor, Port Townsend Bay, and Admiralty Inlet

Access: Land, boat (campgrounds and boat launches closed November 1–February 28)

Facilities: 102 standard campsites, 14 RV sites, 4 bicycle campsites, 2 group camps, Environmental Learning Center, picnic tables, fire grates, picnic shelter, drinking water, restrooms, showers, trailer dump station, hiking trails, nature trail, interpretive display, groceries (limited), snack bar, 2 boat launches (ramp), dock with float, 7 mooring buoys, fishing pier, U.S. Fish and Wildlife marine lab, youth hostel, historic gun emplacements, underwater park, Cascadia Marine Trail campsite

Attractions: Camping, picnicking, boating, paddling, fishing, clam digging, crabbing, beachcombing, windsurfing, hiking, swimming, scuba diving, historical displays

Mile upon mile of goodies—here are beaches, bluffs, woodlands, and the most spectacular sandspit to be found on the inland waters, all flavored with the intrigue of a historic old fort.

To reach the park by land, turn off Highway 104 (which crosses the Hood Canal Bridge) on any major road headed north and signed to Port Townsend. Watch for signs pointing east to Marrowstone Island and Fort Flagler State Park. Once on Flagler Road you can't miss it.

By water the state park is 2 nautical miles from Port Townsend and 11 nautical miles from Port Ludlow, via the Port Townsend Canal. For navigational comments on entering the channel leading into the harbor, see the section on Kilisut Harbor (above). Scow Bay Spit, a ¾-mile-long curving sandbar, nearly blocks the entrance to the harbor. At high tide water covers a low spot midway along the spit—do not attempt to short-cut through this gap in a boat, because it is very shallow.

At moderate to low tides, the full length of the sandbar is exposed for beach roaming or clam digging. Old pilings offshore to the north were used during World War II for holding four antisubmarine nets that stretched across to Port Townsend.

Park facilities are on the east and west edges of the park, with a network of roads and hiking trails connecting them. The ranger's residence and buildings of the old fort are on the east, inside the park entrance. Building 9, across from the headquarters, houses an interesting interpretive exhibit that is open for viewing when personnel are available.

Camping and boating areas are on the west. The upper campground is on a wooded bluff above the water; the lower one is situated on an open, windswept flat near the beach. The docking float on a T-shaped pier has space for about 10 boats. Seven mooring buoys stretched along the shore to the south provide tie-ups for additional boats, with some anchoring space nearby. One of the single-lane boat launch ramps faces on Port Townsend Bay; the second one is on Kilisut Harbor.

From the fort residence campus, a hard turn to the right leads down-hill past a gun emplacement to a parking lot. A trail continues down to a 500-foot-long wharf originally used by the Army Corps of Engineers during construction of the fort, but now serving as a fishing pier. A forest of pastel sea anemones coats the old pilings of the wharf. The underwater park lying on both sides of the wharf is marked by buoys; fishing line near the pier can pose a hazard to scuba divers. Because this is a sanctuary, spear fishing is prohibited.

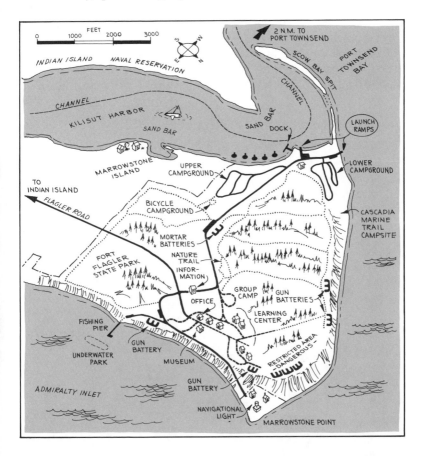

Battery Wansboro, the gun emplacements on the hillside above, is the only one of the Fort Flagler batteries to have guns in place. The original guns were removed long ago; the two 3-inch guns that are here now were placed after the fort became a park. Battery Gratten, at the northeast corner of the park, is down a short trail behind the buildings of the Environmental Learning Center. When passing through this section of the park, notice the buildings—this was the original Officer's Row, but those houses were torn down and replaced with World War II barracks.

The Marrowstone Point lighthouse is reached via a steep, narrow road that goes north from the east side of the residential campus. The automated lighthouse is not open to the public, but at moderate to low tides the shore here opens the way to beachcombing—west for 1½ miles to the park campground, or south for ¾ mile to the fishing pier. Buildings near the lighthouse are occupied by the U.S. Fish and Wildlife Service research laboratory.

Walks can be extended beyond the beaches to include bluff-top routes or forested trails. A complete circuit of the perimeter of the park, following beach, road, and trail, is about 5 miles; exploring inviting side paths can occupy an entire afternoon. Watch for deer, squirrels, raccoons, and bald eagles. Foxes and coyotes also live here but are shyer and harder to spot. The trail that heads south along the east edge of the

Sandy bluffs edge the moorage at Fort Flagler State Park.

park was initially beaten out in the early 1900s by the boots of thirsty soldiers heading for a saloon on the bluff just outside the fort boundary. The saloon hauled its supplies up the steep bluff by means of a winch wrapped around a tree stump, and thus was known as "The Stump."

Along the park road to the west, well inland, are the mortar emplacements of Battery Bankhead. Batteries Downs and Caldwell, situated on the north side of the bluff, can be reached by trail from the park campus or the lower campground. These are quite overgrown, and brush hides the view of the water that the guns once commanded. The main batteries, which are farther east, are dangerous and are posted as off limits.

Flagler was one of the forts that, along with Casey and Worden, guarded the entrance to Puget Sound from foreign invasion. The three forts, facing each other across Admiralty Inlet, formed what was to become known during World War I as the "Triangle of Fire." Construction began on Marrowstone Island in 1897; the fort was named for Brigadier General D. W. Flagler two years later when it was activated. The first troops to arrive had to make do with tent living until the completion of construction of quarters. Armament was placed over the next few years until by 1905 all 10 batteries were completed and armed. At full strength the fort consisted of 18 guns, ranging from 3-inch to 12-inch, and eight 12-inch mortars, aiming death at any enemy ship that dared to poke its prow into view.

It soon became apparent that the fort was poorly situated. The water supply on the island was not adequate to supply such a large installation, although this was eventually solved by running a pipeline from Port Townsend. More serious was the limited sector of fire—Point Wilson obstructed the view of the Strait of Juan de Fuca, and the guns could not engage targets much south of Marrowstone Point.

Initially Fort Flagler was to be headquarters for the Harbor Defense, but pressure by Port Townsend bigwigs who felt their fair city should host the headquarters caused it to be relocated at Fort Worden. The only noticeable change was the transfer of the Artillery Band.

With the onset of World War I, the fort served as a training center for troops, but because there was no threat of naval attack on the sound, the guns were considered unnecessary and many were removed and sent to the European front. At the end of the war the fort languished in a caretaker status until a new global war revitalized it. Antiaircraft guns were installed in World War II to combat the new threat from the skies, and new buildings were constructed to house another generation of trainees.

The final military use of the post was as a base for training an Engineering Amphibious Brigade after World War II. In 1953 the fort was deactivated, and two years later the property was acquired by Washington State for use as a park.

Port Townsend Bay

It is hard to understand why geographers or town founders name cities after waterways, thus causing an endless amount of confusion. The large inlet here is correctly named Port Townsend, but in order to avoid confusion with the more well-known town, we end up referring to it as Port Townsend Bay.

The bay is well protected and without obstructions along its 6-mile length. Some good anchorages can be found at its south end, along the west shore near Hadlock and Irondale.

Hadlock

Facilities: boat launch (ramp), dock and float, Sani-can, *no water*

The small town of Hadlock lies on the bluff above the water at the southwest corner of Port Townsend Bay. Beneath the bluff is a small portion of the community called Lower Hadlock, where there is a public boat launch ramp.

To reach it, turn off Oak Bay Road ¼ mile south of Hadlock onto Lower Hadlock Road, which angles off to the right and drops steeply downhill to the shore.

The launch area has an excellent new dock and boarding float. Overnight moorage is permitted on the float.

South of here, near the entrance to Portage Canal, is the Old Alcohol Plant Marina, Lodge, and Villas, a facility that sat vacant for many years but presently is enjoying a resurrection. The floats, behind a substantial breakwater, offer guest moorage with power and water. The lodge has guest rooms, a restaurant, and a gift shop.

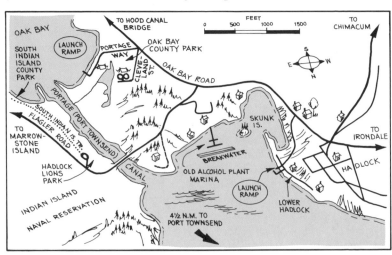

Although one would never guess it from today's quiet demeanor, Hadlock, along with Irondale to the north, was once a hotbed of industry. When the sawmill at Seabeck burned in 1886, it was relocated at Hadlock. In addition to shipping lumber throughout the Pacific, the mill provided lumber for the construction of Forts Worden, Flagler, and Casey.

As its name suggests, Irondale was a major smelting center, in its prime turning out 300 tons of steel daily. When the local ore proved to be of a poor quality, better ore was imported from Texada Island in British Columbia. Eventually, bringing ore from Canada or even farther afield proved too costly and the mill closed. The last fling at industrialism was a wood alcohol plant at Hadlock, but this was short-lived and the area settled back to a quiet residential existence.

Old Fort Townsend State Park

Park area: 377 acres; 3,960 feet of shoreline on Port Townsend Bay
Access: Land, boat. Park closed in winter
Facilities: 40 campsites, 3 primitive campsites, group camp, picnic tables, fireplaces, kitchen, restrooms, RV pumpout, drinking water, mooring buoys, hiking trails, nature trail, interpretive trail, children's play equipment, horseshoe pits, softball field
Attractions: Camping, picnicking, boating, historical displays, hiking, clam digging, crabbing

After you have tramped through numerous World War I and II forts throughout Puget Sound, Old Fort Townsend comes as a surprise—this one is a relic from the time of the Indian Wars. The fort was established in 1856 when settlers in the Port Townsend area became uneasy about the growing hostility of Indians after the government's efforts to move them on to reservations. The Indian uprisings had largely been settled by the time the fort was garrisoned, and troops were left with little to do. The discovery of gold in British Columbia's Fraser River country led to a number of desertions by soldiers more interested in seek-

Spectacular rhododendrons brighten Old Fort Townsend State Park.

ing promised riches than endlessly marching on a parade ground.

The boredom at Fort Townsend was relieved briefly when a company of men from the fort were sent to San Juan Island in 1859 when an altercation over a pig and some potatoes promised some action. The Pig War standoff between the Americans and British led to more waiting and boredom.

As the Civil War was proving a more serious problem, demanding the full attention of the government and its army, all the troops remaining at Fort Townsend were withdrawn in 1861 and the post was manned by local volunteers. Although the military commanders thought the fort was poorly located as a defensive position and should be abandoned, when the San Juan boundary dispute (precipitated by the pig incident) was finally settled, the troops stationed on San Juan Island were relocated to Fort Townsend.

The fort was actively manned for another 20 years, although there was no particular threat from either natives or foreign nations and there were few American citizens in the area who needed protecting. One general declared that, "Instead of the garrison protecting Port Townsend, the town is guarding Fort Townsend!" In 1895 a kerosene lamp caught the barracks on fire and, perhaps fortuitously, it burned to the ground. This proved a good excuse for the Army to decommission the fort and ship out the troops.

In 1907 the site was briefly considered for the placement of eight 12-inch mortars that would be aimed west toward Discovery Bay. The mortars were to be fired across the Quimper Peninsula into the bay to

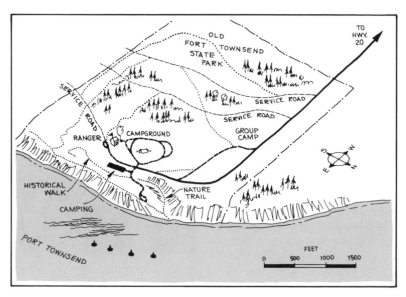

discourage the enemy from a backside attack on Fort Worden. The plan was dropped when it was proved that Fort Worden was capable of defending itself from the rear. The Fort Townsend site was used briefly by the Navy during World War II as an enemy munitions defusing station, and in 1958 it gave up all claim to a military existence when the land was purchased for a state park.

Old Fort Townsend State Park is located 4 miles south of Port Townsend, east of Highway 20. The intersection of the road to the park is well signed.

The only military building remaining at Fort Townsend is the tall, brick, WWII-era Navy Explosives Laboratory located near the park entrance. Near the old parade grounds is a self-guided historical walk past the buildings and facilities of the early fort.

The park sits on a bluff 200 feet above the water, with a commanding view though the trees of Port Townsend Bay and Indian and Marrowstone islands. Beautiful old-growth Douglas-fir and cedar surround the upper campgrounds; in spring rhododendrons in the camp area and along the entrance road bring a splash of blazing pink to the somber green forest. A smaller, lower campground is on an open, level area above the parade ground.

The road snakes downhill, ending in a loop near the edge of the bluff. From here a trail along the old service road continues steeply down to the water. Pilings in the water along the north edge of the park are from the fort's old wharf. There no longer is a dock here, but four mooring buoys are provided for visiting boaters. A nature trail that climbs a forested gully provides a nice alternative return route to the upper parking area. Other trails follow the top of the bluff or wander into the hinterland, back to the group camp.

PORT TOWNSEND

Port Townsend has made a graceful transition into a tourist-oriented town without sacrificing its integrity. This is no Victorian Disneyland, but a real city with genuine old buildings filled with antiques. The antique ambiance is complemented by a cultural one, with shops selling work by the finest Northwest artists, photographers, and craftspeople. Whatever your interest, there is something to lure you here.

Port Townsend lies at the north end of the Quimper Peninsula. It can be reached by driving west 5¼ miles from the Hood Canal bridge and turning north onto Highway 19, which is signed to Port Townsend. The Keystone ferry, which docks at the ferry terminal on the south side of town, reaches the town from Whidbey Island.

Annual events in the town include jogging and bicycling races, a sand castle-building competition, a wooden boat show, a salmon fishing derby, an old-fashioned county fair, a quilt show, both modern and folk dance festivals, a boating regatta, plays, music festivals ranging from Bach to bluegrass to Count Basie, and prose and poetry readings by nationally known writers. Many of the events are sponsored by Centrum, a performing arts foundation located on the grounds of Fort Worden. Upon request the Chamber of Commerce will send prospective visitors a list of events scheduled for the year.

Even if one does not come to Port Townsend to take in a special event, there is still plenty to fascinate you. The town, the best example of a Victorian seacoast town to be found north of San Francisco, has been designated as a National Historical District. Stores in beautifully restored old commercial buildings along Water Street offer hours of wonderful browsing and buying—heavy on the nautical and the Victorian. Food purveyors have everything from homemade ice cream cones to gourmet dinners.

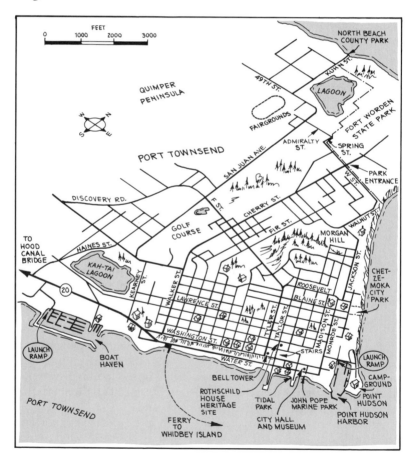

The historic Hastings Building, the most beautiful of downtown Port Townsend's commercial buildings, dates from 1889.

Port Townsend's real jewels are its beautiful old Victorian homes, built when the town seemed destined to be a major center of commerce on Puget Sound. The Chamber of Commerce provides a map describing 70 points of historical interest, including some three dozen private homes built before the turn of the century. Twice yearly—the first weekend in May and the third weekend in September—many of these residences are open for viewing during the city's Historic Homes Tours. Some of the homes operate as bed-and-breakfast inns and can be enjoyed by persons staying there.

Port Townsend is probably the state's most spectacular example of dreams gone awry. The fine, deep harbor was noted (first) by Captain George Vancouver, who gave it its name. Sixty years later, in 1851, it was settled by Alfred Plummer and Charles Bachelder. They and other pioneers were sure that with its strategic location at the entrance to the sound it would become a major point of commerce for boats eager to trade for furs, lumber, and other riches of the Northwest. The wharfs built here soon attracted ships, and when the customs house was transferred to Port Townsend from Olympia in 1854, the city's future seemed assured. Ships from every port in the world stopped here, and the town boosted itself as the "Key City" or "New York of the West." Rock ballast unloaded from ships was used to build the growing number of commercial buildings along Water Street.

Along with its rapid growth came an unsavory reputation. Public drunkenness, prostitution, and brawling were flagrant, and shanghaiing of sailors was a common practice. Because it was unsafe to walk on Water Street, the respected families of the town developed a retail district at the top of the hill, where proper ladies could shop in safety. One journalist called Port Townsend "the town that liquor built": Yankee traders without scruples frequently used liquor in trade with Indians, it was the item in greatest demand by sailors fresh off ships, and it was part of all the other nefarious activities in the town.

Port Townsend continued to boom through the 1880s. What was needed to assure its continued growth and prosperity and keep it abreast with the cities rapidly developing along the eastern shore of the sound was a railroad to link it to markets in the east. In 1887 enterprising citizens solicited funds to lay their own railroad tracks to link with the transcontinental line of the Northern Pacific that had recently been built to Tacoma. The company ran into financial difficulties, compounded by the depression of 1893, and went into receivership. Several other new business ventures, including a drydock and a nailworks, went bankrupt at this same time, throwing the town into a financial tailspin from which it never recovered. Almost overnight the town virtually shut down, going from a city with a population of over 7,000 to less than 2,000.

But some Port Townsend residents hung in there. The presence of the Army at Fort Worden brought some economic relief, and in 1927 the building of the pulp and paper mill south of town finally brought a steady payroll to the area. The current era of tourism began in the late 1950s with the first renovation of the Victorian homes and the inception of an artistic and cultural movement. The carefully cultivated promotion of the town's many assets has proven to be the key to its survival.

Jefferson County Historical Museum and City Parks

Access: Land, boat
Facilities: Picnic tables, children's play equipment, pier with float, tidal display
Attractions: Historical displays, picnicking

The numerous antiques stores provide a history lesson in themselves, but for an added dash of nostalgia, drop in at the Jefferson County Historical Museum, located in City Hall at the corner of Water and Madison streets. The museum is open Monday through Saturday from

11:00 A.M. to 4:00 P.M., and on Sunday from 1:00 to 4:00 P.M.; an admission fee is charged. Guided walking tours of the downtown area, conducted during the summer, begin at the museum.

On the waterfront, across the street from the museum, is John Pope Marine Park. This grassy nook above the beach has a children's play area and a few picnic tables. A huge driftwood log is big enough to have wide bench seats carved into both sides, and a grouping of carved seals frolicking at one end. A pier reaching into the bay boasts a 60-foot-long float on its north side that, in calm weather, can be used for temporary moorage for downtown visits.

Immediately south of the park is more public shoreline. Although officially designated as the "Ruth Seavey Jackson Memorial Art Project," it is more commonly known as "Tidal Park." The block-long park provides visitors a dynamic means of experiencing the rise and fall of the tide in its twice-daily rise and fall of up to 12 vertical feet. A large, enclosed concrete basin, connected to the beach at zero tide level and above, has a series of curved steps on which grow the varied marine life that flourish at the different tide levels. A large wind harp here adds a musical background when winds blow. Picnic tables and a pair of food kiosks share the park.

Tidal Park sits on pilings on the Port Townsend waterfront.

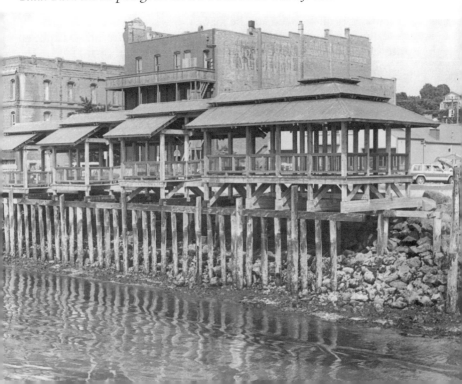

Port Townsend Marinas

Facilities: Complete boat and crew facilities, laundromat, U.S. Customs, boat launch (hoist and ramp), boat rental and charter, restaurants, picnic tables, campsites, shopping (nearby), sewage pump-out station

Two marinas bracket the Port Townsend waterfront. On the south side of town is the larger and more modern of the two facilities, Port Townsend Boat Haven, operated by the Port of Port Townsend; at the north end is Point Hudson Harbor, which is leased to a private company. Both have guest moorage, customs inspections, and full facilities for visiting boaters.

A rock jetty protects the 375 moorages at Boat Haven. The entrance, on the northeast, is clearly marked.

Just inside the breakwater is a small basin for commercial boats, the U.S. Coast Guard installation (where the *Point Bennett* is tied up), and a fuel dock. Once past these, the harbormaster's office and registration dock are immediately on the right. Self-register if the office is closed.

Numerous marine-oriented businesses are located within the basin area. Sling launching is available for trailered boats. A launch ramp at the southwest corner of the harbor is only usable at higher tide levels. The highway between the marina and downtown Port Townsend has recently been filled with a continuous row of new stores—groceries, gas stations, restaurants, and all types of services. The older section of town is about a ¼-mile walk from the marina. Bus service is available.

Point Hudson Harbor is closer to downtown attractions, although the facilities are not as large or as nice as those at the Boat Haven. The dredged basin lies behind a piling jetty immediately south of the point.

A float with numerous finger piers is on the northeast side; a long dock on the southwest has a fuel pump and additional tie-ups. If the harbor is full, rafting is permitted on this long float. At the southwest corner of the basin, a single-lane ramp provides launching for trailered boats. The ramp is not usable at low tide levels.

Behind the harbormaster's office on the northeast shore is a commercially operated RV campground with some tent-camping space, a restaurant, and a small motel. A small shore-side park with picnic tables facing on Admiralty Inlet displays an old Native American longboat. From here, except at high tide, the beach can be walked all the way north to Point Wilson.

Rothschild House Heritage Site

Two of the historic Port Townsend homes are open year-round for touring: the Commanding Officer's Quarters at Fort Worden, and the Rothschild House at the corner of Franklin and Taylor (near downtown).

To reach the house from the business district, climb the stairs that ascend the bluff at the end of Taylor Street; the Rothschild House is one block straight ahead.

The Rothschild House, which is administered by Washington State Parks and staffed by local volunteers, is a simple two-story, four-bedroom home, authentically furnished. It is not as opulent as some of the other Victorian homes locally owned by wealthier families, but it does portray an elegant way of life typical of the time. The house is open for visits daily from 10:00 A.M. to 5:00 P.M. during the summer, but only on weekends during the winter; an admission fee is charged.

The kitchen in the Rothschild House displays housewares typical of the late 1800s.

A block south of the Rothschild House, at the end of Tyler Street, is the old bell tower that once was used to summon volunteer firemen. The tower was built in 1890 and is thought to be the last such standing structure in the United States. In the base of the tower, the county historical society has two historic horse-drawn carriages on display. One is a glass-sided hearse, used in local funerals between 1868 and 1912. The second is a four-passenger Gurney taxi dating from 1890.

Chetzemoka City Park

Park area: 10 acres; 750 feet of shoreline on the Strait of Juan de Fuca
Access: Land, paddle-craft
Facilities: Picnic tables, shelter with fireplace, restrooms, drinking water, bandstand, children's play equipment
Attractions: Picnicking, beachcombing, clam digging, swimming

This small city park pays tribute to the Klallam Indian chief who proved to be a good friend to early Port Townsend settlers. Chetzemoka was derisively called the "Duke of York" by pioneers unable or unwilling to deal with the guttural Klallam tongue. He was portrayed as a buffoon and alcoholic by Theodore Winthrop, who wrote of him in his 1862 book *Canoe and Saddle* (Portland, Ore: Binford & Mort, n.d.). In truth, Chetzemoka got bad press at the time, because it was the whites who regularly supplied the poison for which Native Americans have a genetic weakness. The Indian chief's wisdom in seeing the inevitability of white settlement and his actions as a mediator served both the settlers and his own people very well. During the Indian Wars he was instrumental in discouraging an attack on the whites, an action that surely would have resulted in the loss of far more Indians' lives than whites'.

The city park is on a slight bluff facing Admiralty Inlet, within walking distance of downtown Port Townsend. It can be reached by walking the beach north from Point Hudson for about ¼ mile, or by following Monroe Street northwest and turning right on Blaine Street, which in one block dead-ends at the park.

The park was initially constructed in 1904 when prominent Port Townsend socialites decided that any civilized city should have a public park. With its covered bandstand and formal rose garden, the area is still reminiscent of an old-fashioned park, and one expects to see straw-hatted dandies strolling with their ladies under the blossom-covered arches. During early times it also held a "zoo" consisting of a deer, a peacock, and a bear.

The manicured lawn rolls down to a path that leads to the beach. At high tide the shore is narrow, but low tide exposes an expanse of sandy beach.

North Beach County Park (Jefferson County)

Park area: 1 acre; 310 feet of shoreline on the Strait of Juan de Fuca
Access: Land, paddle-craft
Facilities: Picnic tables, kitchen shelter, fireplaces, latrines, *no water*
Attractions: Swimming, beachcombing

At North Beach the steep bluffs on this side of the Quimper Peninsula briefly dip down to the shore. Early Native Americans landed their canoes here and portaged south across the swampy flat to Kah-tai Lagoon by Port Townsend Bay to avoid tide rips off Point Wilson.

To reach the park by land, drive west out of Port Townsend on any road to its intersection with San Juan Avenue. Follow this street north; at the edge of a large lagoon it turns west and becomes 49th Street. In one block turn north on Kuhn Street and follow it to its end at the park.

Park facilities are rather meager—a few picnic tables and two latrines—but the beach is glorious. The sand slopes gradually into the frothy waters of the straits. Swim if you like, build sand castles, or just let the nearly constant wind off the channel fill your nostrils with brine-scented air. The concrete boat ramp that was once here is badly broken up and nearly covered with sand.

The small county park, which abuts the west side of Fort Worden State Park, provides a handy starting point for beach walks east beneath the 200-foot bluffs of Fort Worden all the way to Point Wilson, 1½ miles away, or even to Port Townsend another 2 miles distance. The way is passable at all times except high tide, so before beginning extended walks check the tide table. Or walk an upland path into meadows at the northwest corner of the state park.

Fort Worden State Park

Park area: 434 acres; 11,020 feet of shoreline on Admiralty Inlet and the Strait of Juan de Fuca
Access: Land, boat
Facilities: 80 campsites with hookups, 3 primitive campsites, picnic tables, water, kitchen shelters, fireplaces, restrooms, showers, bathhouse, vault toilets, drinking water, laundromat, vacation housing, dormitories, youth hostel, dining hall, snack bar/grocery, boat launch (ramp), fishing pier, float, mooring buoys, Coast Artillery Museum, Marine Science Center, underwater marine park, hiking trails, tennis courts, gymnasium, chapel, performance theater, playfields, children's play equipment
Attractions: Camping, picnicking, boating, fishing, scuba diving, arts and crafts, cultural arts, educational and historical displays, hiking, beachcombing

Among the state's many outstanding parks, Fort Worden must rank as one of the grandest. Although it lacks the primeval forest environment (there are plenty of parks elsewhere to provide that), it packs a wealth of activities within its boundaries.

It is located just north of Port Townsend; the 2-mile route from the city center to the park entrance is well marked by signs. By water, the park lies at the confluence of Admiralty Inlet and the Strait of Juan de Fuca. Marine facilities are on the east shore.

The bristling guns of Fort Worden were intended, along with those at Forts Casey and Flagler, to guard the entrance to Puget Sound. Construction on the fort began in 1898 and, as the fortifications neared completion in 1902, the first soldiers were assigned. On the day scheduled for their arrival, the citizens of Port Townsend turned out en masse, complete with a brass band, to welcome them. With dismay and drooping pennants the gentry watched the troop-laden steamer *Majestic* chug by, unaware of the planned celebration, headed for the pier at the fort instead of landing at the town's Union Wharf.

Some small parcels of land within the designated area of the fort had previously been claimed by Port Townsend settlers. The land was needed for fort buildings, and there was also a concern that nonmilitary residents so close to the fort might pose a security risk. When negotiations for the property began there was considerable disagreement between the government and the property owners as to its value. The commandant of the fort took matters into his own hands by beginning the first practice firings of the mortar batteries. As plaster walls cracked from the concussion, and pictures and bric-a-brac came crashing down, real estate values fell with them and homeowners rushed to sell their property.

With 16 12-inch mortars and 25 guns ranging from 3 inches to 12 inches, at full strength Fort Casey was the most heavily fortified of the Puget Sound forts. By 1904 underwater cable communications linked Fort Worden to Forts Casey and Flagler, and the following year it was fully garrisoned with four companies of Coast Artillery troops. With the completion of fire-control stations and five 60-inch searchlight emplacements, the fort stood completed by 1912.

In just five years, with the beginning of World War I, the entire character of the fort changed. As additional troops were sent here to be trained for battle on the European front, more barracks were built, and 18 of the guns were removed for shipment to Europe. At the end of the war the number of troops stationed at Fort Worden decreased drastically. The only new activity was the construction in 1920 of a huge

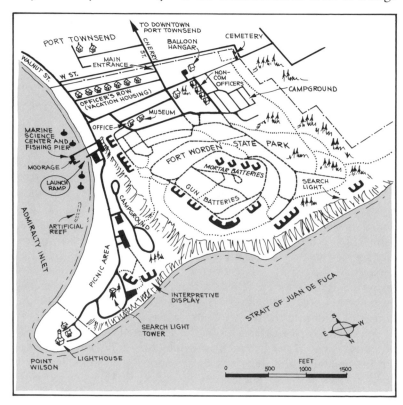

balloon hangar and the addition of two companies of men who experimented, unsuccessfully, with using large balloons for gunfire control and observation stations.

The fort saw some activity during World War II as a Harbor Entrance Control Post to monitor radar sites and new underwater sonar and sensing devices; it also served to coordinate all defensive activities on the inland waters. With the end of World War II, all the remaining guns were removed and scrapped. The last military use was during the Korean conflict when units of an Army engineering regiment were stationed here prior to being shipped to the Far East.

After the deactivation of the post in 1953 the state of Washington used it as a juvenile diagnostic treatment center, and finally in 1972 it was transferred to the state Parks Commission. Since that time

The concrete bunkers at Fort Worden are fascinating for both youngsters and their parents.

the facilities at Fort Worden have seen ever-increasing use, not only for traditional state park purposes, but also as a site for conferences, retreats, workshops, sports and music camps, and festivals. Today it ranks as the most heavily used of the state parks, with over 1.25 million visitors passing through its gates annually.

Twenty-three of the housing units originally used by officers and NCOs, and two other historic buildings, are available at reasonable rates to groups or families for overnight stays. Many have been refurbished with antiques and reproductions of Victorian-era furniture. Optional meal service in the park dining hall is also available. Barracks holding 365 beds now serve as dormitories for use by larger groups. The campus exudes the atmosphere of what it once was as a military installation. Although the grounds are nicely kept, they are not quite as carefully manicured as when a crew of as many as 300 enlisted men mowed lawns, swept walks, and groomed beds of bright flowers.

Meeting rooms of various sizes can be reserved by the day, week, or month; the post chapel is a favorite spot for weddings. Two fully equipped theaters rent performance space; one has a capacity of 275, while the other, a converted balloon hangar, holds between 880 and 1,200.

A stop at the state park office, near the entrance, will arm the visitor with maps and a list of current activities. In summer Centrum, a non-profit arts foundation, may be sponsoring a music festival or a play. One park leaflet guides the way on a historical walk around the fort's many buildings. Several miles' worth of strolls are available: to the fort cemetery, to the gun emplacements, to the beach, to the lighthouse—to wherever impulse leads.

Next to the park office is the Coast Artillery Museum (open Wednesday through Sunday, noon to 5:00 P.M.), which has displays of memorabilia from the fort, and historical information about the coastal fortifications. A video program narrates sequences of photos showing life at the fort in the early 1900s and the firing of the big guns and mortars.

The park road leads past the prim row of officer's quarters, which are available for public rental. The Commanding Officer's House, furnished in Victorian period decor, is open to self-guided tours daily from April through October. From here Harbor Defense Way drops down to the east beach. Here are a large wharf and a float with space for about four boats, where overnight moorage is permitted. The two-lane boat launch ramp is on the north side of the pier, protected by its L-shaped bend and a row of pilings. Eight mooring buoys are spaced along the shore

Battery Ash at Fort Worden State Park

north and south of the wharf, although wind and wave action may make an overnight tie-up uncomfortable.

At the end of the wharf is the building that houses the Port Townsend Marine Science Center, which has hands-on exhibits of marine life and conducts summer weekend beach walks, classes, and a number of other marine-oriented activities. Fishing is permitted from the pier; a fish-cleaning station is next to the building.

The offshore waters are designated as an underwater park. Scuba divers explore the pilings of the old wharf and the sandy bottom along the east shore. North of Point Wilson a reef attracts divers expert enough to handle the swift current on this side of the point. The white rock of the reef makes a dramatic contrast with brightly colored sea anemones and fish. Spear fishing is not permitted in the waters of the park.

Two types of beaches are found here: on the east, facing on Admiralty Inlet, is a gradually sloping sandy beach, partially protected by the curving arm of Point Wilson; on the north, the Strait of Juan de Fuca shoreline is a narrower strip, enclosed by rising bluffs and dropping off quickly into the sea. Winds off the straits frequently batter the shore, making walking difficult but often exhilarating. The beaches can be walked south or west of Point Wilson for some distance, depending on the stamina of the walker. Use care on the north shore not to get trapped by incoming tide.

One of the two park camping areas, with 50 campsites, is in an open grassy field west of Harbor Defense Way. None of these campsites are protected from the wind, which can get quite brisk in this exposed location. An enclosed kitchen shelter is near the beach, and numerous picnic tables are scattered along the shore.

The road continues on to a parking lot near Battery Kinzie. At the battery one can wander through the gun emplacements and rooms where munitions were stored. Still in evidence are the overhead metal tracks that were used for transporting munitions. From the top of the battery is a sweeping 300-degree view of the strait and Admiralty Inlet, blocked only by the hill behind. The rusting metal tower to the east once held a searchlight. Battery Kinzie is the best maintained of the fort's 12 batteries; the others, which are on the hill to the southwest, can be reached by trails from the campground or the residential area.

The second park campground is upland on the west side of the park, west of the NCO houses. Here are two loops with 30 campsites in a wooded section of the park. Three primitive bicycle sites are nearby.

Point Wilson Light Station

The lighthouse at Admiralty Head on Whidbey Island, which began operation in 1879, was one of the earliest to guide boaters on Washington's inland waters. In order to avoid the unmarked shoals at

Point Wilson Lighthouse looks out to Admiralty Inlet and the Strait of Juan de Fuca.

Point Wilson, shippers navigating in the dark or fog kept the light well in sight and stayed to the east side of Admiralty Inlet, following the Whidbey Island shoreline. It was not until almost 20 years later that two more lighthouses, at Point No Point and here at Point Wilson, enabled ships to safely follow the shorter route along the western shoreline.

The original lighthouse at Point Wilson was equipped with the most modern Fresnel lens, consisting of an aggregation of 72 glass prisms and bull's-eye lenses. The light source, a wick-type lamp that nightly burned three gallons of whale oil, kerosene, or lard, was eventually replaced by a 1,000-watt electrical bulb. A 12-inch steam whistle signaled a warning to boats in the fog. The beacon, originally in a tower above the keeper's quarters, was moved to a new building in 1913, and separate housing was built for the personnel.

Until 1939, when the Coast Guard took over lighthouse administration, the U.S. Lighthouse Service operated most stations with civil service personnel. In addition to keeping the light clean, winding the clockworks that rotated it, polishing the brass, trimming the lamp wicks (which prompted the nickname "wickie"), and other maintenance tasks, the keeper was expected to keep a garden and livestock to feed himself and his family. Life at Point Wilson, within a short distance of Port Townsend, was far better than at many of the more remote light stations along the coast.

The beacon is now automated and the grounds are not open to the public.

CHAPTER EIGHT

EASTERN STRAIT OF JUAN DE FUCA

Nearing the end of their northward journey, the waters of Puget Sound pour into the long tongue of the Strait of Juan de Fuca before making the final transition to the open sea. The 100-mile-long strait is a commercial superhighway down which freighters and tankers stream, linking Puget Sound ports with markets throughout the Pacific Rim.

Many pleasure boaters avoid the open stretches of the strait, favoring inland waters or hugging the comforting western shore of Whidbey Island. Stomach-churning swells can be built up by winds sweeping the length of the channel. Fog banks creeping in off the ocean linger in the

Dungeness Spit faces on the Strait of Juan de Fuca.

strait long after they have cleared from inland waters. At such times, when you cannot rely on line of sight, good navigational skills are essential to make the 25-mile crossing from Admiralty Inlet to Victoria or the San Juan Islands.

On clear days and when seas are calm, the strait offers sailors steady winds and joyously endless tacks, while cruisers find numerous bays and beaches to explore. Waters of the strait are legendary for salmon, enormous halibut, and bottomfish; many of the boats seen in the strait are those of anglers intent on landing their limit.

The eastern half of the strait, from Port Townsend to Port Angeles, provides boaters somewhat of a transition from the shelter and civilization of the inland waters to the more rigorous demands of the outer reaches of the passage. Two deep inlets, Sequim Bay and Discovery Bay, offer the only well-protected harbors with good anchorages along this south shore. The only town with marine facilities is Port Angeles, which is somewhat sheltered by Ediz Hook and man-made breakwaters.

PROTECTION ISLAND

Not many boaters take note of the rhinoceros auklet, a black, stubby little bird that has been described as flying with the grace of a "winged brick." It is under water that it moves like a ballet dancer, using its wings for propulsion as it pursues herring or smelt and scoops them into its blunt beak. The auklet hunts open waters during the day, and not until twilight does it return to cliff-edge burrows, with fish for its chicks dangling from its heavy, bony bill.

It took a long time before someone noticed, or cared, that an unusually large number of these birds were living on Protection Island. Stud-

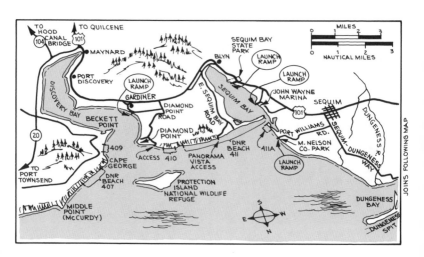

ies eventually revealed that an estimated 17,000 pairs, or about 96 percent of the rhinoceros auklets in the Lower 48 states, nested and raised their young in the sandy cliffs of the 400-acre island. Unfortunately, just at this time bulldozers had begun clearing land for a gargantuan real estate development—and Protection Island itself became desperately in need of protection.

The auklet is only one of the numerous species of birds found here. Loss of breeding habitat in other areas along the sound, due to the encroachment of man, has undoubtedly led to the huge concentration of birds on the island. Hillsides, ledges, sandspits, and open fields are used by nearly three-fourths of the sound's nesting population of seabirds, including pelagic cormorants, glaucous-winged gulls, pigeon guillemots, and black oystercatchers.

Huge flocks of tufted puffins once lived on Puget Sound. Indians killed many, using their brilliant parrotlike beaks as rattles and decoration, but the flocks managed to survive until the arrival of Europeans brought a serious loss of habitat, a depletion of food sources, and eventually the pollution of their environment. All of the tufted puffins now remaining on Puget Sound—some 35 pairs—are believed to nest on Protection Island.

The island was named by George Vancouver, who noted its protective location at the mouth of Discovery Bay. After that no one paid much attention to it for a long time—the government owned it, but gave it away in 1861; an attempt at farming was unsuccessful, and in the late 1940s an unattended beach fire spread and the entire island was burned to a crisp.

The fire-blackened slopes turned green once again, wildflowers bloomed, and life returned to Protection Island. In 1968 some real

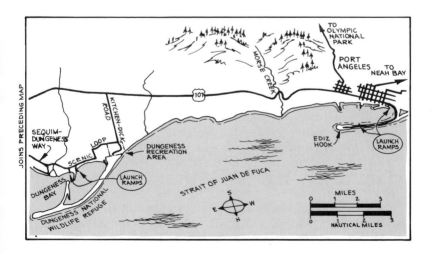

Protection Island as seen from Diamond Point

estate developers bought it and subdivided it into a network of 1,100 lots, including an airstrip and a marina. No matter that storm winds on exposed parts of the bluffs were known to blow away livestock and even overturn tractors, over half the lots were snatched up by persons eager to own part of an island, and construction began.

Panicked environmentalists, including the Audubon Society and The Nature Conservancy, rallied. Their actions brought property sales and construction to a halt. The Nature Conservancy was able to purchase 48 acres of crucial auklet nesting grounds, but the rest of the island was still in danger of eventual settlement. In 1980 Congressman Don Bonker introduced a bill to appropriate $4 million for purchase of land on the island. In August 1988 Protection Island was officially established as a National Wildlife Refuge. The U.S. Fish and Wildlife Service currently owns 316 acres; the remaining 48 acres of land on the west end are owned and managed by the Washington State Department of Fish and Wildlife.

The federally owned portion of Protection Island is closed to all public use year-around. Visits to the state-managed lands at the west end are strongly discouraged from March through September when birds are nesting. These intrusions may also disturb harbor seals, which in spring deliver their pups on sun-warmed sandspits. A 200-yard buffer zone has been established around the island; boaters should stay offshore at least this distance.

DISCOVERY BAY AND MILLER PENINSULA

After his arduous voyage around Africa's Cape of Good Hope and across the Pacific, George Vancouver was pleased to find the sheltered arm of Discovery Bay for a nearly week-long layover to repair his ships and provide the crew some R and R. He wrote glowingly of the beauty of the bay; although the bay is lovely, perhaps his enthusiasm was affected by all those months at sea with only a scruffy crew to look at.

Discovery Bay hasn't changed a great deal since Vancouver dropped anchor here. Only a few communities and homes along the shore mark the arrival of civilization. The sinuous 8-mile-long inlet provides excellent anchorages at numerous spots along the shore, but there is nothing in the way of boating facilities except the launch ramp at Gardiner (see below).

The only public shore lands on the bay are two sections of DNR beach at Cape George. Beach 409, a 1,475-foot strip of tidelands, is about a mile north of Beckett Point; Beach 407, which is just east of the tip of Cape George beneath a sheer 1,500-foot cliff, is 5,035 feet long. Neither beach has upland access, but both can be reached by boat from Gardiner; only the shorelands below mean high water are public.

The Miller Peninsula is flanked by Discovery Bay on the east, and Sequim Bay on the west. Substantial portions of the heart of the wooded peninsula are state property. The state Parks Commission planned to acquire 1,445 acres, managed by the Department of Natural Resources, as funds became available. In 1990 a Japanese developer proposed a complicated land deal: it would buy portions of the state land, and swap other adjacent land it owned on the peninsula, to consolidate enough property to develop a world-class resort on the east side of the peninsula. In turn, the developer would pay costs of building a road into the resulting 920-acre state park property, provide utility hookups within the park, grant public access to the beach below the resort, and spend $1 million to develop the park site.

What looked like a "win-win" situation for both the state Parks Commission and the economy of Jefferson County raised the hackles of environmental groups, which then sued to stop the deal. Although the courts later dismissed the suits, the controversy and changing economic conditions caused the developer to back out of the project. The state still owns the property, and the perpetually cash-strapped state Parks Commission has no funds to develop it in the foreseeable future. The uplands have a few swampy jeep roads through them, but are for all practical purposes inaccessible.

Diamond Point

Historically, Diamond Point is unique. Although this point on the Miller Peninsula originally was one of the many military reservation lands along the sound, in 1894 it became a quarantine station, with a hospital and detention area for ship passengers suspected of having been exposed to contagious diseases such as leprosy and elephantiasis. It operated until 1935, when the facility was moved to Port Townsend. A few of the buildings have been remodeled and are now used as private residences. A deteriorating wharf on the south side of the point was once used by ships undergoing fumigation for vermin and insects, and waiting out the quarantine period.

Unlike other military reservation lands that became parks, Diamond Point now sports row upon row of summer homes. From a small break in the bulkheads along the north shore you can launch a cartop boat to explore the offshore perimeter of Protection Island or to visit two strips of DNR beach to the west.

To reach the public access at Diamond Point, turn north off US Highway 101 8¼ miles northwest of the Highway 20 intersection at the south end of Discovery Bay, turn onto Diamond Point Road, and follow it for 4¾ miles to the junction with Diamond Shore Lane North. In 200 yards this road intersects Beach Drive and Access Road. The latter extends about 300 yards to the north to an opening in the bulkheads and a sign that says PUBLIC ACCESS, NO PARKING. Beaches on either side of the access are private. There is limited parking along the head of the road and Beach Drive, south of the access point. Although this spot once was used to shuttle residents to Protection Island, most of the island is now a National Wildlife Refuge, and shore visits are not permitted.

West of Diamond Point, DNR Beach 410, a 2,710-foot stretch of tidelands, begins just beyond the beach homes, below a wooded bluff. DNR Beach 411 begins ¼ mile beyond the west end of Beach 410 in the middle of Thompson Spit and continues for nearly 5 glorious miles to the end of Travis Spit by Sequim Bay. A commercial RV and camping park at Diamond Point also provides foot and boat access to Beach 410 for persons registered at the park.

Gardiner Boat Launch Ramp

A boat launch site more easily located than the one at Diamond Point is at Gardiner, farther into Discovery Bay.

Turn off US Highway 101 onto Old Gardiner Highway, 4½ miles northwest of the Highway 20 intersection at the end of Discovery Bay. In 2¼ miles, turn east on Gardiner Beach Road and, just after the road bends left to parallel the shore, a single-lane concrete launch ramp is reached. A gravel lot across the road has a vault toilet and parking for a dozen cars.

Continue north on Gardiner Beach Road for less than ¼ mile to drive-by views of Troll Haven, a bizarre regression into the 12th century. Here weirdly carved fence posts line the roadway and a medieval castle, 20-foot-high carved ogres, and demonic defenders of the mythical enclave surround the private holdings of a person with a unique sense of reality.

Panorama Vista Access

DNR Beach 411 (see Diamond Point, above), on the Miller Peninsula, can be reached on foot from a road on the east side of Sequim Bay.

Turn off US Highway 101 onto East Sequim Bay Road at either Old Blyn Road or Blyn Crossing. Follow the road from Blyn Crossing around the east side of Sequim Bay for 4½ miles to Panorama Boulevard. Turn right (east) here, and in ¾ mile turn right (east) again onto Buck Loop. In another ¼ mile, at the intersection of Buck Loop and Deer Court, is a gate at a small Clallam County park; park here and walk down a wide grassy path 500 yards to the beach. Here a staircase below a small clearing

Limpets, snails, and seaweed line a rocky niche at low tide.

drops down to Beach 411. There are no other public facilities.

The public beach, which lies below mean high water and runs for 25,710 feet, extends west to the end of Travis Spit and east to the middle of Thompson Spit near Diamond Point. Protection Island can be seen to the east. Some walkable beach is exposed at all times except extreme high water. At high tide the beach is about 6 feet wide. At low water, clams and geoducks can be dug; however, shellfish should not be taken from Travis Spit because they are hazardous to eat due to a domestic sewage outfall on nearby Gibson Spit.

The beach can also easily be reached by boat from Sequim Bay or from Marlyn Nelson County Park at Port Williams, north of Gibson Spit.

SEQUIM BAY

The continuous action of wind and waves from the Strait of Juan de Fuca wears away the soft glacial-till bluffs and then deposits the material on several long curving sandspits along the north shore of the Olympic Peninsula. A pair of sandspits at the entrance to Sequim Bay nearly join to form an enormous lagoon.

The tidelands of both Travis Spit, which extends from the east, and Gibson Spit, which lies on the west, are public DNR beaches on which small boats can easily be landed. Land access to Beach 411 on Travis Spit is described under Diamond Point (see above). Beach 411A, on Gibson Spit, can also be reached by walking south along the shore from

Port Williams. Keep dogs on a leash (or leave them home) and use special care in walking to avoid disturbing shorebirds and waterfowl nesting in beach grass and driftwood.

Boat access to the inlet is via a dredged channel that starts at the red entrance buoy, runs parallel along the north side of Travis Spit, and then threads along the western shore. Consult a good navigational chart and enter with care, favoring the west side and watching channel markers closely to avoid Middle Ground, a large shoal that lies just inside the entrance; some buoys tow under during strong tides and may not be visible. Once inside there are no navigational hazards, and excellent anchorages can be found throughout the bay in up to 20 fathoms. In addition to the large marina at Pitship Point, a smaller marina midway along the north shore also has fuel and supplies.

Some early maps show the name of the bay as Washington Harbor, but the local settlers preferred the more descriptive Indian name of Sequim, generally thought to mean "quiet water." Today Washington Harbor refers only to the small community at the entrance, where the marine research facilities of Battelle Institute are located.

Stunning displays of nighttime luminescence have been observed in Sequim Bay. When this phenomenon occurs, any disturbance in the water, even the slightest dip of an oar, produces a burst of ghostly radiance. Wake from a churning motor leaves a milky white billow on the black water, and glittery streaks mark the trails of fish swimming just below the surface. Such luminescence is caused by certain dinoflagellates, minute single-celled marine organisms that are part of plankton. Small numbers of these organisms are nearly always present in the water, and many boaters have been startled by nighttime fireworks in their darkened toilets when the heads have been flushed with seawater.

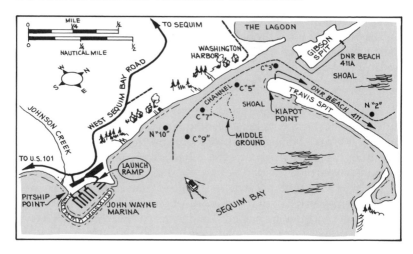

Certain combinations of nutrients, water salinity, and temperature can cause a sudden "bloom," or rapid increase in organisms of a particular kind. Dinoflagellates such as *noctiluca* ("night light") or a species of Gonyaulax noted for its luminescence may be the ones affected, resulting in a remarkable nighttime display. Several kinds of jellyfish also have this quality, but their luminescence shows as specific points of light when they are disturbed, rather than an overall glow of the water.

Pitship Point (John Wayne Marina)

Facilities: Complete boat and crew facilities, restrooms, restaurant, marine supplies, laundromat, public meeting rooms, boat launch (ramp), picnic tables, fireplaces, bait, tackle, fishing pier
Attractions: Boating, fishing, clam digging, swimming

On the west shore of Sequim Bay, where a meager little boat launch and a strip of public beach once existed, now stands a sparkling marina—and it's all due to movie actor John Wayne. Wayne brought his converted mine sweeper, the *Wild Goose,* into Sequim Bay on his frequent visits to Puget Sound and was so fond of the area that he purchased property at Pitship Point. The Port of Port Angeles asked him for land for a marina to serve the needs of Sequim and Port Angeles residents, and he generously donated 23 acres adjoining the port's existing public lands.

The marina snuggles neatly behind a curving rock breakwater on the north side of the point. Picnic tables are on a grassy knoll north of the marina building, and a walkway leads south across a scenic bridge where Johnson Creek empties into the bay. The beach south of the breakwater remains natural, with a long sandy tideflat for clam digging and puddle dabbling.

The first pier inside the marina breakwater is open for transient moorage, public fishing, and crabbing. Next to it are the gas dock and a fine two-lane concrete boat launch ramp. Floats G and H, the first two piers in the moorage area, are guest slips.

John Wayne Marina

To reach Pitship Point by land, turn off US Highway 101 onto Whitefeather Way ½ mile west of Sequim Bay State Park and follow signs to the marina. A commercial RV campground is nearby.

Sequim Bay State Park

Park area: 90 acres; 4,900 feet of shoreline on Sequim Bay
Access: Land, boat
Facilities: 60 standard campsites, 26 RV campsites, 3 primitive campsites, group camp, picnic tables, fireplaces, picnic shelters, group picnic area, restrooms, showers, RV pumpout station, dock and float, 6 mooring buoys, boat launch (ramp), interpretive center, hiking trails, children's play equipment, tennis courts, softball field, horseshoe pits, Environmental Learning Center
Attractions: Boating, fishing, clam digging, crabbing, hiking, scuba diving, field and group sports, marine life study, birdwatching

A wonderful state park for either boaters or land-bound campers! Visitors arriving by water can tie up to the dock, send the kids ashore to work off energy on hiking trails and the tennis courts (or even to camp for the night), and settle back to enjoy some peace and quiet. Or perhaps even the "old folks" would enjoy a ramble through the woods and along the beach.

The state park, which lies 4¾ miles southeast of the town of Sequim on US Highway 101, has one drawback: this major highway runs along the west edge of the park, and in some campsites the drone of traffic is not obscured by the trees.

At the south edge of the park, a long pier has a 50-foot float on the end, where overnight tie-ups are permitted. At mean low water, the float has 6 to 7 feet of water under it, but a piling directly north stands in only 3 feet at the same time; use care approaching or leaving the dock at low tide. Additional moorage is on six state park buoys spread along the shore. A two-lane launch ramp with a boarding float, located farther north along the beach, is steep enough to be used even at minus tides.

The park flows down a series of wooded terraces on the hillside above the bay. A ravine with a cool trickling stream separates the campsites, on the north, from picnic areas and a group camp, on the south. Trees obscure the view of the bay from the campground, but there are water vistas, both high and low, from trails that thread along the embankment and shore.

At the park entrance is a one-room interpretive center that explains the various habitats and characteristics of the marine invertebrates and bivalves found on the beach. It tells of a "Clam Camp," attended by students and teachers, where participants learned about watersheds, marine habitats, and shoreside creatures through field work. A video

*Sequim Bay State Park provides a dock, float, and buoys for the conve-
nience of visiting boaters.*

program with several menus describes such subjects as shellfish identification, harvesting of crabs, watersheds, boating safety, and filleting salmon
and bottomfish.

A tunnel leads under the highway from the main park area to a few
more picnic sites, tennis courts, and a baseball diamond on the west side
of the highway. A separate entrance, a few hundred yards south of the
main park entrance, leads to Ramblewood, the park's Environmental
Learning Center, which may be reserved for group use.

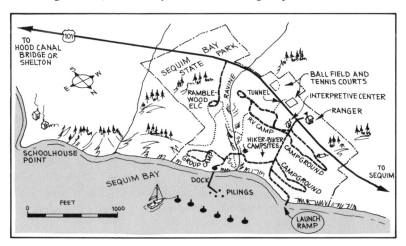

Marlyn Nelson County Park (Clallam County)

Park area: 1 acre; 500 feet of shoreline on the Strait of Juan de Fuca
Access: Land, boat
Facilities: Boat launch (ramp), picnic tables, fire grates, latrine, *no water*

The influence of the little steamers of the early-day Mosquito Fleet extended clear out into the Strait of Juan de Fuca; Port Angeles was one stopover point, and Port Williams, near the entrance to Sequim Bay, was another. Cars followed a rough trail from the villages of Sequim and Port Washington to reach the Port Williams dock, where passengers disembarked and freight was unloaded. Where once there was a post office, hotel, dance hall, and residences, there is now only a tiny county park with a boat launch ramp, some picnic tables, and two fire grates.

Reach the park by land by turning north from US Highway 101 on the east side of Sequim onto Brown Road. At a T intersection in 1 mile, turn right onto Point Williams Road, which leads to the park. Total distance from the highway is 3 miles.

The park opens the way to beach walks below 80-foot-high bluffs of vertical glacial till. The beach walk north is halted in ½ mile by the boundaries of a private game farm. South is Gibson Spit, which encloses a salt-marsh lagoon. The ½-mile section of tidelands wrapping around the tip of the spit is designated as DNR Beach 411A. Shellfish taken from either Gibson Spit or Travis Spit may be hazardous to eat due to a nearby domestic sewage outfall.

DUNGENESS BAY

One of the most spectacular land features on the Strait of Juan de Fuca is Dungeness Spit, the 5-mile-long ribbon of sand at the delta of the Dungeness River. This sandspit, the longest in the U.S., has been built up by action of the wind and water current, which causes silt from the river and eroded material from nearby glacial-till bluffs to be deposited in a long curving sandbar. The spit encloses Dungeness Bay, a broad harbor open on the east. A shoal extending ¾ mile to the northeast from the lighthouse is marked by a lighted bell buoy; however the buoy may tow under during strong currents. Graveyard Spit, a secondary finger of sand, extends from the north, nearly bisecting the bay.

Boaters with local knowledge enter the inner lagoon through a winding, unmarked channel, but much of this lagoon holds less than a fathom of water at mean lower low tide, so great care must be used. Anchorages can be found south of the tip of Dungeness Spit in 5 to 9 fathoms of water. The hook of land affords some protection from swells off the straits, but there is little shelter from strong winds.

Although the spit is called Dungeness, the navigational beacon at its tip is known as the New Dungeness Lighthouse. George Vancouver gave the area its name. It reminded him of Dungeness in the British Channel, so he called this New Dungeness. Over the years local usage shortened it to Dungeness, a name that now applies to the spit, the harbor, the river, the community, and also the tasty crustacean that frequents the bay. Only the lighthouse retains the original name.

The New Dungeness Lighthouse was the first to guard the inland waters of Washington. In 1857, when it was built, it stood 100 feet tall, but over the years the masonry weakened, caused perhaps by a structural flaw. When the Canadian army began practice firing of their cannons from their fortifications on Vancouver Island in 1927, the reverberations caused serious cracks in the lighthouse mortar. It became necessary to remove the upper third of the tower, bringing it down to

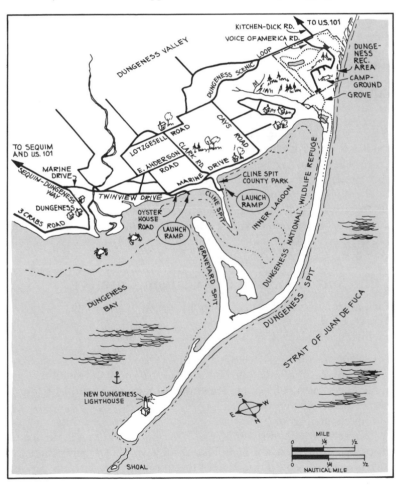

its present height of 63 feet. When this was done the old oil-fired light was scrapped and the electrified Fresnel lens was brought from the decommissioned lighthouse at Admiralty Head. That well-traveled lens is now in the Coast Guard Museum in Seattle.

Graveyard Spit did indeed once serve as a graveyard. A group of Tsimshian Indians from British Columbia who camped here in 1868 were descended upon in the night and massacred by a party of local Klallam Indians. One woman escaped, despite serious wounds, and sought refuge in the lighthouse. The bodies of her companions were buried on the spit.

This is a popular recreation area. The spit itself is a National Wildlife Refuge, and several other public accesses are on the shore, facing on Dungeness Bay. Clam digging and crabbing are permitted on any of the public lands; however, all oysters in Dungeness Bay are private property.

A scenic road north of US Highway 101 leads to all these recreation sites. From the town of Sequim head north on Sequim Avenue, which is signed as the Dungeness Scenic Loop; the western end of this loop drive rejoins US 101 at Kitchen-Dick Road, 4 miles west of Sequim.

Dungeness Boat Launch

As the east end of the Dungeness Scenic Loop, Sequim–Dungeness Way, reaches Dungeness Bay and curves west, it becomes East Anderson Road. At a T intersection, Marine Drive heads north, and in ¼ mile Oyster House Road descends to the beach. At the end of this road is a boat launch facility operated by the Port of Port Angeles.

The single-lane concrete ramp, with a boarding float, faces on a long tideflat that extends outward toward the tip of Graveyard Spit; a dredged channel makes the ramp usable even at minus tides. Restrooms are next to a large gravel parking lot. Adjacent to the ramp is a business that sells fresh oysters, clams, shrimp, and crabs.

Cline Spit County Park (Clallam County)

Park area: 1 acre; 300 feet of shoreline on Dungeness Bay
Access: Land, boat
Facilities: Boat launch (ramp), parking, restrooms

Clallam County has developed a strip of state park property on Cline Spit, facing on the inner lagoon, as a launch ramp and small day-use public access area. The single-lane ramp is quite long, and is usable at lower tides; however, boats leaving the lagoon must negotiate the circuitous channel around the ends of Cline and Graveyard spits.

To reach the park, turn off Marine Drive onto Cline Spit Road, which drops steeply down to the shore. Signs and chain-link fencing mark the park boundary; the extreme end of the spit is private. There is parking here for about a dozen cars and trailers. The ramp provides an ideal put-in for paddle exploration of Dungeness Bay.

Dungeness Recreation Area (Clallam County)

Park area: 216 acres; 2,500 feet of shoreline on the Strait of Juan de Fuca
Access: Land, paddle-craft
Facilities: 67 campsites, picnic tables, group shelter, restrooms, drinking water, RV pumpout station, hiking trails, horse trails, children's play equipment
Attractions: Camping, picnicking, hiking, birdwatching, viewpoints, horseback riding

This fine Clallam County park serves as a companion to the Dungeness National Wildlife Refuge, providing camping and upland recreation for people visiting the spit.

The park, which lies just off the northwest end of Dungeness Scenic Loop road, is most easily reached by driving west out of Sequim on US Highway 101 for 4 miles, then turning north on Kitchen-Dick Road, which is signed to the park. At a sharp turn east in 1½ miles, the road becomes Lotzgesell Road, and the recreation area entrance is reached in another ¼ mile.

The park is on a 100-foot bluff above the water, with no paths leading directly to the shore. However, several cliff-edge picnic areas and a trail that threads between them provide stunning views of the strait and the islands to the north. To the south is an equally breathtaking panorama of snow-draped Olympic peaks.

A large section of the park is open grassland with occasional thickets, providing a home for pheasant, bobwhites, California quail, mourning doves, and songbirds such as western meadowlark. A small pond hidden behind a low ridge attracts ducks and sometimes even whistling swans. The park's

A trail skirts the top of a cliff in the Dungeness Recreation Area.

several horse trails are closed on weekends and holidays between April 15 and October 15.

Facilities here rival the best of the state parks. Spacious, level campsites are separated by a nice buffer of shrubbery, and restrooms are modern and clean. Clallam County uses unique fireplaces throughout its parks—old tire rims fitted with grates serve the purpose admirably. The northern boundary of the park abuts the wildlife refuge; trails through a wooded upland lead down to the spit.

Dungeness National Wildlife Refuge

Area: 755 acres; 45,000 feet of shoreline on Dungeness Bay and the Strait of Juan de Fuca

Access: Land

Facilities: Hiking trails, restrooms, pit toilets, interpretive displays, *no water*

Attractions: Hiking, beachcombing, birdwatching, clam digging, crabbing, swimming

Among birdwatchers Dungeness Spit is legendary, although one doesn't need to be a dedicated ornithologist to appreciate the natural treasures of the refuge. Here is the beach walk to end all beach walks; only the most hardy could explore all the shores in one day—but dawdling is so enjoyable that it doesn't really matter if the end of the spit is reached.

The refuge is reached from the parking lot on the north side of the Dungeness Recreation Area (see above).

Separate trails for horses and hikers leave from here. The $3 per family entry fee to the area is paid at the trailhead. The grove that the trail passes through before descending to the beach offers a chance to enjoy a contrasting environment. Here fir and spruce provide homes for owls, sparrows, chickadees, bald eagles, raccoons, squirrels, and other wildlife common to coniferous forests. Informational displays along the trail descending to the spit describe the variety of life that can be seen along the spit, in the lagoon, or in offshore waters.

The inner shore of Dungeness Spit peters out gradually into tideflats, where clams can be dug, and eelgrass-filled shallows, where crabs can be trapped. The outer, breaker-washed shore of the spit is smooth and slopes more steeply into the water. Silver piles of nature-sculpted driftwood line the high-tide level. For extended walks, pack a lunch, a canteen of water, and spare clothing. If the weather is severe, stay off the spit, because wave-tossed drift logs can be hazardous. The lighthouse near the end of the spit has been deactivated and is controlled remotely; however, a group of volunteers keep the facilities open for tours during summer months. If you are determined to reach the end of the spit, be

Dungeness Spit extends for 5 miles along the Strait of Juan de Fuca.

aware that it is a 5½-mile hike from the parking lot to the lighthouse.

Nearly every species of waterfowl known to the Washington shores can be found here at some time. A display at the refuge compares the spit to a large hotel—some of the residents are permanent, while others check in and out at various times of the year for short stays. The kinds of birds vary somewhat from the inner shore to the outer shore and as one advances along the spit. Some, such as black brant, prefer brackish waters, while gulls and terns favor the outer shore where currents bring small fish to the surface. Shyer species, such as scoters, dunlins, cormorants, and plovers, stay at the outer end of the spit, where fewer hikers stray. Harbor seals may also be seen here, sunning on the shore or popping their heads from breakers to stare curiously.

Hunting is not permitted in the refuge; however, in the fall birds may be shy because of nearby hunting, and may stay out farther and be more difficult to spot. During the spring nesting season, use special care to not disturb the birds or their nests. Visitors may unwittingly distress the wildlife with their activities. Windsurfing disturbs marine mammals, and kite flying frightens birds from their nests, as they mistake the hovering kites for predators. Access to the inner side of the spit, where the most significant nesting grounds are found, is limited to the first ½ mile, and only between May 15 and September 30. Boaters must stay 100 yards off shore.

PORT ANGELES

Although Port Angeles has long been known as a portal to the high peaks of the Olympics, it has rarely been considered as a marine destination. That has begun to change, however, with the opening of its fine new waterfront facilities catering to tourists and pleasure boaters. The city is still distinctly blue collar, with smokestacks dominating the skyline, mountains of logs lining the waterfront, and boat basins filled with far more fishing boats than pleasure craft.

Port Angeles lies on US Highway 101, 17 miles west of Sequim. With a population of 28,000, Port Angeles is the largest city on the Olympic Peninsula. Its stores and businesses offer a full range of services and shopping to visitors. Harbor Towne, a shopping mall in a nicely refurbished turn-of-the-century building, is immediately across the street from the waterfront.

Four mountain streams drain from the Olympic foothills through the town. In early days the business district on the waterfront was subject to frequent flooding during high tides. In 1914 dirt was sluiced down from a hill to the east and the waterfront was filled in, elevating it 10 feet. Existing buildings were raised, or their first floors became basements. A number of these lifted structures, as well as hollow sidewalks built on pillars, can be seen in a walk through town. The basement level of Harbor Towne was once at street level. Raised buildings on pilings can be seen from the alley between Front and First from Oak to Cherry, and an elevated sidewalk can be seen by looking south from Railroad Avenue to Front Street between Laurel and Oak. The Clallam County Historical Museum, housed in the old County Courthouse at Fourth and Lincoln, has displays showing further town history.

In spite of its workaday atmosphere, the city has a dramatically scenic setting. The Olympic Mountains rise abruptly at its back door, on the eastern skyline is the glacier-covered pyramid of Mount Baker, and the gently encircling arm of Ediz Hook guards its waterfront. The 3½-mile-long sandspit of Ediz Hook encloses Port Angeles Harbor, a natural bay broad and deep enough to serve as anchorage for several ocean-going vessels. The only obstruction in the bay is the log-booming sites at the northwest end. Small boats must be watchful for logs and deadheads that sometimes float in the bay, creating a hazard.

Port Angeles Harbor enjoys a colorful flow of commercial boat traffic. Freighters stop here to load logs and lumber products, tankers as well as freighters sometimes anchor in the protected waters of the bay, and the MV *Coho,* a 340-foot-long Black Ball ferry that runs from Port Angeles to Victoria, British Columbia, is berthed on the downtown waterfront.

The city of Victoria, on Vancouver Island, lies directly north across the Strait of Juan de Fuca. Canadian boaters headed for American waters often stop in Port Angeles to check through U.S. Customs.

Port Angeles Boat Haven

Facilities: Transient moorage with power and water, diesel, gas, restrooms, pumpout station, marine supplies and repair, boat launch (ramps), groceries, ice, bait, deli, restaurant, tidal grid, boat rental and charter, shopping (nearby)

The Port Angeles Boat Haven, operated by the Port of Port Angeles, lies in a breakwater-protected basin on the west end of the waterfront.

Guest moorage is on dock F, which is in the middle on the east side. Restrooms and most facilities are on shore at the east end; the marina office and gas float are at the end of the jetty, opposite this dock. Two separate boat ramps are found at the marina. The primary launch facility is on the west side of the basin, where there is a two-lane ramp that empties directly into the bay. Floats are placed here in the summer, but

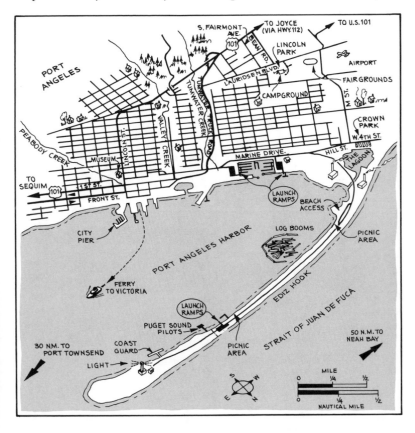

are removed at other times to protect them from weather. A large parking lot is adjoining. At the northeast corner of the basin, well protected by the landfill jetty, are a single-lane ramp and loading float. Maneuvering space and parking on the east side are less generous than those to the west, so the ramp is generally used only when weather makes the other ramp difficult to use. The outboard side of the marina berm is lined with log booms.

City Pier

Area: 4 acres; 300 feet of shoreline on Port Angeles Harbor
Access: Land, boat
Facilities: Transient moorage, U.S. Customs, picnic tables, drinking water, restrooms, marine research laboratory, viewing tower, fishing pier, waterfront trail
Attractions: Fishing, viewpoint, informational display, marine laboratory, boat tour

Focal point of the Port Angeles waterfront is City Pier, a multi-use facility that serves nicely to welcome visiting boaters to the city.

Two floats, one with finger floats, are secured to the inside of the pier. Guest moorage here is limited to craft up to 40 feet, with a maxi-

The viewing tower at the Port Angeles City Pier overlooks harbor activity.

mum stay of 24 hours. At the end of the pier a two-story viewing tower provides a 360-degree view of harbor activity, the strait, Mount Baker, and Hurricane Ridge rising dramatically behind the city. Large ships such as military research vessels and mine sweepers sometimes moor on the outer side of the pier. The U.S. Coast Guard cutter stationed here, when in port, is usually open on Sunday afternoons for curious visitors.

The center of the pier is occupied by the Arthur D. Feiro Marine Lab, run by Peninsula College. Visitors may check it out on weekend afternoons. Open-topped aquarium tanks display local marine life, a touch tank is available for kids to experience marine life intimately, and displays feature marine mammal skeletons and pressed seaweed collections; personnel are on hand to answer questions. The wooden causeway edging the waterfront ends at tiny Hollywood Beach, where there is driftwood and enough sand to keep any toddler happy.

A map display at the pier shows the route of a foot or bicycle scenic waterfront trail beginning here. The trail first follows city streets past the marina, then continues on beside the Ediz Hook road to the launch ramp near its end. An alternate destination is Crown Park, a small city park on the bluff above the lagoon with a fine view of Ediz Hook.

Ediz Hook

Facilities: Boat launch (ramps), restrooms, gas, outboard mix, bait, tackle, snack bar, boat rental and charter, RV parking, picnic areas

Ediz Hook, the 3½-mile-long spit that creates a breakwater for Port Angeles Harbor, is a startling contrast to its sister to the east. While Dungeness Spit has remained largely untrampled, Ediz Hook is a working man's spit—and, boy, has it been trampled! A road traverses the length of the hook, and logging interests, fishermen, boaters, the Coast Guard, and Puget Sound Pilots all make use of this fragile strip. To ensure its continued stability, the outer beach has been built up with gravel and a revetment of enormous boulders to control erosion.

To reach the spit, follow Marine Drive north along the Port Angeles waterfront. A large pulp plant covers the base of the hook, spewing smoke and noise. Logging trucks roar along the road, and the northwest end of the bay is a booming ground filled with logs awaiting the bite of the saw. Just beyond the pulp plant a gravel pull-off strip offers low-bank access to the harbor for kayaking and windsurfing; at its east end is a small grassy park with picnic tables, fire braziers, and drinking water.

Near the end of the spit is a boathouse with ice and bait, two double-lane launch ramps with boarding floats, and another grassy park—this one with five windbreaks protecting picnic tables and fire braziers; restrooms and parking are on the opposite side of the road.

Beyond the gate at the tip of the spit is the U.S. Coast Guard Station and airstrip. Helicopters stationed here are used in rescues and other Coast Guard work throughout the inland waters. Atop the control tower of the air station is a modern automated beacon that serves as a navigational light.

From the time of earliest settlement, pioneers built bonfires on the end of the spit to guide ships. The lighthouse built here in 1865 was replaced by a new, but still traditional, structure in 1908. That light too gave way to progress when it was replaced in 1945 by the current prosaic Coast Guard beacon. The home station for the Puget Sound Pilots is also located here. All vessels traveling east from Port Angeles are required to have a licensed pilot aboard to ensure their safe passage to destination ports within Puget Sound.

Despite the bustle of activity on the spit, the outer beach offers opportunities for long walks, exploration, and even some solitude among the scattered driftwood. Look north to Victoria and the San Juan Islands or west to Striped Peak. Or simply enjoy the play of gulls in wind and wave.

Lincoln Park

Access: Land
Facilities: Sports fields, 25 campsites, water, fireplaces, restrooms
Attractions: Camping, historical structures

From mid-March through November, land-bound travelers can camp at Port Angeles's Lincoln Park. The park lies on the west edge of the town next to the county fairgrounds.

To reach it from downtown, follow Tumwater Truck Road south and turn west on West Lauridsen Boulevard. In 1 mile the park is reached. From Highway 101, turn north on South Fairmont Avenue or Bean Road, which end at West Lauridsen Boulevard immediately east of the park.

The 144-acre wooded park has two entrances off West Lauridsen Avenue. The east entrance leads to the day-use area with sports fields, a replica of an Indian longhouse, and some interesting pioneer cabins. The camping area, reached through the west entrance, holds 25 sites with water and fireplaces, but no electricity. The sites are more suitable for bicyclists and tenters; RV campers may prefer to stay at one of the town's several commercial RV sites.

CHAPTER NINE

WESTERN STRAIT OF JUAN DE FUCA

West of Port Angeles the pulse of the strait quickens. The southern coastline becomes bold, with rock-infested beaches soaring upward in places to rugged, 300-foot bluffs. Waves generated by wind sweeping in from the ocean pound against the shores, making approach by boat difficult and at times dangerous.

The few boating facilities along the strait suffer from the severe environment; launch ramps are sometimes washed out or clogged by debris, and floats must be removed during the off-season to prevent damage by violent storms. The towns of Sekiu and Neah Bay, which have boat basins behind rock breakwaters, are the only harbors of refuge along this section of the strait. The greatest attraction here is for anglers who come from great distances to find exciting action fishing for salmon, halibut, ling-

The Tatoosh Light marks the northwest tip of the contiguous United States.

cod, or rockfish. Most fishing is done from boats as small as 15-foot kicker boats or from moderately sized trailered craft. Halibut caught here range from young 20-pounders called "chicks" up to an occasional 200-pound monster that must be towed to shore behind the boat.

Few pleasure boaters choose this area as a destination; most seen here are in transit to or from ocean voyages. In addition to Neah Bay and Sekiu, a few small bays offer some limited anchorages when seas are calm. When navigating near shore, watch for submerged rocks and reefs. The warmer summer months are often accompanied by dense fog, which usually clears off by midmorning.

Some 40 miles of shorelands at 20 separate locations along this section of the strait are public. Many of these sites are Department of Natural Resources beaches, where the state-owned land is below the mean high-water level; however, at several locations the beaches are paralleled by Highway 112, giving easy access. At other places the beaches can be reached via county parks or commercial resorts. At any of the commercial facilities, beach users must obtain permission from the property owner. In some cases the resorts have rental boats and pay launch ramps; even persons with cartop boats can expect to be charged a fee.

Many beaches are rocky and drop off steeply; when approaching by boat, extreme care must be used, because a wave or surge can throw a boat against the rocks. Landings on these beaches should be attempted only in calm weather and even then with caution.

Land access to this western section of the strait is from state Highway 112. Follow US Highway 101 west out of Port Angeles and 4½ miles west of town, at a major intersection, turn northwest onto Highway 112. Once it reaches saltwater at Twin Rivers, the two-lane road follows

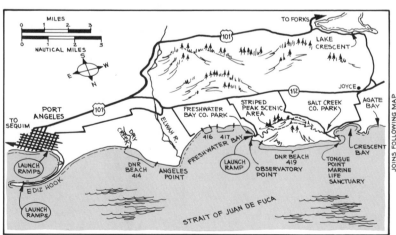

the shoreline much of the way to Neah Bay, turning inland in only a few spots. The twisting road is slow driving, especially if you are pulling a boat trailer, but the scenery is spectacular. Logging trucks may be encountered on weekdays.

STRIPED PEAK

About 12 miles beyond Port Angeles, 1,166-foot Striped Peak is a prominent landmark with its thickly wooded slopes rising abruptly from the strait. The area was the site of Fort Hayden, built in the early 1940s at the outbreak of World War II when the government saw the need to modernize its Coastal Defense System. A second fort was planned for Cape Flattery, near Neah Bay. Land was acquired and excavation was completed, but before the concrete was poured the war had moved far into the Pacific and construction on that fort was halted.

The concrete-canopied, heavily shielded gun batteries at Fort Hayden were designed to withstand direct hits from offshore guns as well as aircraft bombardment. Two 16-inch guns were installed in the battery at Tongue Point, and a second battery, ½ mile east at the 300-foot level of Striped Peak, held two 6-inch guns. The guns were discharged only once—a test-firing. A number of other bunkers used for fire control, observation, and storage are scattered throughout the densely wooded area. Determined exploration may uncover some of them.

With the advent of missiles and other rapid changes in military technology, the fort became obsolete and the multimillion-dollar guns were cut up for scrap. In 1949 the property was declared surplus and shortly after was acquired by state and county agencies for a magnificent recreation area. Striped Peak Scenic Area, Salt Creek County Park, and Tongue

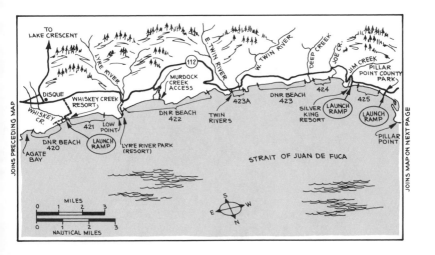

Point Marine Life Sanctuary encompass a total of some 1,700 acres of land and 4 miles of shoreline, with attractions ranging from dense forest to wave-washed rocks to a sublime saltwater estuary.

Freshwater Bay County Park (Clallam County)

Park area: 17 acres; 1,000 feet of shoreline on the Strait of Juan de Fuca
Access: Land, water
Facilities: Boat launch (ramp), restrooms, pit toilets, picnic tables, *no water*
Attractions: Boating, picnicking, beachcombing, clam digging

Launch ramps are infrequent along the western end of the strait, and well-appointed ones are even more rare. This single-lane launch ramp, maintained by Clallam County, is well surfaced and has a spacious parking lot adjoining it. The only disadvantage is that it gradually slopes out onto a long tideflat, making it unusable at low water. The picnic area, uphill near the park entrance, has a number of tables shaded by a magnificent grove of old-growth cedar.

The 4-mile-wide bay, bounded by Angeles Point on the east and Observatory Point on the west, is quite open, but some anchorages can be found in 6 to 10 fathoms. Bachelor Rock, a 20-foot-high sea stack, lies just off Observatory Point.

The launch ramp is reached by turning north off Highway 112 onto Freshwater Bay Road 9 miles west of Port Angeles; don't look for signs directing you to the park—there aren't any. In less than 2 miles the road turns west and becomes Lawrence Road. Turn north on Park Road in a short ½ mile and follow it to the park. The beach immediately north of the ramp is private.

Boats launched at Freshwater Bay have easy access to three DNR

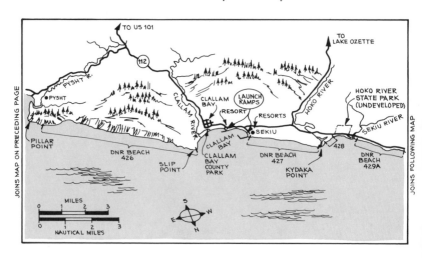

beaches to the east. Beach 417, which is 2,800 feet long, and Beach 416, a 1,345-foot strip, are 1 to 2 miles east, slightly past Colville Creek. Beach 414 lies 5 miles from the launch ramp on the east side of Angeles Point; the eastern edge of this 5,580-foot section of tidelands begins just east of a riprap bulkhead at the Port Angeles city limits. The public land of all three beaches is the area lying below mean high water. At low tide the gravelly shores may yield some horse and butter clams.

Striped Peak Scenic Area

Area: 1,500 acres
Access: Land
Facilities: Viewpoint, hiking trail, *no water*
Attractions: Hiking, mountain biking

This large section of DNR property abuts the eastern boundary of Salt Creek County Park.

At the entrance to Freshwater Bay County Park (see above), Striped Peak Road heads north; bear left at the intersection with Seagull Drive in ½ mile. The road quickly deteriorates to a narrow, twisting, single-lane gravel track. Keep to the right at two intermediate junctions, and in 2¼ miles reach an expansive viewpoint on a shoulder of the mountain. The view here is north across the Strait of Juan de Fuca. A faint trail leaving the east edge of the parking area is the upper end of a path from Salt Creek County Park.

For the adventuresome, hike or take mountain bikes down the lower fork at the first intersection below the viewpoint. This rough, narrow road leads through woods for ¾ mile to another Y at a hairpin turn. Continue right, uphill, along the steep open side of Striped Peak to reach a saddle just below the summit. Here are spectacular views to the

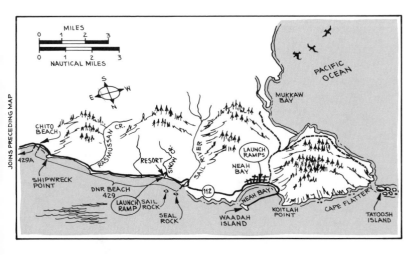

southwest over the lower summit and its radio towers to the rugged face of Mount Angeles in the distance. The road continues on around the peak, meets the spur from the last intersection, then drops downhill to the county park. Four-wheel-drive vehicles can probably negotiate the road. However, it is not maintained, has few turn-around spots, and is gated at the park end, so the route must be retraced to get out.

This route has an added attraction: a glimpse of one of the old gun batteries from Fort Hayden. The concrete bunker, which is just off the end of the first sharp switchback, is not maintained and is heavily overgrown. Two 6-inch guns that sat on concrete pads on either side of the battery were covered with thick armor plate. Use care in the area because broken bottles and trash make it hazardous.

Another alternative is to hike either the road or trail from Salt Creek County Park. Start at the gated road on the east side of the park, just past the entrance information booth. A sign here indicates a hiking trail that leads to a cove in 1 mile and the lower of the two vistas, described above, in 2½ miles. This trail circles the north side of Striped Peak, first reaching a steep spur to a pretty little sheltered cove. The continuation

of the trail climbs along a wooded bench for another mile, then starts a murderous series of switchbacks to reach the viewpoint parking area.

Salt Creek County Park (Clallam County) and Tongue Point Marine Life Sanctuary

Park area: 196 acres; 5,000 feet of shoreline on the Strait of Juan de Fuca
Access: Land, boat
Facilities: 87 campsites, picnic tables, fireplaces, kitchen shelter, restrooms, drinking water, children's play equipment, softball field, horseshoe pits, RV dump station, informational and historical displays, hiking trails
Attractions: Fishing, hiking, beachcombing, scuba diving, swimming, paddling, tidepooling

A treasure of a park, with stunningly beautiful scenery, acres of tidepools to explore, and a sheltered sandy beach for summer lazing.

To reach the park by land, turn north from Highway 112, 12 miles from its junction with US Highway 101, onto Camp Hayden Road. Follow the road for 3½ miles, where it becomes a side loop and the

The concrete gun emplacements of Fort Hayden were quite different from those built at Fort Worden and other World War I forts.

main road becomes Camp Hayden Park Road. In another ¼ mile reach the entrance to Salt Creek County Park.

Inside the park entrance a road to the west leads to the WWII 16-inch gun battery built when this area was a military fort. The construction here is unique to Puget Sound forts, most of which were built before World War I. The concrete canopy was necessary to shield it from airplane attacks as well as bombardment from the large guns onboard ships. Enormous 16-inch guns, 45 feet long and measuring 5 feet thick at the breech, were mounted on revolving turntables inside the bunkers.

Camping at Salt Creek County Park is in two areas. At the east, near the park entrance, RV sites spread around a large open field; tenting sites lie in light timber on a road to the west that loops around a small peninsula. None of the campsites have hookups. Several short trails from the camp areas descend to the beach.

The rocky shoreline east of Tongue Point, along the north edge of the park, drops off abruptly. East of the boundary of the park the public shoreline, designated as DNR Beach 419, continues nearly all the way to Observatory Point. The rock and gravel shore is difficult for casual

Tongue Point Marine Sanctuary is a treasure chest of marine life.

walking, but with some effort at low tide, interesting rock formations and marine life can be seen. At high tide the beach is impassable.

This is a favorite area for scuba divers who explore the submerged rocks and sand channels. Kelp beds, strong currents, and heavy surge conditions are hazards; only expert divers should dive here, and then only on calm days during slack tide.

Tongue Point is a layer of erosion-resistant volcanic basalt that juts out on the east side of Crescent Bay. At low tide a ¼-mile-long tidal shelf is revealed, filled with a dazzling array of marine plants and animals in a jewellike mixture of reds, pinks, purples, and greens hidden in the purple-brown seaweed. A single tidepool may contain as many as a hundred different species, including limpets, hermit crabs, sculpin, nudibranchs, and sea urchins. One tiny golf-ball-sized rock the author picked up had five different kinds of life in its hollows: a sponge, lichens, barnacles, a limpet, and a shore crab. A good field guide on seashore life will help identify the many creatures you may see. This is a marine sanctuary—do not remove or destroy any of the life.

Tongue Point shelters the sandy estuary of Salt Creek, on the east side of Crescent Bay. The estuary can be reached by trails from the campground, or by a road that goes west from the park entrance for ½ mile to a day-use area. Moderate to low tides expose a broad sandy beach punctuated by a remarkable little wooded island of rock that stands as a lonely sentinel on the beach.

The park boundary is down the middle of Salt Creek; land west of here, including the beaches of Crescent Bay, is private; a private resort is on the west end of the bay. Crescent Bay is suitable only for anchoring small boats. Entry to the bay with large boats is hazardous without local knowledge, because rocks lie off Tongue Point and the unnamed point that marks the west end of the bay.

WHISKEY CREEK TO SEKIU

Whiskey Creek Resort and DNR Beaches 420 and 421

Continuing west, public shore accesses become more primitive, offering only basic amenities for the hardy anglers who venture out on the waters of the strait. At Whiskey Creek a commercial resort has beachfront cabins, campsites, hiking trails, and a single-lane concrete launch ramp protected by a short rock breakwater. To reach it turn north off Highway 112, 1¾ miles west of the town of Joyce, onto Schmitt Road, which is signed to the Whiskey Creek Recreation Area. Follow signs 1½ miles to the beach. The resort is open from May to October. Resorts such as this have been hard hit by depleted salmon runs and season closures.

The fish-cleaning station near the beach at Whiskey Creek

Whiskey Creek Resort provides the only land access to DNR Beaches 420 and 421. Because this is a commercial facility, persons wanting to walk the beaches must be guests of the resort or obtain permission from the property owner. DNR Beach 420, which lies east of Whiskey Creek, is 8,750 feet long; Beach 421, west of Whiskey Creek, is 8,010 feet long. The public beach, which is below the mean high water level, is gradually sloping gravel and hard clay, with ample room for beach walking at low tide. Boat landing can be dangerous under severe wave or surge conditions.

Lyre River and DNR Beach 422

The Lyre River was originally called by the local Native Americans "singing waters" for the musical lilt of the water rushing over rocks. Early explorers changed the name to lyre, after the ancient musical instrument that had a similar soothing effect on its listeners.

East of Whiskey Creek a commercial resort at Lyre River caters to family camping. Lyre River Park provides tenting and RV facilities, restrooms with showers and laundromat, a store with ice, groceries, and a fishing tackle. Hand-carried boats can be put in here. The resort is on the eastern edge of DNR Beach 422; however, access to the beach at this point, as well as use of the launch ramp, is restricted to guests of the resort. The lower portion of the Lyre River, which flows through the park, is a popular spot for inner-tube rafting from the upper portions of the park to the mouth at the beach.

The turnoff to Lyre River Park is on Highway 112, 4½ miles west of the town of Joyce. At the sign indicating the Lyre River Recreation Area, turn north onto West Lyre River Road, and follow it ½ mile to its end at the resort. Do not be confused by a sign on the road ½ mile to the east on East Lyre River Road pointing to a DNR campground. While that public forest camp is very pretty, it is on the bank of the river and has no saltwater access.

Murdock Creek Access

DNR Beach 422 can be reached from a logging road 1 mile west of the West Lyre River Road intersection. Turn off Highway 112 onto an unmarked dirt road at the middle of a clearcut. The narrow, steep road twists down around the edge of the clearcut to a branch in the road in ½ mile; here bear right. In 1 mile from the highway a dirt parking area in timber by the beach is reached.

There is space for camping; however, there are no formal campsites and no drinking water. A battered pit toilet is the area's only amenity. The shale intertidal shelf extends out for about ¼ mile, exposing a fascinating assortment of marine life at low tide. Small pools are filled with a variety of chitons, barnacles, starfish, and "Chinese hat"-shaped limpets. Note how different the forms of life found here are than those found on the protected shores of Puget Sound. The beach can be walked east for a mile to the Lyre River or west for 4 miles to the point just east of Twin Rivers. Landing boats should be attempted only when seas are calm.

Twin Rivers

As it journeys west, Highway 112 finally touches the shores of the Strait of Juan de Fuca at Twin Rivers. Suddenly a wealth of sand and shale beaches are revealed, only a jump from the bumper. But don't jump too soon, because the uplands of the first beach encountered are owned by a private camping club that objects to any trespassers.

Twin Rivers lies 22¾ miles west of the intersection of Highway 112 and US Highway 101. Two obscure side roads lead to the private beach; a third road spur (the last to be reached before the bridge over West Twin River) ends at a narrow public access to DNR Beach 423A, where cartop boats can be put in. This access is heavily used in good weather, and parking nearby may be difficult.

Beach 423A, which is a 3,415-foot section lying below the mean high water level, extends from East Twin River west to a landfill jetty owned by a quarry. Some clams may be dug in the sandy beach.

Beyond the quarry property, where the road pulls away from the shore, Beach 423 begins. This section of beach, 15,365 feet in length, is easily accessed from its west end, where the highway returns to the shore by Deep Creek. Some limited parking is available along the road.

Beach 424, 5,925 feet in length, which begins west of the delta of Deep Creek, has no upland access—it must be reached by boat. The closest boat launch is at Silver King Resort, ½ mile away. Unfortunately, boat landing at this or any of the other beaches along the strait can be hazardous. It should be attempted only during calm seas, and even then with great care.

Jim Creek

Silver King Resort, at Jim Creek, offers the only protected moorage for small boats along this section of the strait.

A sign on Highway 112, 8¼ miles west of Twin Rivers, points north to the Jim Creek Recreation Area. Off-season, if the resort is closed, the road may be gated at the highway. The gravel road twists downhill for ½ mile to the resort.

A dredged basin, with floats in summer, is protected by two curving rock jetties; however, it is not suitable for boats of any draft. The surfaced, two-lane boat launch ramp inside the jetty is usable during all but minus tides. The resort offers RV camping with hookups, water, picnic tables, restrooms with laundromat and showers, gas, propane, and a store with some groceries and fishing tackle.

Pillar Point

Pillar Point is rated as one of the fishing "hot spots" along the Strait of Juan de Fuca. In spring and summer king and silver salmon are caught just offshore, and when winter storms permit this is a top area for blackmouth. A county park at Pillar Point and a commercial resort at Jim Creek offer both camping and boat launching facilities.

Pillar Point is a distinctive, 700-foot-high knob with a prominent pillar-shaped sea stack lying off its eastern tip. The point encloses an open shallow bay at the drainage of the Pysht River. Some anchorages can be found in 10 fathoms of water southeast of the point. The surrounding land gives protection from westerly swells; however, there is little shelter from winter storms. Numerous rocks lie offshore east of the county park.

Pillar Point County Park (Clallam County)

Park area: 4 acres; 240 feet of shoreline on the Strait of Juan de Fuca
Access: Land, boat
Facilities: 37 campsites, picnic tables, fireplaces, sewage connections, picnic shelter, boat launch (ramp), restrooms, drinking water
Attractions: Boating, fishing, beachcombing, clam digging

This small county park is primarily used by anglers who launch boats here, although its wide tideflat and scenic location make it popular with anyone who loves the shore.

Pillar Point County Park is just north of Highway 112, 32½ miles west of the junction of Highway 112 and US Highway 101 and 1½ miles west of Jim Creek; the entrance road is well signed. The camping area, on a slight bluff above the shore, is open only from May 15 to September 15, but the park itself is open year-round.

The single-lane boat launch ramp empties onto a shallow flat and is usable only for cartop or small trailered boats. Some fishermen use waders to reach boats launched at high tide and anchored out.

Two nearby DNR beaches can be reached by boat from Pillar Point. Beach 425, which is 4,520 feet long, lies east, midway between the county park and Silver King Resort at Jim Creek. This beach is a continuation of the long tideflat at the mouth of the Pysht River.

To the west, Beach 426 stretches for 42,750 feet from a cove ½ mile west of Pillar Point all the way to Slip Point at the east side of Clallam Bay. This beach lies beneath a 300-foot bluff, and the rocky shores drop off steeply. Landing boats is possible only in a few small coves, and even there the shore should be approached with caution and only during calm seas.

Sometime between March to April, during the brief annual spawning run of smelt, the area from Pillar Point east to Twin Rivers is a prime spot for catching smelt with large long-handled nets. Smelt dippers work from shore on the incoming tide, scooping the little fish from net to bucket to a waiting frying pan.

Clallam Bay

Clallam Bay is the only protected harbor along the Strait of Juan de Fuca between Port Angeles and Neah Bay. The bay has two small communities along its shore—Clallam Bay and Sekiu. A sandbar at the mouth of the Clallam River fronts the town of Clallam Bay, giving it some shelter from storms sweeping in off the strait, but also serving to keep boats at a distance. The major boating center is at Sekiu, on the west side of the bay, where a rock jetty forms a well-protected basin for the fleet of small recreational fishing boats that arrive via trailer in the summer.

The 2-mile-wide bay has some protected anchorages in 6 to 10 fathoms near the Sekiu jetty. The floats within the jetty are primarily for small boats—some are on dry land at low tide.

By land, Clallam Bay is 45½ miles west of US Highway 101 via Highway 112. Both the towns of Clallam Bay and Sekiu have service stations, grocery stores, restaurants, and overnight accommodations. Clallam Bay and points west along Highway 112 can also be reached by driving US 101 west from Port Angeles 45¼ miles to Sappho and turning north on Highway 113; in 10½ miles the road joins Highway 112 and continues on to Clallam Bay. This route eliminates some of the narrow, twisting road along the shore, but is less scenic.

Extensive DNR public beaches flank either side of the bay. Beach

426 (see Pillar Point County Park, above), runs east from Slip Point, which is marked by a light at the east side of the bay. Beach 427, 17,890 feet in length, goes west from Sekiu Point all the way to Kydaka Point near the Hoko River. Both of these beaches lie beneath high bluffs and are accessible only by boat. At low tide Beach 427 has some sandy stretches that hold clams and mussels.

Scuba divers sometimes enter the water at the resort at Sekiu and work their way around the point to Beach 427. With permission, divers can cross Coast Guard property by the Slip Point light to reach Beach 426. The underwater area at Beach 427 is rocky, with ledges and caves containing brightly colored rockfish, anemones, and, in dark corners, octopus and wolf eels. Thick beds of kelp, strong currents, and surge are hazards, making this a dive only for the experienced.

Clallam Bay County Park (Clallam County)

Park area: 36 acres; 9,850 feet of shoreline on the Strait of Juan de Fuca
Access: Land, boat
Facilities: Restrooms, picnic tables
Attractions: Beachcombing, picnicking

As it reaches the strait, the Clallam River meanders westward, paralleling the shore before emptying into Clallam Bay. A wide sandy bar

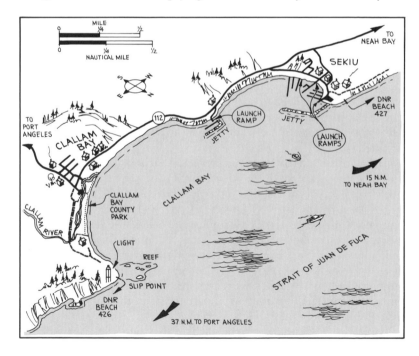

that has been built up at the mouth of the river was owned by Washington State Parks, but has been turned over to the county for its management as a jewel of a day-use park.

Here is the ideal spot to spend a sunny afternoon in the sheltering arms of a driftwood snag, or to let the kids dabble toes in the sand and rolling surf. Beach and river shores call for exploration, and the bordering woodland offers promise of a shy squirrel or twittering birds.

Where Highway 112 enters the town of Clallam Bay from the east and takes a left turn, a stub road at the intersection goes straight ahead to the county park's parking lot by a rail fence and some picnic tables.

Down a short path to the left an arched bridge crosses the river to the beach. An old abandoned road runs west along the bar past picnic sites, some in beach grass right above the high water level, others snugly secluded in bushes and evergreens.

Sekiu Resorts

Facilities: Transient moorage, boat launch (ramps), gas, outboard mix, restrooms, showers, laundromat, camping, RV sites, cabins, motels, restaurants, groceries, ice, fishing tackle and bait, boat and motor rental, charters

Resorts along the shore at Sekiu cater to the hordes of anglers who arrive during the spring and summer to fish for prized salmon or halibut.

Accommodations tend to be plain rather than posh. Reservations are usually necessary during good weather. Some limited charters are available through the resorts; however, many fishermen trailer their own boats or rent kicker boats. Not all the resorts and motels have full facilities; some primarily offer overnight accommodations, while others have full boating services.

While a number of the resorts close off-season and remove their floats to protect them from storms, a few remain open the year around to take advantage of bottom fishing when an occasional break in winter weather permits.

Sekiu lies just north of Highway 112, 2 miles west of the town of Clallam Bay. Another resort at Middle Point, which has a launch ramp and floats protected by its own rock breakwater, is midway between the two towns.

SEKIU TO NEAH BAY

Nearing Neah Bay, the shoreline becomes even more spectacular, with wave-torn beaches, sea stacks, and imposing offshore rocks. Low tide reveals a boulder-strewn shale shelf with cracks and crevices holding tidepools. Abundant marine life inhabits this shelf—some of it bright

Seal Rock, left, and Sail Rock, right, are two spectacular monoliths offshore from Sail River.

and obvious, but much of it blending into the overall purple-brown color scheme. Even flamboyant, bright pastel sea anemones contract into nondescript brown nodules as the tide recedes.

At several places Highway 112 comes close enough to the shore to permit easy access; a few pull-offs provide limited parking. All the beach between the Sekiu River and Sail River is public DNR beach below the mean high water level, with the exception of a narrow strip at Chito Beach. Beach 429A, which is 12,210 feet in length, is east of Chito Beach; Beach 429, 37,440 feet long, is to the west. Chito Beach, a scattering of homes and summer cabins along the highway, has no public access. A commercial RV and camping park may be open in the summer.

Beach 428, at the mouth of the Hoko River, is 2,750 feet long. It is located below a housing development. However, there is no public access through the residential area; the beach must be reached by boat.

Several exquisite sea stacks are next to the highway near the west end of Beach 429. They are not as large or dramatic as those found out on the coast at La Push and Shi-Shi Beach, but they are much more accessible and are equally fascinating. The surrounding beaches are prime areas for tidepooling.

Near Snow Creek and Sail River two massive rocks, nearly 100 feet tall, rise ¼ mile offshore. When seen from the southeast, Sail Rock resembles the mainsail of a giant sloop; Seal Rock is an even larger rectangular-shaped monolith lying to the west. The vast numbers of birds that nest here, including cormorants, gulls, and tufted puffins, have found a spot safe from the encroachment of real estate developers.

Hoko River State Park (Undeveloped)

A quarter mile east of the Sekiu River, Highway 112 skirts a broad sandy beach below a low bank. Although there is no indication of public ownership, the beach and uplands for ½ mile to the east are undeveloped properties owned by the state Parks Commission. Two or three road-side pull-offs permit hand-carried boats to be put in. Boating in the strait during times of waves, surge, or strong current can be hazardous.

Snow Creek

The State Department of Fisheries placed restrooms with showers just off the road at Snow Creek, 3½ miles east of Neah Bay, with the intent of providing a public access at the site of an abandoned resort. Since then the resort has been resurrected, and now offers tent and RV camping, a marine rail launch facility, a dock and float, offshore buoys, and a small store with ice, bait, firewood, scuba air, and a few groceries. The resort provides access to DNR Beach 429 and some sensational views of Seal and Sail rocks, just offshore. Non-guests should ask permission before crossing private property to reach the beach.

NEAH BAY AND CAPE FLATTERY

The town of Neah Bay is the center of the Makah Indian Reservation. These people, who are more culturally allied with the Nootka tribe of Vancouver Island than tribes of the inland waters of Puget Sound, at one time occupied all of the coastal land down to Lake Ozette. Archaeological evidence shows their presence here for around 3,000 years.

The Makahs built large sea-going canoes in which they pursued whales. Using ritualistic preparation and hunting techniques very similar to those of the Eskimos far to the north, they harpooned and killed the whales, then towed the carcasses back to their villages where they were butchered, and the meat smoked and dried. They were also highly skilled at fishing for salmon and bottomfish and hunting seals.

Neah Bay was the site of the first attempt by Europeans to settle what is now the state of Washington. In the spring of 1792 a group of Spanish colonists landed here with instructions to build a fort and clear land, in an attempt to establish a claim to the coast north of California. The Spaniards evidently found the coastal climate too bitter for them, even in the summer, and the fur trade not to their liking; the settlement was abandoned after four months.

Some 50 years later Samuel Hancock, a Yankee pioneer, established a trading post here for storing and shipping oil from whales harpooned by the Indians. At the time of the arrival of white men, the Makah Nation was large, but smallpox, brought in 1853 via a trading ship, ravaged the

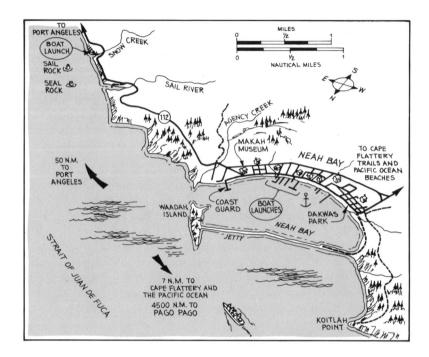

tribe, reducing it to a mere 150 individuals. Hancock wrote of bodies so numerous that he was unable to bury them and had to drag them to the beach to float off on the tide. The terrible epidemic is described in the book *Exploring Washington* by Harry M. Majors (Van Winkle Publishing Co., Holland, Mich.; 1975). Today the tribe numbers about 1,400 members.

In the Neah Bay Treaty of 1855, initiated by Governor Isaac Stevens, the Makah Indians were assigned 23,000 acres of land at this westernmost tip of the state. The present reservation is about 44 miles square, covering about half the original area. During the last weekend of August, at the annual Makah Day celebration held at Neah Bay, tribes from throughout the Northwest gather to celebrate their heritage with traditional dances and costumes, a salmon bake, bone games, athletic contests, and canoe races.

The traditional fishing economy has remained one of the mainstays of the Makah tribe, and today Neah Bay is the center of large commercial and sport fishing industries. The deep natural harbor provides moorage for both large and small fishing boats, while ocean-bound yachtsmen often use the bay as a last stop before hitting open water. Fishing resorts such as this have been hard hit by recent decrease in salmon runs and cutbacks in fishing seasons.

Waadah Island, a ½-mile-long wooded knob, lies on the east side of the bay, off Baada Point. A rock breakwater that stretches for 1½ miles between Waadah Island and the shore shelters the inner bay from all but easterly weather. The low jetty does not give complete protection from severe northerlies, but such storms are rare, especially in summer.

A reef and numerous rocks extend from the southwest side of Waadah Island. The entrance channel, marked by buoys, should be followed carefully all the way into the bay, slightly favoring the south side. Anchorages can be found in 20 to 40 feet of water. Floats for pleasure boats are removed off-season.

By land Neah Bay can be reached by driving either Highway 112 or US Highway 101 west from Port Angeles. If following 101, turn north at Sappho to join Highway 112. The distance is about 70 miles

Cleaning the day's catch at Neah Bay

either route, and much of the way is on narrow, twisting roads.

A small shoreside park in Neah Bay provides a place to munch a sandwich and observe waterfront activity. Dakwas Park is marked by a totem pole surrounded by a low chain-link fence.

Neah Bay Resorts

Facilities: Guest moorage, boat launch (ramps and hoists), gas, outboard mix, camping, RV sites, cabins, motels, restrooms, showers, laundromat, groceries, ice, bait, fishing tackle, restaurants, boat rental and charters, U.S. Customs

Floats for recreational boats are found at marinas and resorts along the south shore of Neah Bay, east of a long pier belonging to a commercial fishing company. Facilities in the town are decidedly utilitarian. A general store offers a range of groceries and supplies. Resorts have fishing tackle and bait. There are no marine repair facilities. Motel and camping accommodations too are rather spartan, appealing primarily to sport fishermen whose main interest is catching a prize salmon.

Makah Museum

A splendid museum at Neah Bay displays artifacts from the Makah Indian culture. Many of the items are from the Ozette archaeological dig, where part of a coastal village had lain buried in a mudslide for over 500 years. The items are beautifully presented, with photos, drawings, and text explaining their use in everyday Makah life.

The museum is on the east side of the town, adjacent to Highway 112.

Displays cover whaling, wood technology, tools, fishing, hunting, gathering, stone and bone technology, tools and games, food preparation, basketry, weaving, and trade. In the heart of the museum is a reproduction of a longhouse based on dimensions of Ozette houses; when your eyes become accustomed to the dark interior, you recognize dried fish hanging from poles from the ceiling, mats decorating the walls, and benches and baskets surrounding the glowing embers of fires. Rushes drying on poles will be used to fashion garments, baskets, and other household items. One door of the longhouse overlooks a diorama of the Ozette beach, with a canoe and view of Cannonball Island. Voices speaking the native Makah language, then singing, drift through the longhouse, like ghosts from an ancient time.

A full-size version of a traditional longhouse has been built on the grounds, adjacent the parking lot. It is used for community gatherings,

Displays at the Makah Museum in Neah Bay (Marge and Ted Mueller photo, © Makah Cultural and Research Center)

ceremonies, potlatches, and other group activities. The museum is open from 10:00 A.M. to 5:00 P.M. daily during the summer, and is closed on Mondays and Tuesdays from mid-September to the end of May. An entrance fee is charged.

Cape Flattery

Cape Flattery marks the northwest tip of the coterminus United States, where the crashing surf of the Pacific Ocean continues to gnaw at the rugged cliffs of this remote point of land. The cape is laced with wave-carved coves separated by high, razor-thin headlands; a myriad of near-shore rocks stubbornly resist the grinding of the powerful surf. These rocks are home or migratory resting place for a variety of marine birds; seals and sea lions also haul out here for sunny respites from the sea. Shoreside trees provide lofty observatories for eagles scanning the beaches for prey.

A half mile offshore is Tatoosh Island, the site of the Coast Guard lighthouse that marks the entrance to the Strait of Juan de Fuca. Before the lighthouse was erected here, the island had been used for centuries by the Makah Indians during summer months for salmon fishing and whaling, and it also served as a native burial ground. The Indians did not take kindly to an invasion of their traditional summer outpost, and regularly harassed crews when construction of the lighthouse began in 1855.

Severe weather and waves, coupled with the difficulty of landing on the harsh shore, presented a major challenge to the undertaking. Despite these problems, the lighthouse was completed and commissioned on December 28, 1857. The remoteness, weather, and Indian problems made it difficult to recruit lighthouse keepers, however. History records many wild tales: an attempted suicide by a keeper depressed by the site's loneliness, fierce storms that seemed to shake the whole island, a diphtheria epidemic, and haunting by ghosts of natives buried there. Like other lighthouses, the Tatoosh light has now been automated, and the station is no longer manned.

Cape Flattery Trail

A short but rough trail permits a visit to this remote section of Cape Flattery shoreline with views of Tatoosh Island and its lighthouse. At the west end of Neah Bay, take the road southwest out of town, signed to Cape Flattery Resort. The resort, a onetime Air Force station, is reached in 2¾ miles. Continue west, then north on the road, which rapidly deteriorates to a two-lane, then lane-and-a-half track laced with teeth-jarring chuckholes. The drivable road ends at a parking area 8 miles from Neah Bay.

A signed trail heads west into the trees. In about 500 yards is a fork;

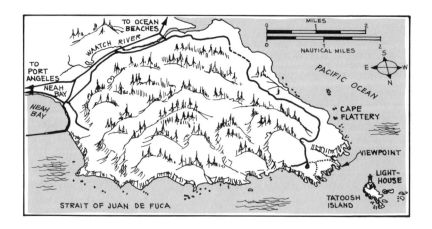

the branch to the north leads to headlands on the north tip of Cape Flattery, the west fork continues on to the end of the head. The ½-mile-long trail is not steep, but it has a wealth of tangled tree roots, mud holes, and swampy areas to challenge hikers. The path finally breaks out in a narrow finger of land with cliff edges lined by low brush. Be careful, a misstep can drop you over one of the 150-foot-high vertical cliffs that ring the point.

The view more than rewards the effort of the trip—jagged sea cliffs, 100 to 200 feet high, stretch along the coast as far as the eye can see. Waves crash against the rocky narrow beach below, bursting into plumes of frothing water as they collide with rough beach. Offshore, Kessiso Rocks and a jumble of other rocks have a legion of gulls and other seabirds perched atop. Offshore is Tatoosh Island, its lighthouse flashing a continual warning to mariners. On the north end of the island note the frame of a derrick stretching out above sea cliffs; over time this proved the easiest way to hoist personnel and supplies aboard the island.

* * *

Our journey along Washington's entrance waters is ended. But where next? A hard turn to port at Tatoosh Island leads south to wave-dashed coastal beaches, La Push, and Grays Harbor. To the north the wild coastline of Vancouver Island beckons. Northeast are the harbor of Victoria and the green maze of the Gulf Islands. Or perhaps (oh, blasphemous thought!) to show our stern to the dank and drizzle of the Pacific Northwest and head for the palm-laden shores of Hawaii—or even the South Seas.

Pago Pago, Afoot and Afloat—it does have a nice ring!

APPENDICES

A. EMERGENCY PHONE NUMBERS AND LIST OF CONTACTS

All numbers listed are area code 360 unless otherwise indicated.

All western Washington counties use 911 as the number for fire and police emergencies. For non-emergency situations contact the local sheriff's department.

Sheriff

Clallam County: (Port Angeles) 417-2259
Island County: (Oak Harbor) 678-4422
Jefferson County: (Port Townsend) 385-3831
Skagit County: (Mount Vernon) 336-9450
Whatcom County: (Bellingham) 676-6650 or 384-5360

Other important agency numbers:

U.S. Coast Guard

Anacortes: 293-9555   Port Angeles: 457-4404
Bellingham: 743-1692   Port Townsend: 385-3070
Neah Bay: 645-2236   Seattle: (206) 217-6000
Cellular Telephone Emergency Access: *CG

U.S. Customs

Anacortes: 293-2331   Port Townsend: 385-3777
Neah Bay: 645-2311   After Hours: 1-800-562-5934
Port Angeles: 457-4311

Radio Contact

Marine VHF: Coast Guard distress or hailing—Channel 16
Marine VHF: Coast Guard liason—Channel 22
Citizens Band: Distress—Channel 9

Other Contacts

Red Tide Hotline: 1-800-562-5632
Whale Hotline (to report sightings or strandings): 1-800-562-8832

Ferries

Washington State Ferries Information: (Seattle) (206) 464-6400 or (toll free) 1-800-843-3779; www.wsdot.wa.gov
Guemes Island Ferry: 293-6356
Lummi Island Ferry: 676-6730 or 398-1310
Victoria Express (passengers only, Port Angeles to Victoria): 1-800-633-1589 or 452-8808
MV *Coho* (cars and passengers, Port Angeles to Victoria): 457-4491

Washington State Parks

General information regarding the state parks is available from Washington State Parks and Recreation Commission, 7150 Cleanwater Lane, P.O. Box 42650, Olympia, WA 98504-2650. 753-2027.
Birch Bay State Park: 5105 Helwig Road, Blaine, WA 98230. 371-2800.
Camano Island State Park: 2269 Lowell Point Road, Stanwood, WA 98292. 387-3031.
Deception Pass State Park: 5157 North State Highway 20, Oak Harbor, WA 98277. 675-2417.
Ebey's Landing State Park: *contact Fort Casey State Park.*
Fort Casey State Park: 1280S Fort Casey Road, Coupeville, WA 98239. 678-4519.
Fort Ebey State Park: 395 North Fort Ebey Road, Coupeville, WA 98239. 678-4636.
Fort Flagler State Park: Nordland, WA 98358. 385-1259.
Joseph Whidbey State Park: *contact Fort Ebey State Park.*
Larrabee State Park: 245 Chuckanut Drive, Bellingham, WA 98226. 676-2093.
Mystery Bay State Park: *contact Fort Flagler State Park.*
South Whidbey State Park: 4128 South Smugglers Cove Road, Freeland, WA 98249. 683-4235.

Other Parks

Clallam County Parks Department: Courthouse, Port Angeles, WA 98362. 417-2291
Dungeness Recreation Area (Clallam County): 683-5847.
Ebey's Landing National Historical Reserve: 908 NW Alexander, Coupeville, WA 98239. 678-4579.
Island County Parks and Recreation: 101 Sixth Street, Coupeville, WA 98239. 679-7373.
Jefferson County Parks and Recreation: Lawrence and Tyler, Port Townsend, WA 98368. 385-2221.
Lighthouse Marine Park (Whatcom County): 811 Marine Drive, Point Roberts, WA 98281. (604) 945-4911.
Pillar Point County Park (Clallam County). 963-2301.
Salt Creek County Park (Clallam County). 928-3441.
Semiahmoo Park (Whatcom County): 926l Semiahmoo Parkway, Blaine, WA 98230; 371-5513.

Skagit County Parks and Recreation: 315 South Third, Mount Vernon, WA 98273. 336-9414.
Washington Park (city of Anacortes): Parks and Recreation Dept., Sixth and Q, Anacortes, WA 98221. 293-1918.
Whatcom County Parks Information: 3373 Mount Baker Highway, Bellingham, WA 98226. 733-2900 or 592-5161.

Wildlife Refuges

Dungeness National Wildlife Refuge Area: 753-9476
Skagit Wildlife Recreation Area: 445-4441

B. Nautical Charts and Maps

Sketch maps for this book are intended for general orientation only. When traveling by boat on any of the Northwest's waters, it is imperative that the appropriate nautical charts be used. The following list of charts covers the area included in this book. They may be purchased at map stores or many marine supply centers.

The following two small-craft folios cover all areas east of Sequim Bay that are included in this book:

NOAA chart folio 18423 SC, *Bellingham to Everett Including San Juan Islands*, is a folio of charts (1:80,000), including some detailed insets. It covers most of the water areas in this book.

NOAA chart folio 18445 SC, *Puget Sound—Possession Sound to Olympia Including Hood Canal* (1:80,000) covers the southern tip of Whidbey Island.

Other charts that may be useful, either because their scale is smaller or because they cover areas outside the small-craft folios, include:

NOAA Chart 18421, *Strait of Juan de Fuca to Strait of Georgia* (1:80,000) and *Drayton Harbor* (1:30,000)
NOAA Chart 18424, *Bellingham Bay* (1:40,000) and *Bellingham Harbor* (1:20,000)
NOAA Chart 18427, *Anacortes to Skagit Bay* (1:25,000)
NOAA Chart 18428, *Oak and Crescent Harbors* (1:10,000)
NOAA Chart 18429, *Rosario Strait—Southern Part* (1:25,000)
NOAA Chart 18430, *Rosario Strait—Northern Part* (1:25,000)
NOAA Chart 18431, *Rosario Strait to Cherry Point* (1:25,000)
NOAA Chart 18432, *Boundary Pass* (1:25,000)
NOAA Chart 18433, *Haro Strait—Middle Bank to Stuart Island* (1:25,000)
NOAA Chart 18434, *San Juan Channel* (1:25,000)
NOAA Chart 18441, *Puget Sound—Northern Part* (1:80,000)
NOAA Chart 18460, *Strait of Juan de Fuca Entrance* (1:100,000)
NOAA Chart 18464, *Port Townsend* (1:20,000)
NOAA Chart 18465, *Strait of Juan de Fuca—Eastern Part* (1:80,000)
NOAA Chart 18468, *Port Angeles* (1:10,000)

NOAA Chart 18471, *Approaches to Admiralty Inlet—Dungeness to Oak Bay* (1:40,000)
NOAA Chart 18484, *Neah Bay* (1:10,000)

A book by Totem Publications (Camano Island), *Street and Road Atlas of Whatcom, Island and Skagit Counties,* has detailed street maps that are useful for locating out-of-the-way nooks and crannies.

USGS topographical maps are not necessary for any of the hiking described in this book; however, the 7½-minute series maps are both useful and interesting. Those covering areas in this book are: Anacortes North, Anacortes South, Angeles Point, Bellingham North, Bellingham South, Birch Point, Blaine, Bow, Camano, Cape Flattery, Carlsborg, Clallam Bay, Coupeville, Crescent Harbor, Cypress Island, Deception Pass, Disque, Dungeness, Ediz Hook, Eliza Island, Ferndale, Freeland, Gardiner, Joyce, Juniper Beach, La Conner, Langley, Lummi Bay, Lummi Island, Maxwelton, Morse Creek, Mukilteo, Neah Bay, Nordland, Oak Harbor, Point Roberts, Port Angeles, Port Townsend North, Port Townsend South, Pysht, Sekiu River, Sequim, Slip Point, Tulalip, Twin Rivers, Utsalady, Waadah Island, and West of Pysht. All are available at hiking or map stores.

C. Selected References

History

Eastwood, Harland, Sr. *Fort Whitman on Puget Sound, 1911–1945.* Lopez, Wash.: Twin Anchors Co., 1983.

Elmore, Helen Troy. *This Isle of Guemes.* Guemes Island, Wash.: Community Club of Guemes Island, 1973.

Faber, Jim. *Steamer's Wake.* Seattle, Wash.: Enetai Press, 1985.

Gibbs, Jim A. *Lighthouses of the Pacific.* West Chester, Pa.: Schiffer Publishing, Ltd., 1986.

Gregory, V. J. *Keepers at the Gate.* Port Townsend, Wash.: Port Townsend Publishing Co., 1976.

Hitchman, Robert. *Place Names of Washington.* Tacoma, Wash.: Washington State Historical Society, 1985.

Meany, Edmond S. *Vancouver's Discovery of Puget Sound.* New York: The Macmillan Co., 1907.

Williamson, Joe, and Joe Gibbs. *Maritime Memories of Puget Sound.* Seattle, Wash.: Superior Publishing Co., 1976.

Beaches and Marine Life

Puget Sound Public Shellfish Sites. Olympia, Wash.: State of Washington Department of Fisheries, n.d.

Sheely, Terry W. *The Complete Handbook on Washington's Clams/Crabs/Shellfish.* Snohomish, Wash.: Osprey Press, n.d.

Your Public Beaches: Strait of Juan de Fuca. Olympia, Wash.: State of Washington Department of Natural Resources, n.d.

Your Public Beaches: North Puget Sound. Olympia, Wash.: State of Washington Department of Natural Resources, 1978.

Nature

Angell, Tony and Kenneth C. Balcom, II. *Marine Birds and Mammals of Puget Sound*. Seattle, Wash.: Washington Sea Grant Program, 1982.

Mac's Field Guide to Water Birds of the Northwest Coast. Seattle, Wash.: The Mountaineers, 1986.

Osborne, Richard, John Calambokidis, and Eleanor M. Dorsey. *A Guide to Marine Mammals of Greater Puget Sound*. Anacortes, Wash.: Island Publishers, 1988.

Paulson, Dennis. *Shorebirds of the Pacific Northwest*. Seattle, Wash.: University of Washington Press, 1993.

Wahl, Terence R. and Dennis R. Paulson. *A Guide to Bird Finding in Washington*. Bellingham, Wash.: T. R. Wahl, 1981.

Yates, Steve. *Marine Wildlife of Puget Sound, the San Juans, and the Strait of Georgia*. Chester, Conn.: The Globe Pequot Press, 1988.

Boating and Paddling

Hale, Robert, ed. *Pacific Northwest Waggoner*. Bellevue, Wash.: Robert Hale and Co., 1994.

Northwest Boat Travel. Mount Vernon, Wash.: Northwest Boat Travel, published annually.

Pacific Boating Almanac: Pacific Northwest and Alaska. Ventura, Calif.: Western Marine Enterprises, Inc., published annually.

United States Coast Pilot: 7 (Pacific Coast: California, Oregon, Washington, and Hawaii). Washington, D.C.: U.S. Department of Commerce, published annually.

Washburn, Randel. *Kayaking Puget Sound, the San Juans, and Gulf Islands*. Seattle, Wash.: The Mountaineers, 1990.

Bicycling

Litman, Todd, and Suzanne Kort. *The Best Bike Rides in the Pacific Northwest*. Old Saybrook, Conn.: The Globe Pequot Press, 1992.

Woods, Erin and Bill Woods. *Bicycling the Backroads of Northwest Washington*. 3d ed. Seattle, Wash.: The Mountaineers, 1992.

Scuba Diving

Fischnaller, Steve. *Northwest Shore Dives*. Edmonds, Wash.: Bio-Marine Images, 1986.

Pratt-Johnson, Betty. *141 Dives in the Protected Waters of Washington and British Columbia*. West Vancouver, Canada: Gordon Soules Book Publishers, 1990.

Weber, Edward. *Diving and Snorkeling Guide to the Pacific Northwest*. Houston, Tex.: Pices Books, 1993.

Fishing

Haw, Frank, and Raymond M. Buckley. *Saltwater Fishing in Washington*. 2d ed. Seattle, Wash.: Stan Jones Publishing, 1981.

Olander, Doug. *Northwest Coastal Fishing Guide*. Seattle, Wash.: The Writing Works, 1984.

D. QUICK REFERENCE TO FACILITIES AND RECREATION

Some kinds of marine recreation—such as boating, fishing, and beach-combing—are found throughout North Puget Sound. Others, however, are more specific to particular areas. The table on the following pages provides a quick reference to facilities and activities in the major areas covered in this book.

- *Marine Services* include marine supplies and repair; in some places they may be of a very limited nature.

- *Shopping/Food* generally includes groceries, cafes, or restaurants, and a varying range of other types of stores. These too may be of a limited nature.

- *Floats/Buoys* refers to marinas that have transient moorage, as well as public facilities at parks.

- *Launch Facilities* may be only a shore access for hand-carried boats. Hoists and slings are always at commercial marinas. Ramps may be at either commercial or public facilities.

- *Point of Interest* includes historical or educational displays, museums, and self-guided nature tours, and exceptional birdwatching opportunities.

Some facilities listed may be entirely at commercial resorts or marinas; some may close off-season. For detailed information read the description of specific areas in the text.

( ) = Nearby; [ ] = Freshwater
Fuel: D = On Dock; S = Service Station
Launch Facilities: R = Ramp; H = Hoist; C = Hand Carry
      MR=Marine Railway
Camping: B = Bicycle Only
Walking/Hiking: BW = Beach Walk

	U.S. Customs	Fuel	Marine Services	Groceries/Shopping	Restaurants	Floats/Buoys	Launch Facilities	Fishing	Shellfish	Paddling	Scuba Diving	Swimming	Camping	Marine Trail Site	Picnicking	Walking/Hiking	Point of Interest
1. THE STRAIT OF GEORGIA																	
Point Roberts Marina	•	•	•	(•)	•	•	H	•							•		
Lighthouse Marine Park					•		R	•		•		•	•		•	•	•
Blaine Marina	•	•	•	(•)	•	•	R	•	•	•					•		
Semiahmoo Marina		•	•	•	•	•	H								•	•	
Semiahmoo County Park								•	•	•					•	•	•
Birch Bay State Park				(•)	(•)		C	•	•	•	•	•	•		•	•	•
2. BELLINGHAM BAY																	
Gooseberry Point		•	•	•	•		H										
Lummi Island Recreation Site								•		•	•		•	•	•	•	
Inati Bay						•		•		•	•		•				
Squalicum Harbor	•	•	•	•	•	•	R/H	•							•		•
Boulevard Park								•	•	•					•	•	
Harris Avenue Launch Ramp							R										
Bellingham Cruise Center				•													•
Marine Park							C			•					•		
Clarks Point Trails																•	
Larrabee State Park							R	•	•	•	•	•	•		•	•	
Strawberry Island Recreation Site										•	•		•	•	•		
Cypress Head Recreation Area						•		•		•	•		•	•	•		
Pelican Beach and Eagle Cliff						•		•	•	•	•		•	•	•	•	
Young County Park and Clark Point							C	•	•	•			•		•	•	
Samish Island Picnic Site								•	•						•		
3. FIDALGO ISLAND AND PADILLA BAY																	
Saddlebag Island Marine State Park								•	•	•	•		•	•	•	•	
Padilla Bay Shore Trail																•	•
Bay View Launch Ramp							R										
Bay View State Park							C	•		•			•	•		•	

	U.S. Customs	Fuel	Marine Services	Groceries/Shopping	Restaurants	Floats/Buoys	Launch Facilities	Fishing	Shellfish	Paddling	Scuba Diving	Swimming	Camping	Marine Trail Site	Picnicking	Walking/Hiking	Point of Interest
Breazeale Interpretive Center																•	•
Swinomish Channel Boat Launch							R								•		
March Point Boat Launch Ramps							R			•							
Anacortes Marinas	•	•	•	•	•	•	H										
Cap Sante City Park and Rotary Park															•	•	
Washington Park							R	•	•			•			•	•	•
Skyline Marina		•	•	•	•	•	H										
Skagit County Historical Museum																	•
La Conner Marina		•	•	(•)	(•)	•	H	•		•			(•)				
Pioneer City Park				(•)	(•)		R			•					•		•
4. SKAGIT DELTA AND CAMANO ISLAND																	
Skagit Wildlife Recreation Area							R	•	•	•						•	•
Utsalady Point Park							R			•					•		•
Onamac Point							•										
Camano Island State Park							R	•		•		•	•	•	•	•	
Cavelero Beach County Park							R			•		•			•		
Kayak Point County Park							R	•	•	•		•	•		•	•	
5. DECEPTION PASS STATE PARK																	
Cornet Bay						•	R	•	•	•	•				•	•	
Goose Rock and the ELC													•	•	•	•	
Hope and Skagit Islands						•		•	•	•	•			•	•	•	
Bowman and Rosario Bays						•	R	•		•	•	•	•	•	•	•	
Cranberry Lake Vicinity							[R]	[•]		[•]		[•]	•		•	•	•
Pass Lake							[R]	[•]		[•]						•	
Heart Lake							[R]	[•]		[•]						•	
6. WHIDBEY ISLAND																	
Joseph Whidbey State Park							C			•					•	•	

	U.S. Customs	Fuel	Marine Services	Groceries/Shopping	Restaurants	Floats/Buoys	Launch Facilities	Fishing	Shellfish	Paddling	Scuba Diving	Swimming	Camping	Marine Trail Site	Picnicking	Walking/Hiking	Point of Interest
Libbey Beach County Park							C			•					•		
Fort Ebey State Park								[•]					•		•	•	•
Oak Harbor Marina		•	•	(•)	(•)	•	R/H			•					•		
Oak Harbor City Parks				(•)	(•)	•	R	•		•		•	•		•		•
Monroe Landing County Park							R			•							•
Coupeville		•		•	•	•	R	•		•					•	•	•
Ebey's Landing State Park							C			•					•	•	•
Fort Casey State Park							R	•	•	•	•		•		•	•	•
Keystone Spit State Park and Driftwood Park								•		•	•				•	•	•
South Whidbey State Park									•				•		•	•	•
Double Bluff State Park Tidelands							C	•	•						•	•	
Dave Mackie County Park							R			•		•			•		
Freeland County Park							R	•	•						•		
Langley Marina and Phil Simon Park		•	•	(•)	(•)	•	R/H	•		•					•		
Columbia Beach						•		•									
Possession Beach County Park							R	•	•	•					•	•	•

7. ADMIRALTY INLET

	U.S. Customs	Fuel	Marine Services	Groceries/Shopping	Restaurants	Floats/Buoys	Launch Facilities	Fishing	Shellfish	Paddling	Scuba Diving	Swimming	Camping	Marine Trail Site	Picnicking	Walking/Hiking	Point of Interest
Oak Bay County Park							R	•	•	•		•	•		•		
Hadlock Lions Park									•						•	•	
South Indian Island County Park							C	•	•	•		•			•	•	
East Beach County Park							C	•	•	•		•			•		
Mystery Bay State Park						•	R	•	•	•					•		
Fort Flagler State Park					•	•	R	•	•	•	•	•	•		•	•	•
Hadlock				(•)	(•)	•	R			•							
Old Fort Townsend State Park						•		•	•	•			•		•	•	•
Port Townsend Marinas	•	•	•	(•)	(•)	•	H/R			•			•		•	•	•
Chetzemoka City Park									•			•			•		•

	U.S. Customs	Fuel	Marine Services	Groceries/Shopping	Restaurants	Floats/Buoys	Launch Facilities	Fishing	Shellfish	Paddling	Scuba Diving	Swimming	Camping	Marine Trail Site	Picnicking	Walking/Hiking	Point of Interest
North Beach County Park							C		•	•					•	•	
Fort Worden State Park			•			•	R	•	•	•	•	•	•		•	•	•

8. EASTERN STRAIT OF JUAN DE FUCA

	U.S. Customs	Fuel	Marine Services	Groceries/Shopping	Restaurants	Floats/Buoys	Launch Facilities	Fishing	Shellfish	Paddling	Scuba Diving	Swimming	Camping	Marine Trail Site	Picnicking	Walking/Hiking	Point of Interest
Gardiner Boat Launch Ramp							R								•		
Pitship Point (John Wayne Marina)		•	•		•	•	R	•	•	•					•		•
Sequim Bay State Park						•	R	•	•	•			•		•	•	•
Marlyn Nelson County Park							R		•						•	•	
Dungeness Recreation Area													•		•	•	
Dungeness National Wildlife Refuge								•	•		•				•	•	•
Port Angeles Boat Haven		•	•	(•)	(•)	•	R									•	
City Pier	•			(•)	(•)	•			•			•			•	•	•
Ediz Hook				•			R	•				•			•	•	•
Port Angeles Lincoln Park				(•)	(•)								•		•	•	•

9. WESTERN STRAIT OF JUAN DE FUCA

	U.S. Customs	Fuel	Marine Services	Groceries/Shopping	Restaurants	Floats/Buoys	Launch Facilities	Fishing	Shellfish	Paddling	Scuba Diving	Swimming	Camping	Marine Trail Site	Picnicking	Walking/Hiking	Point of Interest
Freshwater Bay County Park							R	•	•						•		
Salt Creek County Park and Tongue Point Marine Life Sanctuary							C	•		•	•	•	•		•	•	•
Whiskey Creek							R	•		•			•		•		
Lyre River			•				C	•		•		•	•		•		
Jim Creek							R	•		•			•		•		
Pillar Point County Park							R	•	•	•			•		•		
Clallam Bay County Park				(•)	(•)				•						•	•	
Sekiu Resorts		•	•	•	•	•	R	•							•	•	
Snow Creek			•			•	MR	•							•	•	
Neah Bay Resorts	•	•	•	•	•	•	H/R	•							•	•	•
Cape Flattery Trail																•	•

INDEX

ABOUT THE AUTHORS

MARGE and TED MUELLER are outdoor enthusiasts and environmentalists who have explored Washington State's waterways, mountains, forests, and deserts for nearly 40 years. Ted has taught classes on cruising in Northwest waters, and both Marge and Ted have instructed mountain climbing through the University of Washington. They are members of The Mountaineers and The Nature Conservancy, and Ted is a board member of the Washington Water Trails Association.

Heidi Mueller

THE MOUNTAINEERS, founded in 1906, is a nonprofit outdoor activity and conservation club, whose mission is "to explore, study, preserve, and enjoy the natural beauty of the outdoors...." Based in Seattle, Washington, the club is now the third-largest such organization in the United States, with 15,000 members and five branches throughout Washington State.

The Mountaineers sponsors both classes and year-round outdoor activities in the Pacific Northwest, which include hiking, mountain climbing, ski-touring, snowshoeing, bicycling, camping, kayaking and canoeing, nature study, sailing, and adventure travel. The club's conservation division supports environmental causes through educational activities, sponsoring legislation, and presenting informational programs. All club activities are led by skilled, experienced volunteers, who are dedicated to promoting safe and responsible enjoyment and preservation of the outdoors.

The Mountaineers Books, an active, nonprofit publishing program of the club, produces guidebooks, instructional texts, historical works, natural history guides, and works on environmental conservation. All books produced by The Mountaineers are aimed at fulfilling the club's mission.

If you would like to participate in these organized outdoor activities or the club's programs, consider a membership in The Mountaineers. For information and an application, write or call The Mountaineers, Club Headquarters, 300 Third Avenue West, Seattle, Washington 98119; (206) 284-6310.

Send or call for our catalog of more than 350 outdoor titles:

The Mountaineers Books
1001 SW Klickitat Way, Suite 201
Seattle, WA 98134
1(800)553-4453